Greek Philosophers Cloutier

C. C. W. Taylor is a Fellow of Corpus Christi College and a Reader in Philosophy at Oxford University. His publications include *Plato*, *Protagoras* and (with J. C. B. Gosling) *The Greeks on Pleasure*, both published by Oxford University Press.

R. M. Hare is White's Professor Emeritus of Moral Philosophy at Oxford University, Fellow of Corpus Christi College, and Professor of Philosophy Emeritus at the University of Florida. His other books include *The Language of Morals*, *Freedom and Reason*, *Moral Thinking*, and *Sorting Out Ethics*, all published by Oxford University Press.

Jonathan Barnes is Professor of Ancient Philosophy at the University of Geneva. He has edited the *Revised Oxford Translation of Aristotle*, and he is the author of books and papers on Aristotle and other ancient luminaries.

Greek Philosophers

Socrates
C. C. W. Taylor

Plato
R. M. Hare

Aristotle
Jonathan Barnes

OXFORD
UNIVERSITY PRESS

OXFORD
UNIVERSITY PRESS

Great Clarendon Street, Oxford OX2 6DP

Oxford University Press is a department of the University of Oxford.
It furthers the University's objective of excellence in research, scholarship,
and education by publishing worldwide in

Oxford New York

Athens Auckland Bangkok Bogotá Buenos Aires Calcutta
Cape Town Chennai Dar es Salaam Delhi Florence Hong Kong Istanbul
Karachi Kuala Lumpur Madrid Melbourne Mexico City Mumbai
Nairobi Paris São Paulo Shanghai Singapore Taipei Tokyo Toronto Warsaw

with associated companies in Berlin Ibadan

Oxford is a registered trade mark of Oxford University Press
in the UK and in certain other countries

Socrates © C. C. W. Taylor 1998
Plato © R. M. Hare 1982, 1996
Aristotle © Jonathan Barnes 1982, 1996
This composite volume © Oxford University Press 1999
Foreword © Keith Thomas 1999

First published as an Oxford University Press paperback 1999
Reissued 2001

British Library Cataloguing in Publication Data

Data available

Library of Congress Cataloging in Publication Data

Data available

ISBN 0-19-285422-4

10 9 8 7 6 5 4 3 2 1

Typeset by RefineCatch Limited, Bungay, Suffolk
Printed in Great Britain by
Cox & Wyman Ltd.,
Reading, Berkshire

Foreword

Philosophy, as it is studied in the West today, is an invention of the ancient Greeks. So too, to a great extent, are science and mathematics. But today's science and mathematics so far transcend the achievement of the Greeks that no modern scientist is likely to study Euclid or Hippocrates or Archimedes for other than purely antiquarian reasons. Modern philosophers, by contrast, continue to discuss problems which were first raised some two thousand five hundred years ago, and they often do so in terms which their Greek predecessors would have found fully intelligible. For that reason, the ancient philosophers are not just historical figures; they are part of the living community of philosophical debate; and they have to be studied by anyone with a serious interest in the subject.

Unfortunately, much Greek philosophical writing has been irretrievably lost. The authors whose works survive in greatest bulk are Plato and Aristotle, both of whom left extensive writings which, between them, cover virtually the whole range of philosophical problems. Plato has a greater claim than anyone else to be regarded as the founder of philosophy as we know it. His dialogues remain the starting-point for the study of logic, metaphysics, morals, and politics. He believed it important to separate knowledge from mere opinion; and he held that true knowledge would enable people to live well, for morality could be objective. He also believed that the soul was distinct from the body, and that there was a world of ideas separate from things in this world. His thought is often poetic and imaginative, with a mystical dimension, yet it also relates to highly practical issues in education and politics of a kind which continue to perplex us.

Aristotle was both philosopher and scientist. He was a polymath who provided organizing categories for the whole of human knowledge. He founded biology, reshaped logic and metaphysics, and determined the subsequent character of thinking about ethics, politics, psychology, and literary criticism. By laying down the principles of valid inference and explanation, he erected the foundations of scientific knowledge. His mind was orderly, balanced, and stunningly capacious.

Socrates left no writings whatsoever. He was Plato's teacher and he is known to us primarily as the dominant character in Plato's dialogues, particularly the earlier ones. It is frequently impossible to distinguish between what Socrates thought and what Plato thought, but the individuality of Socrates is nevertheless brilliantly realized. To the modern world, he remains the enduring model of the great teacher, the questioner and sceptic who leads his pupils towards a solution by forcing them to see the inconsistencies in their own unconsidered beliefs and assumptions.

Since the fifth and fourth centuries BC, when these men taught and wrote, there has never been a time when their ideas have been wholly without influence. Plato's thought underlay the Neoplatonic movement of late Antiquity, but then went into a period of relative neglect until it was revived during the Italian Renaissance. It had a deep influence upon the Cambridge Platonists of the seventeenth century and the poets and philosophers of the Romantic period, before entering modern philosophical discourse. Aristotle came into his own in the twelfth and thirteenth centuries, when the scholastic synthesis of his thought with the doctrines of medieval Christianity became the accepted intellectual orthodoxy. The scientific revolution of the seventeenth century shattered this tradition and relegated Aristotle's scientific works to oblivion, but his *Ethics*, *Politics*, and *Poetics* remained deeply influential. The *Ethics*, in particular, is still the indispensable starting-point for anyone wishing to reflect upon morality, human nature, and human fulfilment. As for Socrates, his heroic death became a moving exemplar of intellectual integrity and total commitment to the intellectual life as the supreme human value. His questioning posture shaped the way in which philosophy was subsequently taught, and numerous successive schools of philosophical thought have attempted to appropriate him as their patron saint.

The three self-contained studies which make up this volume were originally written for the Past Masters series, which sets out to expound the ideas of notable thinkers of the past in an authoritative but lucid and accessible manner. Jonathan Barnes brings outstanding scholarly authority to his discussion of Aristotle, while R. M. Hare's account of Plato has the special interest of being the work of one who is himself a distinguished moral philosopher. Years of profound study of the Platonic dialogues lie behind C. C. W. Taylor's memorable portrait of Socrates as one whose thought and personality, though known to us entirely at second hand, constitute an unsurpassed embodiment of the philosophic life. By reprinting these three books together, Oxford University Press has provided a valuable introduction to the work of three thinkers whose arguments and insights continue to engage the liveliest minds of our time.

Corpus Christi College,
Oxford

KEITH THOMAS
General Editor
Past Masters

Contents

Aristotle by Jonathan Barnes   191

References and Further Reading   303

Index   323

Socrates

C. C. W. Taylor

Acknowledgements

Anyone who writes on Socrates must acknowledge his or her indebtedness to the very large amount of scholarly work on that philosopher, most of it written in the later part of this century, and much of it of the highest quality. We are all part of a continuing tradition. Details of some of the most significant modern work on Socrates are given in the section on Further Reading at the end of this book.

In addition to this general indebtedness, certain portions of this book borrow heavily from specific writings by others. The first section in Chapter 2, 'Authors other than Plato', relies particularly on D. Clay, 'The Origins of the Socratic Dialogue', in P. A. Vander Waerdt (ed.), *The Socratic Movement* (Ithaca, NY and London, 1994) and on C. H. Kahn, *Plato and the Socratic Dialogue* (Cambridge, 1996), ch. 1. Chapter 5, 'Socrates and Later Philosophy', relies on a number of authors: in the section on 'Ancient Philosophy' I am indebted above all to A. A. Long, 'Socrates in Hellenistic Philosophy', *Classical Quarterly*, 38 (1988), 150–71, and also to contributions to Vander Waerdt's *The Socratic Movement* by G. Striker, J. G. DeFillipo and P. T. Mitsis, J. Annas, and V. T. McKirahan. (Details of those articles may be found in that volume.) The section 'Medieval and Modern Philosophy' is based in part on P. J. Fitzpatrick, 'The Legacy of Socrates', in B. S. Gower and M. C. Stokes (eds.), *Socratic Questions* (London and New York, 1992).

I am grateful to the General Editor of the series for the invitation to contribute a volume, and to him and an anonymous referee for their helpful suggestions for improvements to the text.

Abbreviations

DL	Diogenes Laertius
Pl.	Plato
Apol.	*Apology (Defence of Socrates)*
Charm.	*Charmides*
Euthyd.	*Euthydemus*
Euthyph.	*Euthyphro*
Gorg.	*Gorgias*
Hipp. Ma.	*Hippias Major*
Lach.	*Laches*
Prot.	*Protagoras*
Rep.	*Republic*
Symp.	*Symposium*
Tht.	*Theaetetus*
Xen.	Xenophon
Apol.	*Apology*
Mem.	*Memorabilia*
Oec.	*Oeconomicus*
Symp.	*Symposium*

1 Introduction

Socrates has a unique position in the history of philosophy. On the one hand he is one of the most influential of all philosophers, and on the other one of the most elusive and least-known. Further, his historical influence is not itself independent of his elusiveness. First we have the influence of the actual personality of Socrates on his contemporaries, and in particular on Plato. It is no exaggeration to say that had it not been for the impact on him of the life and above all of the death of Socrates Plato would probably have become a statesman rather than a philosopher, with the result that the whole development of Western philosophy would have been unimaginably different. Then we have the enduring influence of the figure of Socrates as an exemplar of the philosophic life, of a total moral and intellectual integrity permeating every detail of everyday life and carried to the heroic extreme of steadfastness in the face of rejection and ignominious death. But the figure of Socrates the protomartyr and patron saint of philosophy, renewed in every age to speak to that age's philosophical condition, is the creation, not of the man himself, but of those who wrote about him, above all of Plato. It is Plato's depiction of the ideal philosopher which has fascinated and inspired from his day to ours, and if we attempt to penetrate that depiction in the quest for the historical Socrates we find the latter as elusive as the historical Jesus of nineteenth-century New Testament scholarship.

Again, there are two main reasons for this elusiveness (a situation which reinforces the scriptural parallel); first, Socrates wrote nothing himself, and secondly (and consequently), after his death he quickly became the subject of a literary genre, that of 'Socratic conversations' (*Sōkratikoi logoi*), in which various of his associates presented imaginative representations of his conversations, representations which focused on different aspects of his personality and style of conversation in accordance with the particular interests of the individual author. Plato's dialogues and the Socratic writings of Xenophon are the only examples of this genre to survive complete, while scraps of other Socratic writings, notably those of Aeschines, survive through quotation by later authors. This literature will be discussed in more detail below. For the moment it should be emphasized that, while each of Plato, Xenophon, and the rest presents his own picture of Socrates in line with his particular purpose, each presents a picture *of Socrates*. That is to say, it would be a serious distortion to think of any of these writers as creating a free-standing figure, for example, of the ideal philosopher, or the model citizen, to which figure its author attaches the name 'Socrates'. Socrates is, indeed, depicted by Plato as the ideal philosopher, and in my view that depiction involves at various stages the attribution to him of philosophical doctrines which Plato knew that Socrates never maintained, for the very good reason that Plato had himself invented those doctrines after Socrates' death. But Socrates was in Plato's view the appropriate paradigm of the ideal philosopher because of the kind of person Plato believed Socrates to have been, and the kind of life Plato believed him to have lived. In the sense in which the terms 'fiction' and 'biography' designate exclusive categories, 'Socratic conversations' are neither works of fiction nor works of biography. They express their authors' responses to their understanding of the personality of a unique individual and to the events of that individual's life, and in order to understand them we must seek to make clear what is known, or at least reasonably believed, about that personality and those events.

2 Life

While Socrates' death can be firmly fixed by the record of his trial to the early spring of 399 BC (Athenian official year 400/399), there is an unimportant dispute about the precise date of his birth. The second-century BC chronicler Apollodorus (cited by the third-century AD biographer Diogenes Laertius (2.44)) assigns it with unusual precision (even giving his birthday) to early May 468 (towards the end of the Athenian official year 469/8) but Plato twice (*Apol.* 17d, *Crito* 52e) has Socrates describe himself as seventy years old at the time of his trial. So, either Socrates, still in his sixty-ninth year, is to be taken generously as describing himself as getting on for seventy, or (as most scholars assume) the Apollodoran date (probably arrived at by counting back inclusively seventy years from 400/399) is one or two years late. The official indictment (quoted by Diogenes Laertius) names his father, Sophroniscus, and his deme or district, Alopeke (just south of the city of Athens), and in Plato's *Theaetetus* (149a) he gives his mother's name as Phainarete and says that she was a strapping midwife. That may well have been true, though the appropriateness of the name (whose literal sense is 'revealing virtue') and profession to Socrates' self-imposed task of acting as midwife to the ideas of others (*Tht.* 149–51) suggests the possibility of literary invention. His father was said to have been a stonemason, and there is a tradition that Socrates himself practised that trade for some time; the fact that he served in the heavy infantry, who had to supply their own weapons and armour, indicates that his circumstances were reasonably prosperous. His ascetic life-style was more probably an expression of a philosophical position than the reflection of real poverty. His wife was Xanthippe, celebrated by Xenophon and others (though not by Plato) for her bad temper. They had three sons, two of them small children at the time of Socrates' death; evidently her difficult temper, if real, was not an obstacle to the continuation of conjugal relations into Socrates' old age. An unreliable later tradition, implausibly ascribed to Aristotle, mentions a second wife named Myrto, marriage to whom is variously described as preceding, following, or bigamously coinciding with the marriage to Xanthippe.

Virtually nothing is known of the first half of his life. He is reported to have been the pupil of Archelaus, an Athenian, himself a pupil of Anaxagoras; Archelaus' interests included natural philosophy and ethics (according to Diogenes Laertius 'he said that there are two causes of coming into being, hot and cold, and that animals come to be from slime and that the just and the disgraceful exist not by nature but by convention' (2.16)). The account of Socrates' early interest in natural philosophy put into his mouth in Plato's *Phaedo* (96a ff.) may reflect this stage in his development; if so, he soon shifted his interest to other areas, while any influence in ethics on the part of Archelaus can only have been negative.

It is only with the outbreak of the Peloponnesian War in 432, when he was already over 35, that he begins to emerge onto the historical scene. Plato several times (*Apol.* 28e, *Charm.* 153a, and *Symp.* 219e ff.) refers to his military service at the siege of Potidaea on the north Aegean coast in the opening years of the war, and in the last of these passages has Alcibiades enlarge on his courage in combat and his remarkable endurance of the ferocious winter conditions, in which he went about wearing his ordinary (by implication, thin) clothing and barefoot. The latter detail is of interest in linking Plato's portrayal of Socrates with our only unambiguously independent evidence for his personality and activity, the portrayal of him in fifth-century comedy. Some lines of the comic dramatist Ameipsias, quoted (according to most scholars, from his lost play *Connus*, which was placed above Aristophanes' *Clouds* in the competition of 423) by Diogenes Laertius, refer to his physical endurance, his ostentatiously simple clothing, and his going barefoot 'to spite the shoemakers'; and shoelessness is twice mentioned as a Socratic trademark in *Clouds* (103, 363). Another comic poet, Eupolis, referred to him as a beggarly chatterbox, who didn't know where his next meal was coming from, and as a thief, another detail reproduced in Aristophanes' caricature (*Clouds* 177–9). By the 420s, then, Socrates was sufficiently well known to be a figure of fun for his eccentrically simple life-style and for his loquacity. But, while his individual characteristics undoubtedly provided welcome comic material, it is as representative of a number of important and, in the dramatist's eyes, unwelcome trends in contemporary life that he figures in the only dramatic portrayal to have survived, that in Aristophanes' *Clouds*.

The crucial point is well summarized by W. K. C. Guthrie:

[W]e can recognize in the Socrates of the *Clouds* at least three different types which were never united to perfection in any single person: first the Sophist, who teaches the art of making a good case out of a bad one; secondly the atheistic natural philosopher like Anaxagoras; and thirdly the ascetic moral teacher, ragged and starving through his own indifference to worldly interests.[1]

In the play Socrates presides over an institution where students pay to learn techniques of chicanery to avoid paying their debts; this is called 'making the weaker argument defeat the stronger', a slogan associated with the sophist Protagoras, and the combat between the two arguments, in which the conventional morality of the stronger (also identified as the Just Argument) succumbs to the sophistry of the weaker (the Unjust Argument), is a central scene of the play. But, as well as a teacher of sophistry, the Socrates of the *Clouds* is a natural philosopher with a special interest in the study of the heavens, a study which involves rejection of traditional religion and its divinization of the heavenly bodies in favour of the new deities: Air, Aither, Clouds, Chaos, Tongue, and 'heavenly swirl', which displaces

---

[1] *A History of Greek Philosophy*, iii (Cambridge, 1969), 372.

Zeus as the supreme power of the universe. Naturally, the new 'religion' provides the metaphysical underpinning of the sophistical immoralism, since, unlike the traditional gods (who are not 'current coin with us', as Socrates says (247–8)), the new deities have no interest in punishing wrongdoers. At the conclusion of the play Socrates' house is burnt down specifically as a punishment for the impious goings-on which have taken place in it; 'investigating the position of (peering at the arse of) the moon' and 'offering wicked violence to the gods' (1506–9) are two sides of the same coin.

By 423, then, Socrates was sufficiently well known to be caricatured as a representative of the new learning as it appeared to conservatively minded Athenians, a subversive cocktail of scientific speculation and argumentative gymnastics, with alarming implications for conventional morality and religion. Such a burlesque does not, of course, imply detailed knowledge on the part of either dramatist or audience of the doctrines or activities either of Socrates or of contemporary intellectuals (though a number of commentators have been impressed by parallels between details of the doctrines ridiculed in *Clouds* and some of the doctrines of the contemporary natural philosopher Diogenes of Apollonia). But both dramatist and audience must have had some picture (allowing for a great deal of exaggeration, oversimplification, and distortion) of what sort of thing Socrates on the one hand and 'intellectuals' like Protagoras and Diogenes on the other were getting up to. We have to ask what Socrates had done by 423 to create that picture.

It is totally implausible that he had actually done what Aristophanes represents him as doing, namely, set up a residential institution for scientific research and tuition in argumentative techniques, or even that he had received payment for teaching in any of these areas. Both Plato and Xenophon repeatedly and emphatically deny that Socrates claimed scientific expertise or taught for money (*Apol.* 19d–20c, 31b–c, Xen. *Mem.* 1.2.60, 1.6.5, and 1.6.13), and the contrast between the professional sophist, who amasses great wealth (*Meno* 91d, *Hipp. Ma.*

282d–e) as a 'pedlar of goods for the soul' (*Prot.* 313c), and Socrates, who gives his time freely to others out of concern for their welfare and lives in poverty in consequence (*Apol.* 31b–c), is a central theme in Plato's distancing of the two. It is impossible to believe that Plato (and to a lesser extent Xenophon) would have systematically engaged on that strategy in the knowledge that Socrates was already notorious as exactly such a huckster of learning, but not at all difficult to believe that comic distortion depicts him as such when he was in fact something else. What else? One thing every depiction of Socrates agrees on is that he was, above all, an arguer and questioner, who went about challenging people's pretensions to expertise and revealing inconsistencies in their beliefs. That was the sort of thing that sophists were known, or at least believed, to do, and, for a fee, to teach others to do. It was, therefore, easy for Socrates, who was in any case conspicuous for his threadbare coat (*Prot.* 335d, Xen. *Mem.* 1.6.2, DL 2.28 (citing Ameipsias)), lack of shoes, and peculiar swaggering walk (*Clouds* 362, Pl. *Symp.* 221b), to become 'That oddball Socrates who goes about arguing with everyone and catching them out; one of those sophist fellows, with their damned tricky arguments, telling people there aren't any gods but air and swirl, and that the sun's a red-hot stone, and rubbish of that kind.' Rumours of his early interest in natural philosophy and association with Archelaus and (possibly) of unconventional religious attitudes may have filled out the picture, which the comic genius of Aristophanes brought to life on the stage in 423.

Plato mentions two other episodes of active military service, at Delium in Boeotia in 424 (*Apol.* 28e, *Lach.* 181a, and *Symp.* 221a–b) and at Amphipolis on the north Aegean coast in 422 (*Apol.* 28e). His courage during the retreat from Delium became legendary, and later writers report that he saved Xenophon's life on that occasion. As Xenophon was about six years old at the time the incident is obviously fictitious, doubtless derived from Alcibiades' account of Socrates' heroism in the earlier campaign at Potidaea, which included his

saving Alcibiades' life when he was wounded (*Symp.* 220d–e).
At any rate, it is clear that exceptional physical courage was
an element in the accepted picture of Socrates, along with
indifference to physical hardship, a remarkable capacity to
hold his liquor (*Symp.* 214a, 220a, 223c–d), and, in some
accounts, a strongly passionate temperament, in which anger
and sexual desire were kept under restraint by reason (Cicero,
Tusculan Disputations, 4.37.80, cf. Pl. *Charm.* 155c–e, Symp.
216d) (or were not, according to the hostile Aristoxenus). We
are given a detailed picture of his physical appearance in middle age in Xenophon's *Symposium*, where he describes himself as snub-nosed, with wide nostrils, protruding eyes, thick
lips (5.5–7), and a paunch (2.19), which exactly fits Alcibiades'
description of him in Plato's *Symposium* as like a satyr or
Silenus (215b, 216d; cf. Xen. *Symp.* 4.19). (For the snub nose
and protruding eyes see also *Tht.* 143e.) Two scholia (i.e. mar-
ginal notes in manuscripts, probably written in late antiquity)
on *Clouds* 146 and 223 say that he was bald, but there is no contemporary authority for this, and it may be an inference from
his resemblance to a satyr, as satyrs were often represented as
bald.

Nothing more is known of the events of his life till 406,
when there occurred what was apparently his only intervention, till his trial, in the public life of Athens. Following a
naval victory the Athenian commanders had failed to rescue
survivors, and the assembly voted that they should be tried
collectively, instead of individually as required by law. Most
offices being at that time allocated by lot, Socrates happened
to be one of the committee who had the task of preparing
business for the assembly, and in that capacity he was the
only one to oppose the unconstitutional proposal. (That is the
version of events reported at *Apol.* 32b–c and by Xenophon in
his *Hellenica* (1.7.14–15), but in his *Memorabilia* Xenophon
twice (1.1.18, 4.4.2) gives a different version, in which Socrates
was the presiding officer of the assembly during the crucial
debate, and 'did not allow them to pass the motion' (which,
given that the motion was in fact passed, must be understood

to mean 'tried unsuccessfully to prevent the motion being put'[2]).}

On the final defeat of Athens in 404 the democratic constitution was suspended and power passed to a junta of thirty who, nominally appointed to revise the laws, soon instituted a reign of terror in which thousands were killed or driven into exile. This lasted for eight months until the tyranny was overthrown in a violent counter-revolution and the democracy restored. Socrates had friends in both camps. Prominent among the Thirty were his associates Charmides and Critias (both relatives of Plato), both of whom were killed in the fighting which accompanied the overthrow of the tyranny, while among the democrats his friends included the orator Lysias and Chaerephon, both of whom were exiled and active in the resistance to the tyrants. Socrates maintained the apolitical stance which he had adopted under the democracy. He remained in Athens, but when the tyrants attempted to involve him by securing his complicity in the arrest of one Leon of Salamis he refused to co-operate 'but just went home' (*Apol.* 32d, cf. Xen. *Mem.* 4.4.3). There is no hint of political opposition, but the same simple refusal to be involved in illegality and immorality which had motivated his stand on the trial of the naval commanders. There is no evidence as to whether he took any part in the overthrow of the tyranny; the silence of Plato and, even more significantly, Xenophon on the issue suggests that he did not.

Trial and death

Some time in 400 or very early in 399 an obscure young man named Meletus (*Euthyph.* 2b) brought the following indictment against Socrates:

Meletus son of Meletus of Pitthos has brought and sworn this charge against Socrates son of Sophroniscus of Alopeke: Socrates is

---

[2] See Pl. *Gorg.* 473e, with commentary by E. R. Dodds, *Plato, Gorgias* (Oxford, 1959), 247–8.

a wrongdoer in not recognizing the gods which the city recognizes, and introducing other new divinities. Further, he is a wrongdoer in corrupting the young. Penalty, death.

Two others were associated in bringing the charge: Lycon, also unknown, and Anytus, a politician prominent in the restored democracy. After a preliminary examination (mentioned at the beginning of Plato's *Euthyphro*) before the magistrate who had charge of religious cases, known as the king, the case came to trial before a jury of 500 citizens in the early spring of 399.

No record of the trial survives. In the years following various authors wrote what purported to be speeches for the prosecution or the defence; two of the latter, by Plato and Xenophon, survive and none of the former. After speeches and production of witnesses by both sides the jury voted for condemnation or acquittal. According to *Apol.* 36a the vote was for condemnation by a majority of sixty, presumably approximately 280 to 220. Once the verdict was reached each side spoke again to propose the penalty, and the jury had to decide between the two. The prosecution demanded the death penalty, while (according to Plato) Socrates, after having in effect refused to propose a penalty (in *Apol.* 36d–e he proposes that he be awarded free meals for life in the town hall as a public benefactor), was eventually induced to propose the not inconsiderable fine of half a talent, over eight years' wages for a skilled craftsman (38b). The vote was for death, and according to Diogenes Laertius eighty more voted for death than had voted for a guilty verdict, indicating a split of 360 to 140; Socrates' refusal to accept a penalty had evidently alienated a considerable proportion of those who had voted for acquittal in the first place.

Execution normally followed very soon after condemnation, but the trial coincided with the start of an annual embassy to the sacred island of Delos, during which, for reasons of ritual purity, it was unlawful to carry out executions (*Ph.* 58a–c). Hence there was an interval of a month (Xen. *Mem.* 4.8.2) between the trial and the execution of the sentence. Socrates was imprisoned during this period, but his friends had ready access to him (Crito 43a), and Plato suggests in Crito that he had the opportunity to escape, presumably with the connivance of the authorities, to whom the execution of such a prominent figure may well have been an embarrassment (45e, 52c). If the opportunity was available, he rejected it. The final scene is immortalized in Plato's idealized depiction in Phaedo. The method of execution, self-administration of a drink of ground-up hemlock, was less ghastly than the normal alternative, a form of crucifixion, but medical evidence indicates that the effects of the poison were in fact much more harrowing than the gentle and dignified end which Plato depicts. According to Plato his last words were 'Crito, we owe a cock to Asclepius; pay it and don't forget' (Ph. 118a). Asclepius was the god of health, and the sacrifice of a cock a normal thank-offering for recovery from illness. Perhaps those were in fact his last words, in which case it is interesting that his final concern should have been for a matter of religious ritual. (This was an embarrassment to rationalistic admirers of Socrates in the eighteenth and nineteenth centuries.) But the idealized quality of Plato's description makes it plausible that the choice of these words was determined rather by dramatic appropriateness than by historical accuracy. On that assumption the point may have been to give a final demonstration of Socrates' piety, but that would have been more appropriate to Xenophon's portrayal than Plato's. A recent ingenious suggestion is that the detail refers back to Phaedo's statement (59b) that Plato was absent from the final scene through illness. The offering is in thanks for Plato's recovery, and marks Plato's succession as Socrates' philosophical heir. This degree of self-advertisement seems implausible; the older view (held by Nietzsche among others) that the thanks is offered on behalf of Socrates himself, in gratitude for his recovery from the sickness of life (cf. Shakespeare's 'After life's fitful fever he sleeps well'), seems more likely.

The lack of any record of the trial makes it impossible to reconstruct precisely what Socrates' accusers charged him with. The explicit accusations cited above are sufficiently vague to allow a wide variety of conduct to fall under them, and in addition Athenian legal practice sanctioned the introduction of material which, while strictly irrelevant to the letter of the charges, might be expected to influence the jury for or against the defendant. An ancient tradition holds that the real ground for the condemnation of Socrates was political, namely, his supposed influence on those of his associates who had become notorious for anti-Athenian and anti-democratic conduct, above all Alcibiades and Critias; thus the orator Aeschines asserted categorically that 'You, Athenians, killed the sophist Socrates because he was seen as having educated Critias, one of the thirty who overthrew the democracy' (*Against Timarchus* 173 (delivered in 345 BC); cf. Xen. *Mem.* 1.2.12–16). Given the notoriety of Alcibiades, Critias, Charmides, and other known associates of Socrates such as Phaedrus and Eryximachus, both of whom had been involved (along with others of the Socratic circle) in a celebrated religious scandal in 415 BC, it would have been very odd had the prosecution not brought up their misdeeds to defame Socrates as a corrupter of the young. An amnesty passed in 403 did indeed prevent people from being charged with crimes committed previously, but that was no bar to citing earlier events as indicative of the defendant's character. It seems, then, virtually certain that the charge of corrupting the young had at least a political dimension. It would not follow that the specifically religious charges were a mere cover for a purely political prosecution, or that the alleged corruption did not itself have a religious as well as a political aspect. We have seen that in the 420s Aristophanes had made Socrates a subverter of traditional religion, whose gods are displaced in favour of 'new divinities' such as Air and Swirl, and a corrupter of sound morality and decent education. It is clear from his *Apology* that Plato thought that some of this mud still stuck in 399, and I see no reason to doubt that he was right. Though the evidence of a whole series of prosecutions of free-thinking intellectuals, including Protagoras and Euripides, in the late fifth century is gravely suspect, it is likely that Anaxagoras was driven from Athens by the threat of prosecution for his impious declaration that the sun was a red-hot stone, and the care which Plato takes in the *Apology* to distance Socrates from Anaxagoras (27d–e) indicates that he saw that case as looming large in the attack on Socrates.

There is also some evidence that Socrates' personal religious behaviour and attitudes were seen as eccentric. He famously claimed to be guided by a private divine sign, an inner voice which warned him against doing things which would have been harmful to him, such as engaging in politics (*Apol.* 31c–d), and in the *Apology* (ibid.) he says that Meletus caricatured this in his indictment. Of course, there was nothing illegal or impious in such a claim in itself, but taken together with other evidence of nonconformity it could be cited to show that Socrates bypassed normal channels in his communication with the divine, as Euthyphro suggests in the dialogue (*Euthyph.* 3b, cf. Xen. *Mem.* 1.1.2). Moreover, there is evidence from the fourth century that the Athenian state, while ready enough to welcome foreign deities such as Bendis and Asclepius to official cult status, regarded the introduction of private cults as sufficiently dangerous to merit the death penalty. So any evidence that Socrates was seen as the leader of a private cult would indicate potentially very damaging prejudice against him. We have some hints of such evidence. In *Clouds* Socrates introduces Strepsiades to his 'Thinkery' in a parody of the ceremonies of initiation into religious mysteries (250–74), while a chorus of Aristophanes' *Birds* (produced in 414) describes Socrates as engaged in raising ghosts by a mysterious lake, and his associate Chaerephon, 'the bat' (one of the students of *Clouds*), as one of the ghosts whom he summons (1553–64). We have here the suggestion that Socrates is the leader of a coterie dabbling in the occult, and the episode of his trance at Potidaea, where he stood motionless and lost in thought for twenty-four hours (*Symp.* 220c–d) may have contributed to a reputation for uncanniness. While it may seem to us that the picture of Socrates as an atheistic natural philosopher fits ill with that of a spirit-summoning fakir, that dichotomy may not have seemed so apparent in the fifth century BC; and in any case we are concerned with a climate of thought rather than a precisely articulated set of charges. Socrates, I suggest, was seen as a religious deviant and a subverter of traditional religion and morality, whose corrupting influence had been spectacularly manifested by the flagrant crimes of some of his closest associates.

So much for the case for the prosecution. As for the defence, though there was a tradition (which appears to go back to the fourth century BC) that Socrates offered none at all, the weight of the evidence suggests that he did indeed offer a defence, but one which was by ordinary standards so unusual as to give rise to the belief that he had not prepared it in advance, and/or that he did not seriously expect or even intend it to convince the jury (both in Xen. *Apol.* 1–8). (In all probability the story told by Cicero (*De oratore* 1.231) and others that Lysias wrote a speech for the defence which Socrates refused to deliver as out of character indicates merely that a defence of Socrates was among the speeches attributed to Lysias; see [Plutarch] *Life of Lysias* 836b.) It is natural to enquire how much of the substance of his defence can be reconstructed from the two versions which we possess, those by Plato and Xenophon. The two are very different in character. Plato's, which is over four times as long, purports to be the verbatim text of three speeches delivered by Socrates, the first in reply to the charges, the second, delivered after his conviction, addressed to the question of penalty, and a final address to the jury after their vote for the death penalty. Xenophon's is a narrative, beginning with an explanation of Socrates' reasons for not preparing his defence in advance, continuing with some purported excerpts (in direct speech) from the main defence and the final address to the jury, and concluding with some reports of things which Socrates said after the trial. There are also considerable differences in content. Both represent Socrates as replying in the main speech to the three counts of the indictment, but the substance of the replies is quite different. Xenophon's Socrates rebuts the charge of not recognizing the gods of the city by claiming that he has been assiduous in public worship; he takes the charge of introducing new divinities to refer only to his divine sign, and replies by pointing out that reliance on signs, oracles, etc. is an established element in conventional religion. The charge of corruption is rebutted primarily by appeal to his acknowledged practice of the conventional virtues, backed up by his claim (admitted by Meletus) that what is actually complained of is the education of the young, which should rather be counted benefit than harm. The tone throughout is thoroughly conventional, to such an extent that the reader might well be puzzled why the charges had been brought at all.

Plato's Socrates, by contrast, begins by claiming that the present accusation is the culmination of a process of misrepresentation which he traces back to Aristophanes' caricature, in which the two cardinal falsehoods are (i) that he claims to be an expert in natural philosophy and (ii) that he teaches for pay. (In rebutting the second point he contradicts Xenophon's Socrates in denying that he educates anyone.) In response to the imagined question of what in his actual conduct had given rise to this misrepresentation he does indeed claim that it is possession of a certain kind of wisdom. The explanation of what this wisdom is takes him far beyond Xenophon's Socrates, since it involves nothing less than a defence of his whole way of life as a divine mission, but one of a wholly unconventional kind.

This mission was, according to Plato's Socrates, prompted by a question put by his friend Chaerephon to the oracle of Apollo at Delphi. Chaerephon asked whether anyone was wiser than Socrates, to which the oracle replied that no one was. Since Socrates knew that he possessed no expertise of any sort, he was puzzled what the oracle could mean, and therefore sought to find someone wiser than himself among acknowledged experts (first of all experts in public affairs, subsequently poets and craftsmen). On questioning them about their expertise, however, he found that they in fact lacked the wisdom which they claimed, and were thus less wise than Socrates, who was at least aware of his own ignorance. He thus came to see that the wisdom which the oracle had ascribed to him consisted precisely in this awareness of his ignorance, and that he had a divine mission to show others that their own claims to substantive wisdom were unfounded. This enterprise of examining others (normally referred to as 'the Socratic elenchus', from the Greek *elenchos*, 'examination'), which was the basis of his unpopularity and consequent misrepresentation, he later in the speech describes as the greatest benefit that has ever been conferred on the city, and his obligation to continue it in obedience to the god as so stringent that he would not be prepared to abandon it even if he could save his life by doing so.

This story poses a number of questions, of which the first, obviously, concerns the authenticity of the oracle. Is the story true, or, as some scholars have suggested, is it merely Plato's invention? There are no official records of the Delphic oracle against which we can check the story; the great majority of the oracular responses which we know of are mentioned in literary sources whose reliability has to be considered case by case. The fact that Xenophon too mentions the oracle is no independent evidence, since it is quite likely that he wrote his *Apology* with knowledge of Plato's, and it is therefore possible that he took the story over from him. Certainty is impossible, but my own inclination is to think that the story is true; if it were not, why should Plato identify Chaerephon as the questioner, rather than just 'someone', and add the circumstantial detail that, though Chaerephon himself was dead by the time of the trial, his brother was still alive to testify to the truth of the story? More significant than the historicity of the story is the different use which Plato and Xenophon make of it. According to Xenophon what the oracle said was that no one was more free-spirited or more just or more self-controlled than Socrates, and the story then introduces a catalogue of instances of these virtues on his part, in which wisdom is mentioned only incidentally. According to Plato what the oracle said was that no one was wiser than Socrates, and Socratic wisdom is identified with self-knowledge. Xenophon uses the story to support his conventional picture of Socrates' moral virtue, Plato to present Socratic cross-examination as the fulfilment of a divine mission and therefore as a supreme act of piety.

Another striking feature of Plato's version of the oracle story is the transformation of Socrates' quest from the search for the meaning of the oracle to the lifelong mission to care for the souls of his fellow-citizens by submitting them to his examination. By 23a the meaning of the oracle has been elucidated: 'In reality god [i.e. god alone] is wise, and human wisdom is worth little or nothing. . . . He is the wisest among you, O humans, who like Socrates has come to know that in reality he is worth nothing with respect to wisdom.' But this discovery, far from putting an end to Socrates' quest, makes him determined to continue it: 'for this reason I go about to this very day in accordance with the wishes of the god seeking out any citizen or foreigner I think to be wise; and when he seems to me not to be so, I help the god by showing him that he is not wise.' Why is Socrates 'helping the god' by showing people that their conceit of wisdom is baseless? The god wants him to reveal to people their lack of genuine wisdom, which belongs to god alone; but why? It was traditional wisdom that humans should acknowledge their inferiority to the gods; dreadful punishments, such as Apollo's flaying of the satyr Marsyas for challenging him to a music contest, were likely to be visited on those who tried to overstep the gulf. But the benefits accruing from Socratic examination are not of that extrinsic kind. Rather, Socrates' challenge is to 'care for intelligence and truth and the best possible state of one's soul' (29e), since 'it is as a result of goodness that wealth and everything else are good for people in the private and in the public sphere' (30b). There is, then, an intimate relation between self-knowledge and having one's soul in the best possible state; either self-knowledge is identical with that state, or it is a condition of it, necessary, sufficient, or perhaps necessary and sufficient. That is why no greater good has ever befallen the city than Socrates' service to the god.

The details of the relation between self-knowledge and the best state of the soul are not spelled out in the *Apology*. What is clear is that here Plato enunciates the theme of the relation between knowledge and goodness which is central to many of the dialogues, and that that theme is presented in the *Apology* as the core of Socrates' answer to the charge of not recognizing the gods of the city. Unlike Xenophon, Plato says nothing about Socrates' practice of conventional religious observance, public or private. Instead he presents the philosophic life itself as a higher kind of religious practice, lived in obedience to a god who wants us to make our souls, that is, our selves, as perfect as possible. Each author has Socrates reply to the charge in the terms of his own agenda, Xenophon's of stressing Socrates' conventional piety and virtue, Plato's of presenting him as the exemplar of the philosophic life.

Plato's version of the replies to the other charges shows the power of Socratic questioning. The charge of introducing new divinities is rebutted by inducing Meletus to acknowledge under cross-examination that his position is inconsistent, since he maintains both that Socrates introduces new divinities and that he acknowledges no gods at all, while the charge of corruption is met by the argument that if Socrates corrupted his associates it must have been unintentionally, since if they were corrupted they would be harmful to him, and no one harms himself intentionally. As the latter thesis is central to the ethical theses which Socrates argues for in several Platonic dialogues, we see Plato shaping his reply to the charges against Socrates by reliance, not merely on Socrates' argumentative technique, but also on Socratic ethical theory. Plato sees the accusation of Socrates as an attack, not just on the individual, but, more significantly, on the Socratic practice of philosophy, which is to be rebutted by showing its true nature as service to god and by deploying its argumentative and doctrinal resources. Xenophon's reply, by contrast, has little if any philosophical content.

It is clear, then, that the hope of reconstructing Socrates' actual defence speeches at the trial by piecing together the evidence of our two sources is a vain one, since each of the two presents the defence in a form determined by his own particular agenda. The question of whether any particular statement or argument reported by either Plato or Xenophon was actually made or used by Socrates seems to me unanswerable. Looked at in a wider perspective, it seems to me that Plato's version may well capture the atmosphere of the trial and of Socrates' defence more authentically than Xenophon's, for two reasons. First, the prominence which Plato gives to Aristophanes' caricature and its effects (entirely absent from Xenophon's version) sets the accusation in its historical background and gives much more point to the accusations of religious nonconformity and innovation than does Xenophon. Secondly, the presentation of Socrates' elenctic mission as service to the god and benefit to the city expresses much better than Xenophon's bland presentation the unconventional character of Socrates' defence, and, ironically enough, displays much more forcefully than his own version the arrogance which he says all writers have remarked on and which he sets out to explain.

3 Socratic literature and the Socratic problem

The account of Socrates' life and death attempted in the previous chapter has already involved us in grappling with the so-called 'Socratic problem', that is, the question of what access our sources give us to the life and character of the historical Socrates. Every statement in that chapter has involved some assumptions, explicit or implicit, about the character and reliability of the source on which it relies. In particular, the account of Socrates' trial emphasizes the different apologetic stances which shape the presentations of Socrates' defence by Plato and Xenophon, concluding that, while we can identify with some plausibility the main lines of the attack on Socrates, our sources merely suggest to us the general tenor of his defence, while leaving us agnostic about the detail. It is the task of this chapter to put that result into context by giving a brief sketch of the extant ancient literature dealing with Socrates and of the genres to which it belongs.

Authors other than Plato

On the first kind of Socratic literature, the depiction of Socrates in fifth-century comedy, I have nothing to add to the previous chapter. It is the only Socratic literature known to have been written before Socrates' death, and its depiction of Socrates cannot have been influenced by Plato. It gives us a contemporary caricature, which associates Socrates with some important aspects of contemporary intellectual life, and which we have every reason to believe contributed substantially to the climate of suspicion and hostility which led eventually to his death.

*

In the opening chapter of his *Poetics* Aristotle refers to 'Socratic conversations' (*Sōkratikoi logoi*) as belonging to an as yet nameless genre of representation together with the mimes of Sophron and Xenarchus, two fifth-century Sicilian writers (apparently father and son). The 'mimes' were dramatic representations of scenes from everyday life (we have a few titles such as *Mother-in-Law* and *The Tuna Fishers*), fictional and apparently comic, classified into those with male and those with female characters; there is no suggestion that the characters portrayed included actual historical individuals. Though Aristotle counts them as belonging to the same genre as Socratic conversations, and Plato was said to have introduced them to Athens and to have been influenced by them in his depictions of character, we should not exaggerate the degree of resemblance, which consists essentially in the fact that both are representations in prose of conversations from (roughly) contemporary life. In particular, we should not jump to the conclusion that because the mimes are wholly fictional, and because Socratic conversations belong to the same genre as the mimes, therefore Socratic conversations are wholly fictional. There is at least one respect in which they are not wholly fictional, in that their characters are mostly taken from real life. The extent to which the depiction of those characters is fictional is a further question.

Ancient sources credit different authors with the invention of the 'Socratic conversation', but there is no dispute that the composition of such conversations was widespread among Socrates' associates, at least nine of whom, in addition to Plato and Xenophon, are mentioned by one source or another as having written them. There is no good evidence that any of this literature was written before Socrates' death, and it is reasonable to assume that its authors shared the intention, explicit in Xenophon, to commemorate Socrates and to defend his memory both against the charges made at the trial and against hostile accounts such as the *Accusation of Socrates*, a pamphlet (now lost) written by a rhetorician named Polycrates some time after 394 BC. Some friends of Socrates are reported by Diogenes Laertius to have made notes of his conversations, and there is no reason to reject that evidence, but just as we must not assume that 'Socratic conversations' were wholly fictional, so we must avoid the opposite error of thinking of them as based on transcripts of actual conversations. The function of note-taking was not to provide a verbatim record for later publication, but to preserve authentically Socratic material for incorporation into broadly imaginative reconstructions.

Apart from the writings of Plato and Xenophon, very little of this literature has survived. For most authors all that we have are titles and occasional snippets. Some of the titles indicate thematic interconnections, including connections with Platonic dialogues. Thus, Crito is said to have written a *Protagoras* and a defence of Socrates; Aeschines, Antisthenes, Eucleides, and Phaedo all wrote an *Alcibiades*; Aeschines and Antisthenes each wrote an *Aspasia* (Aspasia was the celebrated mistress of the statesman Pericles and the inspiration of Plato's *Menexenus*); and Antisthenes wrote a *Menexenus*. A particularly interesting survival is an anonymous papyrus fragment now in Cologne;[1] this contains part of a dialogue between Socrates and an unnamed person in Socrates' cell after his sentence (recalling Plato's *Crito*) in which Socrates is asked why he did not defend himself at the trial. In his answer Socrates is represented as maintaining, as in *Protagoras*, that pleasure is the supreme end of life, a position taken by the Cyrenaic school founded by Socrates' associate Aristippus (also an author of dialogues). It has been plausibly suggested that the author may have belonged to that school. Another possible association with Plato's *Protagoras* is provided by Aeschines' *Callias* (whose house is the setting for Plato's dialogue, as well as for Xenophon's *Symposium*). In addition to his *Alcibiades*, Eucleides of Megara wrote an *Aeschines*, a *Crito*, and an *Eroticus* (the last on a characteristically Socratic theme, as evidenced by Plato's *Phaedrus* and *Symposium* and by Aeschines' *Alcibiades*). The prominence of the name of Alcibiades in this

[1] For details see J. Barnes, 'Editor's Notes', *Phronesis*, 32 (1987), 325–6.

catalogue is not accidental. As we saw in the previous chapter, Socrates' association with Alcibiades had certainly fuelled the accusation of corruption of the young and was probably still being used to blacken his reputation after his death; in Xenophon's words (*Mem*. 1.2.12), 'The accuser [perhaps Polycrates] said that Critias and Alcibiades, associates of Socrates, did the greatest harm to the city. For Critias was the most covetous and violent of all the oligarchs, and Alcibiades the most wanton and licentious of all the democrats.' It then became a central theme of Socratic literature to show that, far from encouraging Alcibiades in his wantonness, Socrates had sought to restrain him, and that his crimes (which included sacrilege and treason) had issued from his neglecting Socrates' advice and example, not from following them. Xenophon argues prosaically in *Mem*. 1.2 that (like Critias) he was well behaved as long as he kept company with Socrates and went to the bad only after he ceased to associate with him, and that in any case his motive for associating with Socrates had from the beginning been desire for political power rather than regard for Socrates. (A dangerous argument, for why should desire for power lead him to associate with Socrates, unless he believed that Socrates would help him to attain it?) Plato's depiction in the *Symposium* of Alcibiades' relations with Socrates, presented in the first person by the dramatic character of Alcibiades himself, is intended to make the same point. Socrates' courage and self-control (which withstands the sexual blandishments of the otherwise irresistible Alcibiades) fill him with shame and the recognition that he should do as Socrates bids him, but when he is apart from him he falls under the influence of the flattery of the multitude, so that he would be glad to see Socrates dead (216b–c). The theme of the probably pseudo-Platonic *First Alcibiades* is similar. Alcibiades, convinced that his capacity is greater than that of any of the acknowledged political leaders, is proposing to go into politics, and Socrates' task is to convince him that he is unqualified because he lacks the necessary knowledge, namely, knowledge of what is best. The dialogue ends with Alcibiades promising to be submissive to Socrates, to

which Socrates replies, clearly with reference to their respective fates, that he is afraid that the city may prove too strong for
them both.

Ambition, shame, and knowledge are similarly central
themes in the *Alcibiades* of Aeschines of Sphettus, of which we
possess some substantial fragments. Socrates narrates to an
unnamed companion a conversation with Alcibiades, beginning
by observing how Alcibiades' political ambitions are prompted
by emulation of Themistocles, the great statesman who had led
Athens in the Persian war of 480. He then points out how
Themistocles' achievements were based on knowledge and
intelligence, which were yet insufficient to save him from final
disgrace and banishment. The point of this is to bring home to
Alcibiades his intellectual inferiority to Themistocles and the
consequent vanity of his pretensions to rival him, and the strategy is so successful that Alcibiades bursts into tears, lays his
head on Socrates' knees, and begs him to educate him. Socrates
concludes by telling his companion that he was able to produce
this effect not through any skill on his part but by a divine gift,
which he identifies with his love for Alcibiades: 'and so although
I know no science or skill which I could teach anyone to benefit
him, nevertheless I thought that by keeping company with
Alcibiades I could make him better through the power of love.'
This excerpt combines two themes prominent in Plato's depiction of Socrates: the denial of knowledge or the capacity to teach
and the role of love in stimulating relationships whose goal is the
education of the beloved (see esp. *Symposium* and *Phaedrus*).

The only other Socratic dialogue of which any substantial excerpts survive (apart from the dialogues of Plato and
Xenophon) is Aeschines' *Aspasia*. This also connects with
themes in other Socratic writings. It is a dialogue between
Socrates and Callias, whose opening recalls Plato's *Apology*
20a–c, but in reverse, since there Socrates reports a conversation in which Callias recommends the sophist Euenus of Paros
as a tutor for his sons, whereas in Aeschines' dialogue Callias
asks Socrates whom he would recommend as a tutor, and is
astonished when Socrates suggests the notorious courtesan

Aspasia. Socrates supports his recommendation by instancing two areas in which Aspasia has special expertise: rhetoric, in which she instructed not only the famous Pericles but also Lysicles, another prominent politician, and marriage guidance. The former topic is common to this dialogue and Plato's *Menexenus*, in which Socrates delivers a funeral oration which he says was written by Aspasia who, he adds, had taught rhetoric to many, including Pericles, and had written the famous funeral speech reported by Thucydides in book 2 of his history. The topic of marriage guidance provides an interesting link with Xenophon, for the recipients of Aspasia's wise advice described by Socrates are none other than Xenophon and his wife. (The style of the advice is characteristically Socratic, since Aspasia proceeds by a series of instances in which both husband and wife want to have the best of any kind of thing, dress, horse, etc., to the conclusion that they both want the best spouse, from which she infers that each of them has to make their partnership perfect.) It can hardly be coincidence that Xenophon twice refers to Aspasia's expertise in matchmaking and the training of wives (*Mem*. 2.6.36, *Oec*. 3.14). We should not, of course, suppose that Xenophon had actually benefited personally from Aspasia's expertise, as Aeschines depicts; the point is that this was a common theme in the Socratic literary circle, and that whoever treated it later (a question which the evidence seems to leave open) probably did so with the earlier treatment in mind. We must remain equally agnostic about the relative priority of Plato's *Menexenus* and the *Aspasia*s of Aeschines and Antisthenes, and of that of the various *Alcibiades*es. In general, there seems little if any ground for the attempt to assign relative priority among Socratic works, with the exception of a few cases where Xenophon seems fairly clearly to refer to works of Plato.

The Socratic writings of Xenophon and Plato's Socratic dialogues are the only bodies of Socratic literature to have survived complete. In addition to Xenophon's version of Socrates' defence, we have his *Memorabilia*, four books of reports, mostly in direct speech, of Socrates' conversations; *Symposium*, a lively account of a dinner-party at which Socrates is a guest, similar to and certainly containing references to Plato's *Symposium*; and *Oeconomicus*, a moralizing treatise on estate-management in the form of a Socratic dialogue. The opening of the *Memorabilia* makes it clear that its purpose is primarily apologetic. Xenophon begins by citing the accusation against Socrates and introduces the conversations by elaborating in the first two chapters the themes of his *Apology*, that Socrates was exceptionally pious, of exemplary virtue, and a good influence on his younger associates, some of whom, unfortunately, went to the bad through neglecting his advice. In the rest of the book these themes are developed in a series of conversations, normally between Socrates and one other person, though sometimes it is said that others were present; the interlocutors are mostly familiar figures from the Socratic circle, such as Aristippus, Crito and his son Critobulus, and Xenophon himself, but also including others, such as one of the sons of Pericles, the sophists Antiphon and Hippias, and a high-class prostitute named Theodote. The final chapter returns to the theme which opens the *Apology*, that Socrates did not prepare a defence because his divine sign had indicated to him that it was better for him to die then than to decline into senility, concluding with a eulogy of Socrates as the best and happiest of men, who not only excelled in all the virtues but promoted them in others.

The work is then essentially a fuller, illustrated version of the *Apology*. In keeping with the character of the latter, the content of the conversations is heavily slanted towards piety, moral uplift, and good practical advice. For example Socrates gives an irreligious acquaintance called Aristodemus a little lecture on the providential ordering of the world, pointing out among other things how the eyelashes are designed to screen the eyes from the wind (1.4), and he encourages the hedonist Aristippus to self-control by telling him a story from the sophist Prodicus of how Heracles chose the sober joys of virtue in preference to the meretricious attractions of vice (2.1). He discusses the role of a general with a series of interlocutors (3.1–5), helps a friend in financial difficulties by persuading him to put the women-folk of his large household to work making clothes (2.7), and gives advice on the importance of physical fitness (3.12) and on table manners (3.14). This is not to say that the work has no philosophical content. We find Socrates using methods of argument familiar from Plato, such as inductive arguments to establish a conclusion from an array of similar cases (e.g. 2.3), frequently derived from the practice of practical crafts, and there are instances of cross-examination with a view to show-ing that the person examined lacks the appropriate knowledge (notably 3.6 and 4.2, where the examinations of the respective pretensions to political leadership of Glaucon, Plato's elder brother, and of a young associate named Euthydemus, recall the similar examinations of Alcibiades in Aeschines' *Alcibiades* and the pseudo-Platonic *First Alcibiades*). Two chapters, 3.9 and 4.6, are devoted to philosophical topics familiar from the Platonic dialogues; the former begins with discussion of whether courage is a natural gift or acquired by teaching, a spe-cific instance of the question which begins *Meno* and is prom-inent in *Protagoras*, and in the course of the chapter (sections 4–5) Xenophon reports that Socrates identified wisdom first with self-control and then with justice and the rest of virtue. That too links this chapter with *Meno* and *Protagoras*, in both of which Socrates defends the thesis that virtue is knowledge. In 4.6 the topic is definition; as in several Platonic dialogues Socrates identifies the question 'What is such-and-such?' (e.g. 'What is justice?') as the primary philosophical question, illus-trating the general point by the examples of piety (discussed in *Euthyphro*) and courage (discussed in *Laches*). In section 6 he asserts the 'Socratic paradox' familiar from *Meno*, *Gorgias*, and *Protagoras* that no one knows what he should do but fails to do it, and in section 11 he makes the related claim that those who know how to deal properly with danger are courageous and those who make mistakes cowardly, a thesis which Socrates argues for at *Protagoras* 359–60.

We can sum up by saying that while philosophy takes second

place in the *Memorabilia* to piety, morality, and practical advice, the philosophy which the work does contain is recognizably common to other Socratic writings, especially those of Plato. This raises the question whether we should treat Xenophon as an independent source for those elements of philosophical doctrine and method, thus strengthening the case for their attribution to the historical Socrates, or whether we should conclude that Xenophon's source is those very Socratic writings, above all Plato's. We have to tread cautiously. There are indeed some indications in Xenophon's writings of dependence on Plato. *Symposium* 8.32 contains a pretty clear reference to the speeches of Pausanias and Phaedrus in Plato's *Symposium*, and it is at least likely that the many earlier writings on the trial of Socrates, whom Xenophon refers to in *Apology* 1, include Plato's *Apology*.[2] There is nothing in the *Memorabilia* which so clearly points to a specific Platonic reference, and we are not justified in concluding that any similarity of subject-matter must be explained by Xenophon's dependence on Plato, rather than influence in the reverse direction, or reliance on a common source, including memory of the historical Socrates. (We have very little information about the dates of composition of the works of either Plato or Xenophon.) On the other hand, Xenophon left Athens two years before Socrates' death and did not return for more than thirty years. The bulk of his Socratic writings were written during this period of exile, in which he was cut off from personal contact with Athens and must therefore have relied on the writings of other Socratics, including Plato, to refresh his memory and deepen his knowledge of Socrates. Since the philosophical overlaps mentioned above could all be explained by Platonic influence, and since we must assume that Xenophon made some use of Plato's writings in his absence from Athens, the most prudent strategy is to acknowledge that the philosophical elements

---

[2] For details see P. A. Vander Waerdt, 'Socratic Justice and Self-Sufficiency: The Story of the Delphic Oracle in Xenophon's *Apology of Socrates*', *Oxford Studies in Ancient Philosophy*, 11 (1993), 1–48.

in the *Memorabilia* should not be treated as an independent source for the philosophy of the historical Socrates. Equally, we have no reason to suppose that either Xenophon's portrayal of Socrates' personality or his presentation of the content of his conversations is any more historically authentic than that of any other Socratic writer. He is indeed himself the interlocutor in one conversation (1.3.8–15), and in some other cases he says that he was present (e.g. 1.4, 2.4–5, 4.3), but in most cases he makes no such claim, and in any case the claim to have been present may itself be part of literary convention; he says that he attended the dinner-party depicted in his *Symposium* (Symp. 1.1), whose dramatic date is 422, when he was at most eight years old. Some of the conversations are clear instances of types current in Socratic literature, such as discussions with sophists (1.6, 2.1, 4.4) and cross-examinations of ambitious young men (3.1–6, 4.2–3). The presentation of Socrates' conversations in the *Memorabilia* may indeed owe something to memory of actual Socratic conversations, either Xenophon's own or the memory of others, but (a) we have no way of identifying which elements in the work have that source, and (b) it is clear that any such elements contribute to a work which is shaped by its general apologetic aim and by the literary conventions of the Socratic genre.

I conclude this section by considering another writer who, though not a writer of Socratic dialogues, has been held to be a source of independent information on the historical Socrates, namely Aristotle. (Aristotle did write dialogues, now lost, but there is nothing to suggest that they were Socratic in the sense of representing conversations of Socrates.) Unlike the others whom we have discussed, Aristotle had no personal acquaintance with Socrates, who died fifteen years before Aristotle was born. He joined Plato's Academy as a seventeen-year-old student in 367 and remained there for twenty years until Plato's death in 347. It is assumed that in that period he had personal association with Plato. There are numerous references to Socrates in his works; frequently the context makes it clear that he is referring to the character of Socrates portrayed in some Platonic work, for example, *Politics* 1261^{a}5–8, where he refers to Plato's *Republic* by name, saying 'There Socrates says that wives and children and possessions should be held in common'. Sometimes, however, the context indicates that Aristotle's intention is to refer to the historical Socrates, and it is with regard to some of these passages that we have to consider whether his presentation of Socrates may plausibly be thought to be independent of Plato's portrayal.

The crucial passage is *Metaphysics* 1078^{b}27–32, where Aristotle, discussing the antecedents of Plato's theory of Forms, says the following:

There are two things which may justly be ascribed to Socrates, inductive arguments and general definitions, for both are concerned with the starting-point of knowledge; Socrates did not, however, separate the universal or the definitions, but they [*i.e. Plato and his followers*] did, calling them the Forms of things.

Since Plato represents Socrates as maintaining the theory of separately existing Forms in several dialogues, notably *Phaedo* and *Republic*, and referring to it as something which is familiar to everyone taking part in the discussion (*Ph.* 76d, *Rep.* 507a–b), the information that Socrates did not in fact separate universals from their instances cannot have been derived from Aristotle's reading of Plato, and the inference is irresistible that its source was oral tradition in the Academy stemming ultimately from Plato himself. We do not have to suppose either that Aristotle was personally intimate with Plato, his senior by over forty years (though he is said to have been a favourite pupil, and he wrote a poem in praise of Plato), or that personal reminiscences of Socrates were a staple topic of discussion in the Academy. All that we need suppose is that some basic facts about the role of Socrates *vis-à-vis* Plato were common knowledge in the school. It would have been astonishing had that not been so, and the scepticism of some modern scholars on this point is altogether unreasonable. How much this tradition included, beyond the fact that Socrates did not separate the Forms, it is impossible to say. I find it plausible that it included the two positive assertions which Aristotle associates with that negative one, namely, that Socrates looked for universal definitions and that he used inductive arguments.

Plato

Socrates appears in every Platonic dialogue except the *Laws*, universally agreed to be Plato's last work. So, strictly speaking, all of Plato's writings, with the exception of the *Laws*, the *Apology* (which is not a dialogue), and the *Letters* (whose authenticity is disputed) are Socratic dialogues. There are, however, considerable variations in the presentation of the figure of Socrates over the corpus as a whole. In two dialogues acknowledged on stylistic grounds to be late works, the *Sophist* and the *Statesman*, Socrates appears only in the introductory conversation which serves to link those two dialogues to one another and to *Theaetetus*, while the role of the principal participant in the main conversation, normally assigned to Socrates, is assigned to a stranger from Elea (i.e. to a representative of the philosophy of Parmenides). The same situation occurs in two other late dialogues, *Timaeus* and its unfinished sequel *Critias*; in each case Socrates figures briefly in the introductory conversation and the main speaker is the person who gives his name to the dialogue. In *Parmenides* Socrates appears, uniquely, as a very young man, whose main role is to be given instruction in philosophical method by the elderly Parmenides. Even the dialogues where Socrates is the main speaker exhibit considerable variation in portrayal. Some give prominence to events in Socrates' life, notably *Symposium* and those works centred on his trial and death (*Euthyphro*, *Apology*, *Crito*, and *Phaedo*), but also (to a lesser extent) *Charmides*. Some, including those just mentioned, contain lively depictions of the personality of Socrates and of argumentative interchanges between him and others, with particular prominence given to sophists and their associates. In this group, besides those just mentioned, fall *Protagoras*, *Gorgias*, *Euthydemus*, *Meno*, *Republic* 1, *Hippias*

Major, Hippias Minor, Ion, Laches, and *Lysis*. In others again, though Socrates is the principal figure in the sense of directing the course of the discussion, he is much less of an individual personality, and more of a representative figure of philosophical authority, replacable, for all the difference it would make to the course of the discussion, by another; for example, the Eleatic Stranger (or, perhaps, Plato). Such seems to me (though this is a matter for individual judgement) the role of Socrates in *Republic* (except book 1), *Phaedrus, Cratylus, Theaetetus*, and *Philebus*. How is this plasticity in Plato's portrayal of Socrates to be accounted for, and what are its implications for the relation between that portrayal and the historical Socrates?

In the nineteenth century investigations of stylistic features of the dialogues by various scholars converged independently on the identification of six dialogues: *Sophist, Statesman, Philebus, Timaeus, Critias*, and *Laws*, as the latest works in the corpus, identified as such by resemblance in respect of various stylistic features to the *Laws*, which is attested by ancient sources to have been unfinished at Plato's death. This research also identified a further group of four dialogues: *Parmenides, Phaedrus, Republic*, and *Theaetetus*, as closer than other dialogues to the style of the late group, leading to the hypothesis that these constituted a middle group, written before the late group and after the others. Subsequent stylometric research, while confirming the division into three groups, has not succeeded in establishing any agreed order of composition within any group.[3] This discussion assumes the validity of these results.

For our purpose the most significant feature is the virtual disappearance of Socrates from the late group; he is absent from the *Laws* and from the main discussions of all the others except *Philebus*. His role in that dialogue is similar to that in the dialogues of the middle group with the exception of the anomalous *Parmenides*, where he is assigned the role of interlocutor to Parmenides. In *Philebus, Phaedrus, Republic*, and *Theaetetus*,

---

[3] For a useful summary of the evidence see C. H. Kahn, *Plato and the Socratic Dialogue* (Cambridge, 1996), ch. 2.

though he has the leading role, it is rather as a mouthpiece for philosophical theory and an exponent of argumentative technique than as an individual in debate with other individuals. These distinctions are of course matters not only of judgement but also of degree. This is not to suggest that the figure of Socrates in the middle dialogues has no individual traits, or to deny that some of these link him with the figure portrayed in the early dialogues; thus, Socrates in the *Phaedrus* goes barefoot (229a) and hears his divine voice warning him against breaking off the discussion prematurely (242b–c). Moreover, even in the early dialogues the figure of Socrates has a representative role, that of the true philosopher. But what is quite clear is that Plato's interest in the personality of Socrates as the ideal embodiment of philosophy changes in the course of his career as a writer. At the outset that personality is paramount, but gradually its importance declines, and the figure of Socrates comes to assume the depersonalized role of spokesman for Plato's philosophy, to the point where it is superseded by avowedly impersonal figures such as the Eleatic Stranger and the Athenian of the *Laws*. What follows will be concerned primarily with the depiction of Socrates in the dialogues of the early period.

That depiction, it must be re-emphasized, belongs to the genre of 'Socratic conversations', and our earlier warnings against the assumption of naïve historicism apply to it as much as they do to the writings of Xenophon and the other Socratics. Unlike Xenophon, Plato never claims to have been present at any conversation which he depicts. He does indicate that he was present at Socrates' trial (*Apol.* 34a, 38b), which I take to be the truth, but we saw that that did not justify taking the *Apology* as a transcript of Socrates' actual speech. In one significant case he says explicitly that he was not present; when at the beginning of the *Phaedo* Phaedo tells Echecrates the names of those who were with Socrates on his last day he adds 'Plato I think was ill' (59b). The effect of this is to distance Plato from the narrative; the eye-witness is not the author himself, but one of his characters, Phaedo, hence that eye-witness's claims are to be interpreted as part of the dramatic context. It follows that what is narrated, for example, that Socrates argued for the immortality of the soul from the theories of Forms and of Recollection, is part of the dramatic fiction. I am inclined to think that Plato's claim to have been absent from Socrates' final scene is as much a matter of literary convention as Xenophon's claims to have been present at Socratic conversations, and that in all probability Plato was actually present.

In some cases (*Charmides, Protagoras*) the conversation is represented as having taken place before Plato was born, and in others (*Euthyphro, Crito, Symposium*) the *mise-en-scène* precludes his presence. Mostly the dialogues contain no claim that they are records of actual conversations, and where that claim is made in particular cases, as in the *Symposium* (172a–174a), the claim is itself part of an elaborate fiction, in which the narrator explains how he is able to describe a conversation at which he was not himself present. The central point is that, for Plato's apologetic and philosophical purposes, historical truth was almost entirely irrelevant; for instance, the main point of the dialogues in which Socrates confronts sophists is to bring out the contrast between his genuine philosophizing and their counterfeit, and in so doing to manifest the injustice of the calumny which, by associating him with the sophists, had brought about his death. For that purpose it was entirely indifferent whether Socrates ever actually met Protagoras or Thrasymachus, or, if he did, whether the conversations actually were on the lines of those represented in *Protagoras* and *Republic* 1. As with Xenophon, it may be that Plato makes some use of actual reminiscence; but we cannot tell where, and it does not in any case matter.

So far we have considered as a single group all those dialogues which stylometric criteria indicate as earlier than the 'middle group': *Parmenides, Phaedrus, Republic*, and *Theaetetus*. Within that group any differentiation has to appeal to non-stylometric criteria. Here Aristotle's evidence is crucial. Accepting as historical his assertion that Socrates did not separate the Forms, we can identify those dialogues from the stylistically early group in which Socrates maintains the theory of

Forms, viz. *Phaedo*, *Symposium*, and *Cratylus*, as dialogues where, in that respect at least, the Socrates of the dialogue is not the historical Socrates. This result can now be supplemented by some conjectures about the likely course of Plato's philosophical development which have at least reasonable plausibility.

It is reasonable to see in the attribution of the theory of Forms to Socrates a stage in the process of the transformation of Socrates into an authoritative figure who speaks more directly for Plato than does the Socrates of his earlier writings. This is indicated by some other features of these dialogues. The *Symposium* puts a good deal of emphasis on the individual personality of Socrates, starting with his unusually smart turn-out for the dinner-party (174a) and his late arrival as a result of having stopped on the way to think out a problem (174d–175b, a mini-version of the trance at Potidaea referred to later in the dialogue (220c–d)), and culminating with Alcibiades' eulogy, which puts it squarely in the Socratic 'Alcibiades dialogue' tradition. But Socrates has another role in the dialogue, that of a spokesman who reports the speech of a wise woman, Diotima, to whom belongs the account of the educational role of love, culminating in the vision of the Form of Beauty (201d–212c). So, strictly, Socrates does not himself maintain the theory, but speaks on behalf of someone else who does. I think that Plato uses this device to mark the transition from the Socrates of historical fact and of the tradition of the Socratic genre (not explicitly distinguished from one another) to what we might call the Platonic Socrates. Socrates speaking with the words of Diotima is a half-way stage to the Socrates of *Phaedo* and *Republic*, who has now incorporated the theory of Forms as his own. As regards *Phaedo*, we saw that Socrates' death depicted there was not his actual death, and it was suggested that Plato has signalled that the narrative does not reproduce what Socrates actually said. Another indication of this is the concluding myth of the fate of the soul after death, where Socrates steps out of his own person to tell what 'is said thus' (107d). The subject-matter of *Cratylus*, in particular its interest in linguistic meaning and Heraclitean theories of flux, links it firmly to *Theaetetus* and *Sophist*, to which it can plausibly be seen as a prelude.

Besides the theory of Forms, two other doctrines which it is reasonable to ascribe to Plato are those of the tripartite soul, which does not appear earlier than the middle period *Republic* and *Phaedrus*, and the theory of recollection, which is plausibly ascribed to Pythagorean influences encountered on his first visit to Sicily in 387 and which is closely linked to the theory of Forms, explicitly in *Phaedo* and *Phaedrus* and, arguably, implicitly in *Meno*. Also closely linked to recollection is the theory of reincarnation, which is the central topic of the great myths of the afterlife which conclude *Phaedo* and *Republic*, is indicated, though not particularly prominently, in the myth in *Gorgias*, is prominent in the myth in *Phaedrus*, and occurs in some of the arguments of *Meno* and *Phaedo*. My suggestion is that the Socrates who maintains these doctrines is a figure through whom Plato speaks, to a steadily increasing degree, his own words in the voice of Socrates.

This leaves us with a group of stylistically early dialogues in which Socrates does not maintain any of the doctrines which I have identified as specifically Platonic: the theory of Forms, the tripartite account of the soul, recollection, and reincarnation. Leaving out of account the two *Alcibiades* dialogues as probably spurious, and *Menexenus* on account of the fact that it is in essence not a Socratic dialogue but a parody of a funeral oration, these are: *Apology, Euthyphro, Crito, Charmides, Laches, Lysis, Ion, Euthydemus, Protagoras*, and the two *Hippias* dialogues (of which the authenticity of *Hippias Major* is also disputed). To these should be added *Gorgias* and *Meno* as, probably, transitional works containing features linking them both to the early group and to the middle 'Platonic' dialogues. This is not to say that the Socrates of these dialogues *is* the historical Socrates. Plato, like every other Socratic writer, has from the outset concerns to which historical truth is incidental; in Plato's case these are the defence of Socrates and the presentation of Socratic argument as a paradigm of philosophy. These dialogues do, however, present a picture of Socrates which is coherent both psychologically and (to a reasonable extent, though not wholly) doctrinally. Moreover, that picture is closer to the historical reality to this extent: first, that the kind of discussion which is there presented is probably more like actual Socratic conversations than the more technical argumentation of, say, *Theaetetus*, and secondly, that the Socrates in these dialogues carries a lighter burden of Platonic doctrine.

As far as Plato's portrayal of Socrates is concerned, there is no sharp line to be drawn between 'the historical Socrates' and 'the Platonic Socrates'. The Platonic Socrates is simply Plato's presentation of Socrates in his writings. That presentation, as I hope the foregoing sketch has indicated, undergoes an intelligible development from the portrayal of a highly individual personality engaged in a highly characteristic kind of philosophical activity to the mere ascription of the label 'Socrates' to the lay figure which represents Plato's opinions. The earliest stage of that process, though closer to historical reality, is never a simple depiction of it, and the transition from that stage to a more 'Platonic' stage is continuous, not a sharp cut-off.

The next chapter examines the content of that early stage of the presentation of Socrates. Two presuppositions of this discussion should be made explicit. The first is that, while critical examination of the views of others is Socrates' principal method of enquiry, the aim of that method is at least sometimes to provide arguments in support of certain theses which Socrates maintains, not merely to reveal inconsistency among the beliefs of those to whom he is talking.[4] The second is that the dialogues should not be read in isolation from one another. Some contemporary scholars, reviving the view maintained in the nineteenth century by Grote, suggest that there should be no greater expectation of consistency of doctrine or of the pursuit of common themes in the Platonic dialogues than in

[4] I argue briefly for this general claim in *Plato, Protagoras* (2nd edn.; Oxford, 1991), pp. xiv–xvi, and more fully for specific instances of it in ch. 4 of this volume.

the corpus of a dramatist such as Sophocles. I believe, on the contrary, that Plato throughout portrays Socrates engaged as a philosopher in the search for truth and understanding, and that the individual works which make up that portrayal may therefore be expected to give a coherent picture of his philosophical activity. That is not, of course, to deny that Plato can represent Socrates as changing his mind, or to deny that his portrayal of Socrates changes to reflect shifts in his own philosophical standpoint (some such changes are discussed in the next chapter). All that I am maintaining is that Plato presents Socrates as seeking to work out a broadly coherent position, against the background of which changes and developments have to be seen and explained.

4 Plato's Socrates

As indicated at the end of the last chapter, we shall be considering the portrayal of Socrates' doctrines and methods of argument in twelve dialogues plus *Apology*. The following features are common to all or most of these dialogues.

i. *Characterization of Socrates*. Socrates is predominantly characterized, not as a teacher, but as an enquirer. He disclaims wisdom, and seeks, normally in vain, elucidation of problematic questions from his interlocutors, by the method of elenchus, that is, by critically examining their beliefs. In some dialogues, notably *Protagoras* and *Gorgias*, the questioning stance gives way to a more authoritative tone.

ii. *Definition*. Many of the dialogues are concerned with the attempt to define a virtue or other ethically significant concept. *Euthyphro* asks 'What is holiness or piety?', *Charmides* 'What is temperance?', *Laches* 'What is courage?', *Hippias Major* 'What is fineness or beauty?' Both *Meno*, explicitly, and *Protagoras*, implicitly, consider the general question 'What is virtue or excellence?' In all these dialogues the discussion ends in ostensible failure, with Socrates and his interlocutor(s) acknowledging that they have failed to find the answer to the central question; in some cases there are textual indications of what the correct answer is.

iii. *Ethics*. All these dialogues are concerned with ethics in the broad sense of how one should live. Besides those dialogues which seek definitions, *Crito* deals with a practical ethical problem: should Socrates try to escape from prison after his sentence; and both *Gorgias* and *Euthydemus* examine what the aims of life should be. The only ostensible exception is *Ion*, which is an examination of the claim of a professional reciter of poetry to possess wisdom. But even that ties in closely with the general ethical interest of these dialogues, since the debunking of Ion's claims to wisdom has the implication that both poets and their interpreters are directed, not by wisdom, but by non-rational inspiration, and hence that poetry has no claim to the central educational role which Greek tradition ascribed to it. This little dialogue should be seen as an early essay on the topic which preoccupies much of Plato's writing, namely, the aims of education and the proper qualifications of the educator.

iv. *Sophists.* In several of these dialogues, namely, the *Hippias* dialogues, *Protagoras*, *Gorgias*, *Euthydemus*, and *Meno*, that topic is pursued via the portrayal of a confrontation between Socrates on the one hand and various sophists and/or their pupils and associates on the other. These dialogues thereby develop the apologetic project enunciated in the *Apology*.

These topics will now be considered in more detail.

Socrates' disavowal of wisdom

That Socrates denied having any knowledge, except the knowledge that he had no knowledge, became a catchword in antiquity. But that paradoxical formulation is a clear misreading of Plato. Though Socrates frequently says that he does not know the answer to the particular question under discussion, he never says that he knows nothing whatever, and indeed he makes some emphatic claims to knowledge, most notably in the *Apology*, where he twice claims to know that abandoning his divine mission would be bad and disgraceful (29b, 37b). What he does disavow is having any wisdom (*Apol.* 21b), and consequently he denies that he educates people, clearly understanding education as handing on a body of wisdom or learning (19d–20c). Given his assertions in the *Apology* that only god is truly wise and human wisdom is nothing in comparison to that true wisdom (23a–b), the denial of wisdom might be understood as simply the acceptance of human limitations. To possess wisdom would be to have the complete and totally perspicuous understanding of everything which is the prerogative of god. Neither Socrates nor anyone else can hope to aspire to that, and in denying that he has it Socrates is simply setting his face against a human arrogance which is none the less blasphemous for being virtually universal.

But while the devaluation of human wisdom as such is indeed a strain in the *Apology*, in denying that he possesses wisdom and, consequently, that he teaches people, Socrates is contrasting his own condition, not with the divine wisdom, but with a human paradigm of wisdom. This paradigm is realized by craftsmen such as builders and shoemakers who, he acknowledges (22d–e) do possess wisdom in the sense that they are masters of their craft, though they go wrong in thinking that their special expertise extends to matters outside the scope of the craft. This expertise is a structured body of knowledge which is systematically acquired and communicated to others, by possession of which the expert is able reliably to solve the practical problems posed by the craft and to explain the grounds of their solution. The sophists claimed to possess, and to teach to others, such an expertise applying to overall success in social and personal life, the 'political craft' (*politikē technē*) (*Prot.* 319a, *Apol.* 19d–20c). Though Socrates rejects these claims, it is not on the ground that such expertise is not available to human beings, but on the ground that the sophists' activity fails to meet the ordinary criteria for being a genuine expertise, for example, that of being systematically learned and taught (*Prot.* 319d–320b, *Meno* 89c–94e). He denies that he possesses this expertise himself (*Apol.* 20c), but does not say that it is impossible that he, or anyone, could possess it.

There is, then, no ground to assume that Socrates' disavowal of knowledge is an instance of what has become known as 'Socratic irony', that is, pretended ignorance for dialectical purposes. Socrates does indeed frequently pose as admiring the supposedly superior knowledge of the person he is talking to (e.g. *Euthyph.* 5a–b, where he says that he ought to take instruction from Euthyphro on how to defend himself against Meletus' accusation), but the reader, at any rate, is clearly not supposed to be taken in; on the contrary, these avowals serve to point up the particularly controversial character of what the interlocutor has said, or the dubiousness of his claim to authority. The context of the *Apology*, however, rules out any such dialectical function for the disavowal of knowledge. Socrates is not there posing as deferring to a supposed, but actually bogus, epistemic authority; he is with perfect sincerity matching his own epistemic state against an appropriate paradigm, and finding it wanting.

If the disavowal of knowledge is in fact the disavowal of wisdom or expertise, we can see how that disavowal is compatible with the particular claims to knowledge which Socrates makes. The non-expert can know some particular things, but not in the way that the expert knows them; specifically those particular items of knowledge do not fit into a comprehensive web of knowledge which allows the expert to provide explanations of their truth by relating them to other items and/or to the structure as a whole. But how does the non-expert know those things? Usually, by having been told, directly or indirectly, by an expert. Socrates does not, however, recognize any experts, at least human experts, in matters of morality. So how does he know, for example, that he must not abandon his mission to philosophize, whatever the cost? A possible answer is that he has been told this by god, who is an expert in morality. But, leaving aside questions (suggested by *Euthyphro*) of how he knows that god is an expert in morality, that is not in fact an answer which is given or even suggested in *Apology* or elsewhere.

One might attempt to dissolve the problem by suggesting that Socrates does not intend to claim knowledge of these things, but merely to express his beliefs. But Plato makes him *say* that he knows them, so why should we suppose that Plato does not represent him as meaning what he says? As we have seen, Socrates does indeed recognize an ideal epistemic paradigm which he fails to satisfy, yet he claims knowledge in particular cases. The suggestion being considered amounts to this, that satisfaction of the paradigm is to be equated with knowledge, while the epistemically less satisfactory state which Socrates is in is to be relegated to that of belief. But the distinction between paradigm-satisfying and epistemically inferior states can be maintained without denying the latter the title of knowledge, by using the distinction between the expert's integrated knowledge and the non-expert's fragmentary knowledge. (We might, if we choose, talk of the former as knowledge 'strictly speaking' and the latter as knowledge 'for ordinary purposes' or 'in a loose and popular sense'. Plato does not in fact use such locutions, but the essential distinction is unaltered.) We are, then, still left with the question how Socrates, an avowed non-expert in matters of morality, knows the particular moral truths which he claims to know.

The straightforward, though perhaps disappointing, answer is that Socrates does not say how he knows those truths. Consideration of his argumentative practice may give us some clues. Often his arguments seem intended to do no more than reveal that his interlocutor has inconsistent beliefs about some matter on which he purports to have knowledge, and thereby to undermine that claim to knowledge, as Socrates describes himself in the *Apology* as doing. But at least sometimes he clearly thinks that, provided his interlocutor maintains nothing but what he sincerely believes, the critical examination of those beliefs will reveal, not merely inconsistency among them, but the falsehood of some belief. A particularly clear case is the claim of Polus and Callicles in *Gorgias* that it is better to do wrong than to suffer it. Socrates claims (479e) that the critical arguments by which he has led Polus to accept the contrary thesis that it is worse to do wrong than to suffer it have proved that the latter is true, and asserts even more emphatically at the end of the argument with Callicles (508e–509a) that that conclusion has been 'tied down with arguments of iron and adamant' (i.e. of irresistible force). Yet this very strong claim is conjoined with a disavowal of knowledge: 'My position is always the same, that I do not know how these things are, but no one I have ever met, as in the present case, has been able to deny them without making himself ridiculous.'

Here we have a contrast between expert knowledge, which Socrates disavows, and a favourable epistemic position produced by repeated application of the elenchus. There are some propositions which repeated experiment shows no one to be capable of denying without self-contradiction. Commitment to these is always in principle provisional, since there is always the theoretical possibility that someone might come up with a new argument which might allow escape even from the 'arguments of iron and adamant', as Socrates acknowledges (509a2–4). But realistically, Socrates clearly believes, the arguments rely on principles which are so firmly entrenched that there is no practical possibility of anyone's denying them. Might the truths which Socrates knows non-expertly be truths which he has thus established via the elenchus? While that is an attractive suggestion, we have to acknowledge that it has no clear textual confirmation. In *Crito* (49a) the fundamental proposition that one must never act unjustly is said to be one which Socrates and Crito have often agreed on, and that agreement is to bind them in considering the propriety of Socrates' attempting to escape from prison. The implication is, surely, that the agreement was based on reasons which are still in force; otherwise why should Socrates and Crito not change their minds? But there is nothing to suggest that those reasons took the form of elenchus of Socrates' and Crito's beliefs.

Our conclusion has to be that, though Socrates treats elenchus of the interlocutor's belief as sometimes revealing truth, and though the achieving of truth by that means provides a possible model for non-expert knowledge, we are not justified in attributing to Socrates the claim that all non-expert moral knowledge is in fact achieved via that method. He gives some indication that he knows some moral truths on the strength of having a good argument for them, but he gives no general account of the conditions for non-expert moral knowledge.

Gorgias is the dialogue which provides the clearest cases in which the elenchus is seen as leading to the discovery of truth, and it is probably not coincidental that in the same dialogue we find Socrates abandoning his stance as a non-expert questioner and claiming expertise. One of the themes of the dialogue is the role of rhetoric in education, that is, in promoting the good life. Socrates sets up a taxonomy of genuine crafts concerned respectively with the good of the soul and that of the body, and of counterfeits corresponding to each (463a–465a). The generic name for the craft concerned with the good of the soul is *politikē*, the art of life, subdivided into legislation, which promotes the good of the soul (as gymnastics promotes the good of the body), and justice, which preserves it (as medicine preserves the good of the body). Rhetoric is the bogus counterpart of *politikē*, since the aim of the orator is not to promote people's good, but to pander to their wishes by enabling them to get what they want through the power of persuasion. It thus promotes, not the genuinely good life, but a spurious appearance of it, as cosmetics is the skill, not of making people actually healthy, but of making them look healthy (465c). *Politikē* is thus a genuine expertise, and in striking contrast to his stance in the *Apology* we find Socrates not merely claiming that he practises it, but that no one else does (521d), since he alone cares for the good of his fellow-citizens.

This conception of Socrates as the only genuine practitioner of *politikē* recurs in an image at the conclusion of *Meno* (99e–100a), where Socrates sums up the conclusion of the argument that goodness cannot be taught, but is acquired by a divine gift without intelligence 'unless there were one of the *politikoi* who was capable of making someone else *politikos*' (i.e. unless there were someone who could pass his expertise in the art of life on to another, as conventional politicians have shown themselves incapable of doing). He goes on to say that such a man would be like Homer's description of Tiresias in the underworld (in the *Odyssey*): 'He alone of those in Hades is alive, and the rest flit about like shadows.' This reference to Odysseus' visit to the underworld in *Odyssey* 11 picks up the description of Socrates' meeting with the sophists in *Protagoras*, where Socrates refers to the sophists by quoting the words of Odysseus (315b–c), thereby casting himself as a living man and the sophists as shadows (i.e. ghosts). He is then the real expert in the art of life 'the real thing with respect to goodness, compared with shadows' (*Meno* 100a), who has (in *Meno* and *Protagoras*) a positive conception of the nature of goodness and (in *Meno*) a new method of transmitting that conception to others. This is the method of recollection, in which knowledge which the soul has possessed from all eternity but forgotten in the process of reincarnation is revived via the process of critical examination.

The development of this more authoritative figure of Socrates is a feature of dialogues which we identified as transitional between the earlier 'Socratic' dialogues and the dialogues of Plato's middle period. It is a particular instance of the gradual metamorphosis of the figure of Socrates into the representative of Plato which we noted earlier.

Definition

Socrates' interest in definitions arises from his quest for expertise. The expert knows about his or her subject, and according to Socrates the primary knowledge concerning any subject is precisely knowledge of what that subject is. The connection with expertise is made explicit in *Hippias Major* (286c–d), where Socrates tells Hippias how, when he was praising some things as fine and condemning others as disgraceful, he was rudely challenged by someone who said, 'How do you know what sorts of thing are fine and what sorts disgraceful? Tell me, could you say what fineness is?' Being unable to meet this challenge he consults Hippias, whose universal expertise includes, as 'a small and unimportant part', knowledge of what fineness is; if Hippias were unable to answer that question his activity would be 'worthless and inexpert' (286e).

The primacy of the 'What is such-and-such?' question is emphasized in a number of dialogues. The general pattern of argument is that some specific question concerning a subject, which is the actual starting-point of discussion, for example, how one is to acquire goodness, is problematic in the absence of an agreed conception of what that subject, in this case goodness, is. Hence, though the specific question is psychologically prior, in that that is where one actually begins the enquiry, the 'What is X?' question is epistemologically prior, in the sense that it is impossible to answer the former without having answered the latter, but not vice versa. The problematic question may be of various kinds. In *Laches* (189d–190d) it is how a particular virtue, courage, is to be inculcated, while in *Meno* (70a–71b) and *Protagoras* (329a–d, 360e–361a) it is the generalization of that question to goodness as such. In *Republic* 1 (354b–c) it is whether justice is advantageous to its possessor. In *Euthyphro* (4b–5d) it is whether a particular disputed case, Euthyphro's prosecution of his father for homicide, is or is not an instance of piety or holiness. Similarly, at *Charm.* 158c–159a the question of whether Charmides has self-control is treated as problematic, and therefore as requiring prior consideration of what self-control is.

The pattern exhibited by the last two examples, in which the question 'Is this an instance of property F?' is said to be unsettleable without a prior answer to the question 'What is F?' has given rise to the accusation that Socrates is guilty of what has been dubbed 'the Socratic fallacy', namely, maintaining that it is impossible to tell whether anything is an instance of any property unless one is in possession of a definition of that property. That thesis would be disastrous for Socrates to maintain, not merely because it is open to countless counter-examples (e.g. we can all tell that a five-pound note is an instance of money even if we are unable to give a definition of money), but because Socrates' approved strategy for reaching a definition is to consider what instances of the kind or property in question have in common (e.g. *Meno* 72a–c). Obviously, if we cannot tell which are the instances of the kind or property in question in advance of giving the definition that procedure is futile, as is the procedure of rejecting a definition by producing a counter-example, for if you cannot tell whether any instance is an instance without a definition, equally you cannot tell whether any instance is not an instance without a definition. But since the production of counter-examples is one of the standard procedures of Socratic elenchus, the fallacy would be wholly destructive of Socrates' argumentative method.

In fact, Socrates is not committed to that methodologically self-destructive position. The most that the examples in *Euthyphro* and *Charmides* commit him to is that there are some, disputed, instances, where the question 'Is this an instance of F?' cannot be settled without answering the prior question 'What is F?' That claim does not commit him to maintaining that there are no undisputed cases, and so leaves it open to him to look for a property present in all the undisputed cases of F and absent from all the undisputed cases of non-F, and then to settle the disputed cases by determining whether that property applies to them. (In fact that procedure is bound to leave the dispute unsettled, because the original dispute is now transformed into a dispute over the propriety of widening the extension of the property from the undisputed to the disputed cases. That, however, is another question.)

Socrates' rude challenger in *Hippias Major* does, however, appear to go so far as to claim that it is impossible to tell whether any particular thing is fine before one has given a definition of fineness. When all Socrates' and Hippias' attempts at defining fineness have failed, Socrates imagines himself being confronted again by the challenger and asked, 'How will you know whether any speech has been finely put together, or any action whatever finely done, if you are ignorant of fineness? And if you are in that state, do you think you are better off alive than dead?' (304d–e). We cannot avoid the difficulty by saying simply that this is someone else's view, not Socrates', since Socrates makes it clear that the rude challenger is an alter ego; 'he happens to be very nearly related to me and lives in the same house' (304d). Yet the rude challenger's view is not one which Socrates simply endorses, for he concludes (304e) by saying that he thinks he knows that the proverb 'Fine things are difficult' is true; but on the challenger's account he could not be in a position to know even that. The challenger's view, then, is not after all Socrates' own; it is very closely related to it, indeed (and thereby likely to be confused with it), and constitutes a challenge in that, if accepted, it would overthrow Socrates' entire argumentative methodology. Hence the challenge is to distinguish that view from Socrates' actual, more modest view that there are some difficult cases which cannot be settled without the ability to give a definition. To be an expert in an area is to be able to tell reliably, for disputed and undisputed cases alike, whether any case is an instance of the property or kind in question, and for that, according to Socrates, it is necessary, as well as sufficient, to be able to say what the property or kind is.

The examples from *Laches*, *Meno*, *Protagoras*, and *Republic* 1 exhibit another pattern; here the question which gives rise to the quest for the definition of a property is not whether a given, disputed, instance falls under it, but whether that property itself has some further property, specifically whether justice is beneficial to its possessor, and whether courage and overall goodness (i.e. the possession of all the virtues, courage, self-control, justice, wisdom, etc.) can be taught. At *Meno* 71b Socrates gives an analogy for this pattern of the priority of definition which suggests that it is the most basic platitude. If I don't know at all who Meno is, I can't know whether he has any property, for example, whether he is rich or handsome. Similarly, if I don't know at all what goodness is, there is no possibility of my knowing anything about it, including how it is to be acquired.

Understood in a particular way, this is indeed a platitude. If I have never heard of Meno, the appropriate reply to the question 'Is Meno handsome?' is 'Sorry, I don't know whom you mean.' Similarly, if I have no idea what goodness is, the appropriate reply to 'Can goodness be taught?' is 'Sorry, I don't know what you're talking about.' Here we have cases where a prerequisite of intelligible speech about a subject, that one should be able to identify the subject, is not fulfilled. Clearly, that prerequisite of intelligible speech does not require the ability to give a definition of the subject. In the case of an individual subject such as Meno one does not have to be in possession of any specification

of Meno which uniquely specifies him independently of context;
one might, for instance, be able to identify him only ostensively
as 'That man over there', or indefinitely as 'Someone I met in a
pub last year'. The analogue in the case of a universal such as
goodness is no more than the minimal requirement to know
what we are talking about when we use the word; but that again
does not presuppose the ability to give a verbal specification (i.e.
a definition) of the universal. To return to our earlier example, I
can know what I am talking about when I use the word 'money',
even if I am unable to give a definition of money; it is clearly
enough that I can, for instance, recognize standard instances.
Now, in that sense it is clear that Meno knows what he is talking
about from the very start; otherwise he could not even raise his
initial question 'Can goodness be taught?' So the platitude that
intelligible speech about any subject requires the ability to
identify that subject does not point towards the priority of
definition. Why, then, does Socrates insist on that priority
even though the condition which the platitude specifies is
satisfied?

To answer that question we need to observe that in *Laches*,
Meno, and *Protagoras* the search for the definition of particular
virtues and inclusive goodness is prompted by the practical
question of how those qualities are to be acquired. What kind of
definition of those qualities is demanded by the practical question? Clearly, something more than the bare ability to know
what one is talking about is demanded, because, as we have
seen, that ability is presupposed by the asking of the practical
question itself. It is tempting to suggest that what more is
required is just the ability to elucidate the dictionary meaning
of the term designating the quality under discussion. In the case
of the Greek term which I have rendered distributively as 'virtue' and collectively as 'goodness' (*aretē*), a reasonably accurate
specification of its meaning would be:

1 An attribute of an agent, one of a set of attributes severally
   necessary and jointly sufficient for the attainment of overall
   success in life;
2 The set of attributes specified under 1.

How is the ability to give that elucidation demanded by the practical question? It does indeed advance the enquiry to the extent of making it clear that the search is for properties which promote success in life, but it gives no indication what properties those are, nor, crucially, how those properties are to be acquired. People could agree on that definition but disagree radically in their answers to the practical question, if, for instance, some thought that the properties which bring success in life are all gifts of nature such as intelligence and noble lineage, while others thought that they could all be acquired through practice like practical abilities. The practical question thus appears to demand a different kind of definition from the elucidation of the meaning of the term which designates the property; it demands a substantive specification of what that property is. A substantive specification will include both the decomposition of a complex of properties into the components of that complex (e.g. goodness consists of justice, self-control, etc.) and explanatory accounts of those properties (e.g. self-control consists in the control of the bodily appetites by reason). That is to say, it provides a theory of goodness, which explains it by identifying its constituents and causes, and thereby indicates appropriate methods of acquiring it.

That the definitions sought are of this substantive kind chimes in well with the demand that the giving of definitions is what characterizes the expert. The expert on goodness should be able to explain what goodness is with a view to providing reliable guidance on how to acquire and maintain goodness, just as the expert on health should be able to explain what health is with a view to providing reliable guidance on how to become and stay healthy. The texts of the dialogues mentioned above provide some confirmation that the definitions sought are of this kind, though it would be an oversimplification to pretend that they are distinguished with total clarity from elucidations of the meanings of the terms designating the properties in question.

That Socrates' search is for substantive rather than purely

conceptual or 'analytic' definitions is indicated by those dialogues which either explicitly identify or suggest the identification of goodness with knowledge or some other cognitive
state. The most detailed discussion occurs in *Meno* (suggested
above to be transitional between 'Socratic' and 'Platonic'). At
75–6 Socrates attempts to explain to Meno that he is looking
not for lists of specific virtues such as courage and self-control
but for a specification of what those virtues have in common,
and illustrates this by giving two model specifications, first of
shape and then of colour. Of these, the former is a conceptual
elucidation, namely, that shape is the limit of a solid, and the
second a 'scientific' account of colour (based on the theory of
the fifth-century philosopher Empedocles) as a stream of particles flowing out from the perceived object, of appropriate
size and shape to pass through channels in the eye to the
internal perceptive organ. Socrates gives no clear indication
that he regards these specifications as of different kinds;
he says that he prefers the former, but does not indicate
why, except that he describes the latter as 'high-flown',
perhaps indicating that it is inferior because it is couched in
over-elaborate technical terminology. Despite this expressed
preference for what is in fact a conceptual elucidation over a
substantive definition, Socrates then goes on to propose an
account of goodness of the latter kind, namely, that goodness
is knowledge. This is not itself an elucidation of the concept
of goodness, as specified above, though it does depend on a
conceptual thesis, that goodness is advantageous to its possessor (in Greek, that *aretē* is *ōphelimon*, 87e). Rather, it is the
identification of knowledge as that state which is in fact
necessary and/or sufficient for success in life, and it is arrived
at not purely by considering the meanings of words but by the
adducing of a highly general thesis about how success is
achieved. The thesis is that since every other desirable property, such as strength or boldness, can lead to disaster, the
only unconditionally good thing is that which provides the
proper direction of those qualities, namely, intelligence,
which is equated with knowledge (87d–89c). Again, Socrates is

led ostensibly to abandon that account in favour of the revised suggestion that goodness is not knowledge but true belief (89c–97c) by consideration of the alleged empirical fact that there are no experts in goodness, as there would have to be if goodness were some kind of knowledge (another conceptual thesis). In Socrates' arguments conceptual theses and general empirical claims about human nature mesh to provide the best available theory of what goodness really is, that is, of what property best fits the specification set out in the elucidation of the concept given above.

In *Meno*, then, the practical question of how goodness is acquired leads to a substantive account of goodness as a cognitive state. It is no coincidence that the two other dialogues which begin from that question, either about goodness in general (*Protagoras*) or about a particular virtue (courage in *Laches*), exhibit a similar pattern of development. In *Protagoras* Socrates' young friend Hippocrates begins by assuming that the way to acquire goodness is to be taught it by Protagoras, but the sophist's conception of goodness as a cluster of only contingently connected attributes is rejected in favour of what is in effect a version of the theory proposed in *Meno*, that goodness is knowledge. In *Laches* the question of how courage is to be acquired leads, after the rejection of various alternative suggestions, to a specific version of the theory that goodness is knowledge, namely, that courage is knowledge of what is and what is not to be feared (194e–195a). This is eventually rejected on the grounds that, since what is and what is not to be feared is identical with what is and what is not bad, courage will then just be the knowledge of what is and what is not bad. But since, on this cognitive account, that is precisely what goodness as a whole is, courage will be identical with goodness as a whole, instead of a part of it, as was the original hypothesis (198a–199e). Hence the dialogue ends with the admission that the participants have failed in their search for what courage is. Commentators disagree on whether this inconclusive outcome is to be taken at face value, and, if not, which of the assumptions which lead to it should be abandoned. The significant point to observe is that here again the practical question leads not merely to a substantive account of the property in question but towards the same account as is canvassed in *Meno* and *Protagoras*.

I do not wish to suggest that at the time of writing these dialogues Plato had a clear grasp of the distinction between purely conceptual definitions and the substantive type of account exemplified by the cognitive theory. The fact that even in the dialogue which discusses definition in greatest detail, *Meno*, which I assume to have one of the latest of the dialogues I discuss, he gives as model definitions an example of either kind without any explicit differentiation suggests that he had not arrived at any theoretical discrimination between the two. My suggestion is rather that his practice shows him favouring a kind of definition which we can characterize as substantive rather than conceptual, and that the practical orientation of the discussions leading to those definitions provides an explanation of that fact.

Sometimes the course of the dialogue is even less clearly indicated. In *Euthyphro* the initial question is 'What property is it in virtue of which things (especially kinds of actions) are holy?' When Euthyphro suggests (6e–7a) that it is the property of being approved of by the gods (which is very close to an elucidation of the ordinary Greek conception of *to hosion*), Socrates elicits from him the assertion that the gods approve of holy things *because they are holy* (10d). This excludes the possibility that holiness should be that very property of being approved of by the gods, and points the rest of the discussion in the direction of a search for the kind of conduct which attracts the gods' approval. Here too we may say that Socrates is groping towards a substantive account of holiness, in that the answer would have to be given in terms of a theory of human nature and its relation to the divine, but the dialogue provides no more than hints as to the detailed form of such a theory. The situation in *Charmides* is even less clear-cut, partly because the virtue under discussion, *sōphrosunē* (conventionally translated 'self-control', but sometimes better rendered 'soundness of mind'), is genuinely indeterminate between a style of behaviour and the mental and motivational state directing it. Hence the various suggestions that it is one kind or another of knowledge are less easy to classify as either conceptual elucidations or substantive accounts than the suggested definitions in *Laches*, *Meno*, and *Protagoras*.

Ethics

The search for definitions, then, is the search for expertise, and the possessor of expertise possesses a theory of the subject-matter of that expertise, a grasp of its nature which delivers answers to further questions, both theoretical and practical, about it. In the dialogues discussed in the previous section we see Socrates searching for such a theory applied to human goodness, in some cases a theory of one of the constituents of goodness, that is, an individual virtue (piety in *Euthyphro*, courage in *Laches*, and self-control in *Charmides*), in others (*Meno*, *Protagoras*) a theory of goodness as a whole. In all of these the search is, at least ostensibly, unsuccessful, in that each dialogue ends with the acknowledgement by Socrates and his interlocutors that they have not arrived at the account of goodness or of its parts which they were seeking. But there are some discernible differences. In the three dialogues dealing with individual virtues the discussion is more tentative, Socrates is not readily identified with any positive position, and it is at least plausible to accept the final impasse at its face value. In *Meno* and *Protagoras*, on the other hand, Socrates argues firmly for the thesis that virtue is knowledge, and it is plausible to think that the ostensibly aporetic conclusions are to be interpreted as not detracting from his commitment to that thesis. In these dialogues, it seems to me, Plato depicts Socrates not indeed as possessing the fully developed theory of goodness which is his goal but at least as having a grasp of its general shape. There is, then, even within the dialogues of definition, a development in the portrayal of Socrates from that of purely critical searcher to the proponent of theory (though not expert in the fullest sense). It is an open question whether this development is one within Plato's perception of the historical Socrates, or the first stage of a development from that perception to a presentation containing more of his own views.

The basis of the theory is the combination of the conception of goodness as that property which guarantees overall success in life with the substantive thesis that what in fact guarantees that success is knowledge of what is best for the agent. This in turn rests on a single comprehensive theory of human motivation, namely, that the agent's conception of what is overall best for him- or herself (i.e. what best promotes *eudaimonia*, overall success in life) is sufficient to motivate action with a view to its own realization. This motivation involves desire as well as belief; Socrates maintains (*Meno* 77c, 78b) that everyone desires good things, which in context has to be interpreted as the strong thesis that the desire for good is a standing motive, which requires to be focused in one direction or another via a conception of the overall good. Given that focus, desire is locked onto the target which is picked out by the conception, without the possibility of interference by conflicting desires. Hence all that is required for correct conduct is the correct focus, which has to be a correct conception of the agent's overall good.

On this theory motivation is uniform, and uniformly self-interested; every agent always aims at what he or she takes to be best for him- or herself, and failure to achieve that aim has to be explained by failure to grasp it properly, that is, by a cognitive defect, not by any defect of motivation. Socrates spells this out in *Protagoras*, on the assumption, which he attributes to people generally, that the agent's overall interest is to be defined in hedonistic terms, as the life which gives the best available balance of pleasure over distress. Given that assumption, it is nonsense to explain doing wrong by being overcome by pleasure or by any kind of desire; one must simply have made a mistake in one's estimation of what would bring the most pleasure. As Socrates says (358d), 'It is not in human nature to be prepared to go for what you think to be bad in preference to what is good.' There is considerable disagreement among commentators as to whether Socrates is represented as accepting the hedonistic assumption himself or merely as assuming it *ad hominem* to show that Protagoras has no view other than common opinion, but there is no doubt that, independently of that question, the view that the agent's conception of the good is the unique focus of motivation (maintained also in *Meno*) is Socrates' own. This account of goodness as knowledge thus issues directly in one of the claims for which Socrates was notorious in antiquity, the denial of the possibility of action against the agent's better judgement (*akrasia*); in Aristotle's words (*Nicomachean Ethics* 1145^{b}26–7) Socrates used to maintain that 'no one acts contrary to what is best in the belief that he is doing so, but through error', a thesis expressed more concisely in the slogan 'No one goes wrong intentionally' (*oudeis hekōn hamartanei* (*Prot.* 345e)).

Thus far the theory identifies goodness with the property which guarantees overall success in life, and identifies that property, via the motivational theory just described, with knowledge of what is best for the agent. But that theory lacks moral content; nothing in it shows or even suggests that what is best for the agent is to live a morally good life, as defined by the practice of the traditional virtues, including justice, with its implications of regard for others, and self-control, with its implications of the sacrifice of self-gratification. But if anything is characteristic of Socrates it is his insistence on the pre-eminence of morality. We saw that in the *Apology* he says that he knows that, come what may, he must not do wrong by disobeying the divine command to philosophize, and in *Crito* the fundamental thesis that one must never do wrong (or 'commit injustice' (*adikein*)) is the determining principle of his decision not to attempt escape from prison (49a–b). The link with the motivational thesis is established by the thesis that the best life for the agent is a life lived in accordance with the requirements of morality. Given that thesis, the slogan that no one goes wrong intentionally takes on the moral dimension that 'no one willingly does wrong (or 'acts unjustly'), but all who do wrong do so involuntarily' (or 'unintentionally') (*Gorg.* 509e), the full moral version of what has become known as the 'Socratic paradox'.

The thesis that the moral life is the best life *for the agent* thus has the central role of linking Socrates' intuitions of the pre-eminence of morality with the theory of uniform self-interested motivation which is the foundation of the identification of goodness with knowledge. It is the keystone of the entire arch. Given that centrality, it is surprising how little argumentative support it receives. At *Crito* 47e justice and injustice are described as respectively the health and sickness of the soul; hence, just as it is not worth living with a diseased and corrupted body, so it is not worth living with a diseased and corrupted soul. But that is not an argument. Even granted that health is an intrinsically desirable and disease an intrinsically undesirable state, the crucial claims that justice is the health of the soul, and injustice its disease, require defence, not mere assertion.

Plato supplies some arguments in *Gorgias*, but they are weak. Against Polus Socrates argues that successful tyrants, who, it is agreed, manifest the extremes of injustice, do not secure the best life for themselves, as Polus claims. On the contrary, they never get what they really want, because what they want is to do well for themselves, whereas their injustice is bad for them. The proof that it is bad for them (473a–475c) starts from Polus' admission that acting unjustly, while good (*agathon*) for the agent, is disgraceful (*aischron*). Socrates then secures agreement to the principle that whatever is disgraceful is so either because it is unpleasant, or because it is disadvantageous. Acting unjustly is clearly not unpleasant; hence by the above premisses it must be disadvantageous. Hence a life of injustice is bad for the agent. Of the many weaknesses of this argument the crucial one is its neglect of the relativity of the concepts. To be acceptable the first premiss must be read as 'Whatever is disgraceful to anyone, is so either because it is unpleasant to someone or because it is disadvantageous to someone.' Given that premiss, it obviously does not follow that, because injustice is not unpleasant to the unjust person it must be disadvantageous to that person; it could be disadvantageous to someone else, and its being so could be the ground of its being disgraceful to the unjust person. (Indeed, one of the main reasons why we think that injustice *is* disgraceful to the perpetrator is that it is typically harmful to someone else.) Later in the dialogue (503e–504d) Socrates argues against Callicles that, since the goodness of anything (e.g. a boat or a house) depends on the proper proportion and order of its components, the goodness of both body and soul must depend on the proper proportion and order of their components, respectively health for the body and justice and self-control for the soul. The parallelism of bodily health and virtue, which was simply asserted in *Crito*, is here supported by the general principle that goodness depends on organization of components, but that principle is insufficient to establish the parallelism. For the proper organization of components is itself determined by the function of the kind of thing in question; it is by considering that the function of a boat is to convey its occupants safely and conveniently by water that we determine whether its parts are put together well or badly. So in order to know which arrangement of psychological components such as intellect and bodily desires is optimum we need first to know what our aims in life ought to be. One conception of those aims may indeed identify the optimum organization as that defined by the conventional virtues, but another, for example, that of Don Juan or Gauguin, may identify a quite different organization, such as one which affords the maximum play to certain kinds of self-expression, as optimum.

The doctrine that virtue is knowledge is the key to understanding the so-called thesis of the Unity of the Virtues, maintained by Socrates in *Protagoras*. In that dialogue Protagoras assumes a broadly traditional picture of the virtues as a set of attributes distinct from one another, as, for example, the different bodily senses are distinct. A properly functioning human being has to have them all in proper working order, but it is possible to have some while lacking others; most notably, it is possible to possess conspicuous courage while being grossly deficient in respect of the other virtues (329d–e). Socrates suggests that, on the contrary, the names of the individual virtues, courage, self-control, etc., are all 'names of one and the same thing' (329c–d), and later in the dialogue makes it clear how that is to be understood by claiming (361b) that he has been 'trying to show that all things, justice, self-control, and courage, are knowledge'. The sense in which each of the virtues is knowledge is that, given the motivational theory sketched above, knowledge of what is best for the agent is necessary and sufficient to guarantee right conduct in whatever aspect of life that knowledge is applied to. We should not think of the individual virtues as different species of a generic knowledge; on that model piety is knowledge of religious matters and courage is knowledge to do with what is dangerous, and the two are as different as, for example, knowledge of arithmetic and knowledge of geometry, which are distinct species of mathematical knowledge, allowing the possibility that one might have one without the other. The Socratic picture is that there is a single integrated knowledge, knowledge of what is best for the agent, which is applied in various areas of life, and to which the different names are applied with reference to those different areas. Thus, courage is the virtue which reliably produces appropriate conduct in situations of danger, piety the virtue which reliably produces appropriate conduct in relation to the gods, etc., and the virtue in question is the same in every case, namely, the agent's grasp of his or her good.

It has been objected[1] that this integrated picture is inconsistent with Socrates' acceptance in *Laches* and *Meno* that the individual virtues are parts of total virtue. In *Laches*, indeed, the proposed definition of courage as knowledge of what is fearful and not (194e–195a) is rejected on the ground that on that account courage would just be the knowledge of what is good and bad. But then courage would be identical with virtue as a whole, whereas *ex hypothesi* courage is not the whole, but a

---

[1] The objection is urged by G. Vlastos in 'Socrates on "The Parts of Virtue"', in his *Platonic Studies* (2nd edn.; Princeton, NJ, 1981).

part of virtue (198a–199e). Given the aporetic nature of the dialogue, it is unclear whether at the time of writing Plato himself believed that the definition of courage was incompatible with the thesis that courage is a part of virtue, and, if so, whether he had a clear view on which should be abandoned. It is perfectly conceivable that he himself believed that they were not incompatible, and that the reader is being challenged to see that the rejection of the definition is not in fact required. What is clear is that the talk of parts of virtue can be given a straightforward interpretation which is compatible with the integrated picture. This is simply that total virtue extends over the whole of life, while 'courage', 'piety', etc. designate that virtue, not in respect of its total application, but in respect of its application to a restricted area. Similarly, coastal navigation and oceanic navigation are not two sciences, but a single science applied to different situations. Yet they can count as parts of navigation, in that competence in navigation requires mastery of both.[2]

The theory that virtue is knowledge is, as we have seen, flawed, in that one of its central propositions, that virtue is always in the agent's interest, is nowhere adequately supported in the Socratic dialogues. It also has a deeper flaw in that it is incoherent. The incoherence emerges when we ask 'What is virtue knowledge of?' The answer indicated by *Meno* and *Protagoras* is that virtue is knowledge of the agent's good, in that, given the standing motivation to achieve one's good, knowledge of what that good is will be necessary if one is to pursue it reliably, and sufficient to guarantee that the pursuit is successful. But that requires that the agent's good is something distinct from the knowledge which guarantees that one will achieve that good. 'Virtue is knowledge of the agent's good' is parallel to 'Medicine is knowledge of health'. Given that parallel, the value of virtue, the knowledge which guarantees the achievement of the good, will be purely instrumental, as the value of medicine is, and

---

[2] The example is borrowed from T. C. Brickhouse and N. D. Smith, *Plato's Socrates* (New York and Oxford, 1994), 69–71.

derivative from the intrinsic value of what it guarantees, that is, success in life (*eudaimonia*). But Socrates, as we saw, regards virtue as intrinsically, not merely instrumentally, valuable, and explicitly treats it as parallel, not to medicine, but to health itself. Virtue is, then, not a means to some independently specifiable condition of life which we can identify as *eudaimonia*; rather, it is a constituent of it (indeed, one of the trickiest questions about Socratic ethics is whether Socrates recognizes any other constituents). So, far from its being the case that virtue is worth pursuing because it is a means to a fully worthwhile life (e.g. a life of happiness), the order of explanation is reversed, in that a life is a life worth living either solely or at least primarily in virtue of the fact that it is a life of virtue.

The incoherence of the theory thus consists in the fact that Socrates maintains both that virtue is knowledge of what the agent's good is and that it is that good itself, whereas those two theses are inconsistent with one another. It could of course be the case both that virtue is knowledge of what the agent's good is, and that the agent's good is knowledge, but in that case the knowledge which is the agent's good has to be a distinct item or body of knowledge from the knowledge of what the agent's good is. Otherwise we have the situation that the knowledge of what the agent's good is is the knowledge that the agent's good is the knowledge of what the agent's good is, and that that knowledge (i.e. the knowledge of what the agent's good is) is in turn the knowledge that the agent's good is the knowledge of what the agent's good is, and so on *ad infinitum*. So, if Socrates wishes to stick to the claim that virtue is knowledge he must either specify that knowledge as knowledge of something other than what the agent's good is, or he must give up the thesis that virtue is the agent's good.

Plato represents Socrates as grappling with this problem in *Euthydemus*. This dialogue presents a confrontation between two conceptions of philosophy, represented respectively by Socrates and by a pair of sophists, the brothers Euthydemus and Dionysodorus. The latter demonstrate their conception by putting on a dazzling display of the techniques of fallacious argument which enable them to 'combat in argument and refute whatever anyone says, whether it is true or false' (272a–b). For his part Socrates seeks to argue for the central role of wisdom in the achievement of *eudaimonia*. The first part of his argument (278e–281e) is in essence the same as that used in *Meno* 87d–89a to establish that virtue is knowledge; knowledge or wisdom (the terms are interchangeable) is the only unconditionally good thing, since all other goods, whether goods of fortune or desirable traits of character, are good for the agent only if they are properly used, and they are properly used only if they are directed by wisdom. Thus far Socrates reproduces the position of *Meno*, but in the second part of his argument (288d–292e) he goes beyond it. Here he points out that the previous argument has shown that the skill which secures the overall good of the agent is one which coordinates the production and use of all subordinate goods, including the products of all other skills. It is thus a directive or governing skill, which is appropriately termed the political or kingly (*basilikē*) art. But now what is the goal of the kingly art? Not to provide goods such as wealth or freedom for people, for the previous argument has shown that those are good only on the condition that they are directed by wisdom. So the goal of the kingly art can only be to make people wise. But wise at what? Not wise (= skilled) at shoemaking or building, for the same reason, that those skills are good only if they are directed by the supreme skill. The goal of the kingly art can therefore be none other than to make people skilled in the kingly art itself. But, as Socrates admits (292d–e), that is completely uninformative, since we lack any conception of what the kingly art is.

Socrates leaves the puzzle unresolved, and it may well be that at that point Plato did not see his way out of the puzzle. What this dialogue does show is that Plato had become aware of the incoherence of the system of Socratic ethics whose two central tenets are that virtue is knowledge (sc. of human good) and that virtue is human good. If human good is to be identified with both knowledge and virtue, then that knowledge must have some object other than itself. Plato's eventual solution was to develop (in the *Republic*) a conception of human good as consisting in a state of the personality in which the non-rational impulses are directed by the intellect informed by knowledge, not of human good, but of goodness itself, a universal principle of rationality. On this conception (i) human good is virtue, (ii) virtue is, not identical with, but directed by, knowledge, and (iii) the knowledge in question is knowledge of the universal good. It is highly plausible to see *Euthydemus* as indicating the transition from the Socratic position set out most explicitly in *Meno* to that developed Platonic position.

Protagoras may be seen as an exploration of another solution to this puzzle, since in that dialogue Socrates sets out an account of goodness whose central theses are: (i) virtue is knowledge of human good (as in *Meno*); (ii) human good is an overall pleasant life. The significance of this is independent of whether Socrates is represented as adopting that solution in his own person, or merely as proposing it as a theory which ordinary people and Protagoras ought to accept. Either way, it represents a way out of the impasse which blocks the original form of the Socratic theory, though not a way which Plato was himself to adopt. Having experimented with this theory, which retains the identity of virtue with knowledge while abandoning the identity of virtue with human good, he settled for the alternative just described, which maintains the latter identity while abandoning the former.

Socrates and the sophists

The confrontation of Socrates with sophists is central to Plato's apologetic project. Socrates, as we have seen, had been tarred with the sophistic brush, and it was therefore central to the defence of his memory to show how wide the gap was between his activity and that of the sophists. Since Socrates represents in Plato's presentation the ideal philosopher, the confrontation can also be seen more abstractly, as a clash between genuine philosophy and its counterfeit.

Plato depicts Socrates in confrontation with sophists and

their associates in the three longest and dramatically most complex dialogues of the group which we are considering: *Gorgias*, *Protagoras*, and *Euthydemus*. I shall consider those together with *Republic* 1, which may originally have been a separate dialogue; even if it was not, it certainly looks back to the aporetic and elenctic style of the earlier dialogues, while there are obvious similarities between the positions of Callicles in *Gorgias* and Thrasymachus in *Republic* 1. As well as these major dramatic dialogues, Socrates is presented in one-to-one discussion with a sophist in the two *Hippias* dialogues.

The Greek word *sophistēs* (formed from the adjective *sophos* 'wise' or 'learned') originally meant 'expert' or 'sage'; thus the famous Seven Sages were referred to as the 'Seven *Sophistai*'. In the fifth century it came to be applied particularly to the new class of itinerant intellectuals, such as Protagoras and Hippias, whom we find depicted in the Socratic dialogues. We saw earlier that sophists were regarded in some quarters as dangerous subversives, overthrowing conventional religion and morality by a combination of naturalistic science and argumentative trickery. Plato presents a much more nuanced picture. There are indeed elements of subversion, in that both Callicles and Thrasymachus mount powerful attacks on conventional morality. As for argumentative trickery, Euthydemus and Dionysodorus are shameless in their deliberate bamboozling of opponents. But Plato is far from presenting sophists as a class as either moral subversives or argumentative charlatans, much less as both. In *Protagoras* the sophist represents his own teaching of the art of life not as critical of conventional social morality but as continuous with it, since he takes over where traditional education leaves off. He defends traditional morality, and in particular the central role which it assigns to the basic social virtues of justice and self-control, by a story designed to show how it is a natural development, determined by the necessity of social co-operation if humans are to survive in a hostile world. He argues sensibly and in some places effectively for his views. Interestingly, neither his claim to make the weaker argument the stronger nor his agnosticism on the existence and nature of the gods gets any mention in this portrayal. Prodicus, who also appears in *Protagoras* and is mentioned fairly often in other Platonic dialogues, is said to have given naturalistic accounts of the origin of religion and was accounted an atheist by some ancient writers, but this is nowhere mentioned by Plato, whose primary interest is in making fun of his penchant for nice verbal distinctions. Hippias is presented both in *Protagoras* and in the *Hippias* dialogues as a polymath, whose interests range from science and astronomy to history, literary criticism, and mnemonics. In *Hippias Major* he has little capacity for following an argument, and there is no suggestion in any of these dialogues of radical views on anything. Gorgias starts out by claiming that rhetoric, his field of expertise, is a value-free discipline (455a), but is trapped by Socrates into acknowledging that a good orator must know what is just and unjust, and that if his pupils do not know this already they will learn it from him (460a). There is no indication of what his substantive views on justice and injustice may have been; specifically, there is no suggestion in the dialogue that Callicles has derived his immoralism from Gorgias. It would give a better fit with what is plainly meant to be Gorgias' real position if any influence that Gorgias may have had on Callicles were restricted to the rhetorical force which he manifests in such abundance in expressing his atrocious views. In Plato's eyes that influence was no less dangerous than positive indoctrination.

It is worth pointing out that Plato's presentation of the personalities of the sophists is as nuanced as his treatment of their doctrines. At least, they are not portrayed in a tone of uniform hostility. Thrasymachus, indeed, is a thoroughly nasty piece of work: arrogant, rude, and aggressive (he even tells Socrates to get his nurse to wipe his nose and stop his drivelling (343a)), and Hippias is a learned and conceited blockhead, but the others are treated more gently. The charlatanry of the brothers in *Euthydemus* is so transparent as to be almost endearing, while Prodicus is a figure of rather gentle fun. Protagoras, on the other hand, is a much more considerable figure; he is certainly pompous and complacent, and he does get ruffled when he loses the argument, but he quickly recovers his poise and concludes with a generous, if slightly patronizing, compliment to Socrates. More significantly, Plato presents him as someone to be taken seriously intellectually. The speech which sets out his defence of social morality and his role as an educator is a serious piece of work, and up to the concluding argument he is represented as holding his own in debate with Socrates. When we add to this the lengthy critique of his doctrines in *Theaetetus* (something which has no parallel in the case of any other sophist) it is clear that Plato took him very seriously indeed.

Plato's Socrates is not interested in the religious unorthodoxy of the sophists. (Later, in book 10 of the *Laws*, Plato argues strongly that atheism leads to immorality, and recommends institutional means of suppressing it—including the death penalty for those who persist in it—but that is a stance foreign to the Platonic Socrates.) He faces a serious challenge from one strand of sophistic moral thinking, represented by Thrasymachus, who is himself a sophist, and Callicles, who is an associate of Gorgias. The basis of those views, explicit in Callicles, implicit in Thrasymachus, is the dichotomy between what is natural and what is merely conventional. Both assume an egoistic view of human nature, maintaining that, in common with other animals, humans have a natural tendency to seek the maximum self-gratification, from which they conclude that, for the individual, success in life (*eudaimonia*) consists in giving that tendency free play. Law and morality they see as conventional devices for restricting that natural tendency with a view to promoting the good of others; their effect is to force people to sacrifice their own *eudaimonia* in favour of that of others. But since everyone has more reason to favour their own *eudaimonia* over that of others, the rational course for everyone is to free themselves from the shackles of law and morality. (Callicles goes a step further in claiming that that is not merely rational but in reality right or just (*phusei dikaion*), since the individual who is strong enough to exploit others is thereby entitled to do so, and is wronged by laws or conventions which seek to prevent him.)

The moral theory sketched in the previous chapter provided a response to this challenge, though a weak one, since the crucial link between morality and the agent's good was not established. But in addition to this radical challenge to conventional morality, the sophistic tradition provided an argument in support of it, and thereby an answer to the challenge, in the form of the theory of the social origin of morality expounded by Protagoras in the dialogue (see above). This theory rejects the fundamental thesis of the radicals that nature and convention are opposed. On the contrary, convention, in the form of social morality, is itself a product of nature, since it naturally comes about when human beings are obliged to adapt (by forming communities) in order to survive. So far from its being the case that convention stultifies the development of human nature, it is only via convention that human nature is able to survive and flourish, in the sense of developing civilization.

To the extent that Protagoras upholds conventional morality, especially justice and self-control, he is an ally against Callicles and Thrasymachus. For all that, Socrates finds his theory inadequate. He could have made the point, though he does not in fact, that Protagoras's account makes justice and self-control only instrumentally instead of intrinsically desirable; their value lies in their necessity as prerequisites for the benefits of communal life, but what is necessary is that those virtues should be generally, rather than universally, cultivated. Hence someone who can get away with wrongdoing on a particular occasion without endangering the social fabric has no reason not to do so (the 'free-rider' problem). That issue is addressed in book 2 of the *Republic*. In *Protagoras* Socrates' criticism is that, in assuming the separateness of the individual virtues (see above), Protagoras manifests an inadequate grasp of the nature of goodness. Hence his claim to expertise about goodness (in other words, to teach *politikē technē* (319a)) is fraudulent, and those, like Hippocrates, who flock to him in the expectation of acquiring goodness, are not merely wasting their time and money, but are risking the positive harm of acquiring a mistaken view of goodness and hence a mistaken conception of their proper goal in life (312b–314b).

Sophists, then, are dangerous, but not in the way that they are conceived in the popular caricature. They are a threat, not primarily because they peddle atheism or immorality (though some sophists did promote one or the other), but because they set themselves up as experts on the most important question, 'How is one to live?' without actually having the requisite knowledge. This is the recurrent theme of Socrates' confrontations with them. Protagoras claims to teach people how to acquire goodness, but proves to have no grasp of what it is. Euthydemus and Dionysodorus make precisely the same claim (275a), but all they actually have to teach is verbal trickery. (Protagoras is clearly represented as making his claim in good faith, but the same can hardly be said for the brothers. The point is immaterial; whether or not the sophist believes his claim, the important point is that it is unfounded.) Hippias claims universal expertise, including expertise on the nature of the fine or beautiful, an aspect of goodness, but his claim proves as hollow as those of the others. Socrates, by contrast, does not normally claim to have expertise. What he represents is the true conception of the task of philosophy, which is to search for genuine expertise in the art of life. What that expertise is is the possession of the true account of goodness, and hence the true account of our proper aim in life.

This conception of philosophy is emphasized in *Gorgias* via the contrast with rhetoric. The art of life (*politikē*) seeks the good, which requires knowledge of what the good is, whereas rhetoric aims merely at gratifying the desires of people who lack knowledge of whether the satisfaction of those desires is good or not. Hence the true expert in the art of life is the philosopher, represented by Socrates, who here, exceptionally, does claim expertise. If, instead of being guided by philosophy, people's lives are ruled by rhetoric, the result is the substitution of the pursuit of pleasure for that of the good, a situation which can lead to the moral chaos represented by Callicles, for whom the good is the indiscriminate pursuit of every pleasure. Gorgias, it seems, does not himself claim to teach goodness, unlike the sophists; the dialogue is then, unlike the others we have discussed, a critique not of an unfounded claim to expertise, but of the misguided practice (characteristic, in Plato's view, of Athenian democracy) of assigning to the technique of persuasion the role which properly belongs to philosophical enquiry, that of identifying fundamental values.

5 *Socrates and later philosophy*

Ancient philosophy

From the modern perspective by far the most important legacy of Socrates was his influence on Plato. But we have seen that Plato was one of a number of associates who wrote about him in the generation immediately after his death and were themselves influenced by him in one way or another. In this section I shall trace briefly the main ways in which the influence of Socrates was transmitted to later generations, by personal association and via the writings of Plato and others.

We may begin with two personal associates of Socrates, Antisthenes and Aristippus. Antisthenes is said to have been originally a pupil of Gorgias who transferred his allegiance to Socrates. He appears to have been a sophist in the traditional style, who wrote on a wide range of subjects, many of them remote from the interests of Socrates, who concentrated on ethics. His interests in the nature of language and its relation to reality, and in particular his denial of the possibility of contradiction, link him rather with Socrates' sophistic opponents, notably Prodicus and Protagoras, both of whom are said to have maintained that thesis. He thus appears as an eclectic figure, in whom the specifically Socratic influence is manifested in his adherence to some of Socrates' ethical doctrines and in his austere style of life. He maintained that goodness can be taught and that it is sufficient for happiness, adding the significant rider 'requiring nothing more in addition than Socratic strength' (DL 6.10–11). The rider suggests a shift from the Socratic denial of the possibility of *akrasia* (action against one's better judgement); knowledge of the agent's good does not by itself guarantee pursuit of it, as Socrates had held, but in addition the agent must acquire sufficient strength to adhere to his or her judgement of what is best, which implies that that judgement needs to be defended against the possibility of erosion by conflicting desires. (Plato indicates a similar modification at *Rep.* 429c, where he defines courage as 'retention, amid pleasures and desires and fears, of the belief inculcated by law and education about what is fearful and what is not'.) Socratic strength was to be promoted by a life of physical austerity, eschewing all pleasures except those appropriate to such a life. It thus appears that that aspect of Socrates' life-style was as significant an influence on Antisthenes as his doctrines. Subsequently, extreme austerity became the trademark of the Cynics, who combined it with rejection of normal social conventions as an expression of their central tenet that the good was life in conformity with nature. Later Antisthenes was said to have been the founder of the Cynic sect. Rather than any doctrinal or organizational influence, of which there is no evidence, this reflects the tradition of the transmission of the Socratic lifestyle, as Diogenes Laertius explicitly reports (6.2): Antisthenes, he says, 'taking over his endurance from him [i.e. Socrates] and emulating his immunity from feeling became the founder of Cynicism'.

Aristippus was a native of Cyrene in North Africa who was attracted to Athens by the reputation of Socrates. He, too, wrote in a number of areas, including ethics, theory of language, and history, and is said to have been the first of Socrates' associates to follow the sophists' practice of charging fees for teaching. He is reputed to have been the founder of the Cyrenaic school, which was influential in the fourth and third centuries BC, but since all our information about Cyrenaic doctrine dates from after the foundation of the school there is no reliable indication whether any of its doctrines were maintained by Aristippus himself. The principal tenets of the school were the ethical doctrine that the sensory pleasure of the present moment is the supreme good, and the epistemological doctrine that the only things that can be known are present sense-impressions. These are connected by the sceptical implications of the latter. By that doctrine the past and the future are equally inaccessible; hence the only rational aim is some feature of present experience. The claim of pleasure to be that feature was supported by the argument that all living things pursue pleasure and shun pain. Uniquely among Greek philosophers the Cyrenaics rejected the claim of *eudaimonia* to be the supreme good, on the strength of this sceptical argument; *eudaimonia* involves assessing life as a whole, but such assessment is impossible given the unknowability of anything but the present. Hence the wise person's goal should be, not *eudaimonia*, but the pleasure of the moment.

It is hard to see much trace of Socratic influence in these doctrines. The doctrine that the supreme good is the pleasure of the moment is closer to the view of Callicles than to that of Socrates, and though some later sceptics claimed Socrates as their ancestor, that was not on the strength of the thesis that the only knowable things are current sense-impressions, which is a version of the Protagorean position criticized in *Theaetetus*. On the other hand, some evidence of the views of Aristippus preserved by Eusebius suggests something closer to recognizably Socratic positions. According to this, he taught that pleasure is to be pursued, not unconditionally, but provided it does not endanger self-control, which results from education, self-knowledge, study, and endurance (*karteria*), the very word which was the key term in Antisthenes' ascetic morality. It is then plausible to suggest that the doctrine that momentary pleasure is the supreme good represents a position developed by the school, subsequent to the time of Aristippus himself, when the influence of sceptical doctrines had become more prominent.

Most of the ancient biographical evidence about Aristippus concerns his luxurious mode of life, and he appears in that aspect in Xenophon's *Memorabilia*, where Socrates admonishes him by telling him Prodicus' fable of the Choice of Heracles (2.1). The moral of this is the broadly Antisthenean one that a life of simplicity and hard toil brings greater pleasure in the long

run than a life of luxury. The appeal is to long-term considerations, and there is no suggestion that Aristippus has any
theoretical grounds for rejecting that appeal. We might then
suggest that the contrast between Antisthenes and Aristippus
may not have been an extreme doctrinal antithesis, but rather a
matter of temperament, Antisthenes being attracted by the
ascetic aspects of Socrates' life to the extent of elevating them
to the status of a moral ideal, while Aristippus may have felt
that the Socratic ideals of self-knowledge and self-control could
be accommodated to a more easy-going way of life. It is worth
recalling some less stern aspects of the figure of Socrates, such
as his exceptional capacity to enjoy food and drink (Pl. *Symp.*
220a), and his erotic reputation. The hedonistic Socrates presented in *Protagoras* may have been taken by some to represent
his actual views, as is suggested by the papyrus mentioned
above, where Socrates is counted among those who think that
pleasure is the best goal in life. It is a striking fact (commented
on by Augustine (*City of God* 8.3)) that the figure of Socrates
was sufficiently plastic to allow two such contrasting life-
styles as those of Antisthenes and Aristippus both to count as in
certain respects Socratic.

The connection of Socrates with the Cynics via Antisthenes
developed into a connection with Stoicism, since the Stoics saw
themselves as heirs both of the Cynics and of Socrates. The
succession of leaders of the schools drawn up by Hellenistic
historians (exhibited in the order of lives in DL 6–7) runs from
Antisthenes via Diogenes of Sinope (who was described as
'Socrates gone mad' (DL 6.54)) and Crates to Zeno of Citium,
the founder of Stoicism; Zeno is said to have been converted to
philosophy by reading Xenophon's *Memorabilia* on a visit to
Athens, and to have asked where he could find someone like
Socrates, in answer to which he was advised to associate with
Crates. From the Cynics the Stoics took the central doctrine of
the life according to nature as the supreme human good. It was,
however, Socrates rather than the Cynics whom they took to
reveal what the life according to nature consisted in. For the

Stoics, the life according to nature was the life appropriate to each kind of living thing, whereby it fitted into its place in the perfect order of nature as a whole. Human beings are rational creatures, and life according to nature for humans is therefore life in accordance with reason. Since there is no distinction of rational and non-rational elements in the human soul, there is no distinction between moral virtue and rationality. The Stoics thus accepted the cardinal doctrines of Socratic ethics, that virtue is knowledge, and that virtue is sufficient for *eudaimonia*. The doctrine of *Meno* and *Euthydemus* that virtue (= knowledge) is the only unconditional good they interpreted in the strong sense that virtue is the only good, everything else being 'indifferent', that is, neither good nor bad. Aristo, a follower of Zeno, maintained the thesis of the Unity of the Virtues, interpreting it as the thesis that the names of the different virtues are alternative characterizations of the knowledge of good and bad, differentiated by reference to the relation of that knowledge to different circumstances.

The Stoics thus held both the doctrines which we saw to lead to an impasse in Socratic ethics, that virtue is knowledge (sc. of the good) and that virtue is the only good, and their critics were not slow to claim that they too had no escape: Plutarch alleges (*Common Notions* 1072b) that when asked what the good is they say 'Nothing but intelligence' and when asked what intelligence is say 'Nothing but knowledge of goods', referring directly to the passage in *Euthydemus* (292e) where the difficulty was originally raised. But their doctrine that human goodness is conformity with the perfect order of nature gives them an escape-route. Human goodness is knowledge of goodness indeed, but it is not thereby knowledge of nothing other than human goodness, that is, knowledge of itself. It is knowledge of the goodness of the universe, i.e. conformity to the goodness of the universe by the realization of perfect rationality in the soul. But now it seems that the difficulty has been merely postponed; for rationality has to consist in making the right choices, that is, choices of what is good in preference to what is bad, and if nothing is good or bad but virtue and vice respectively we have after all no informative account of what goodness is. This problem exercised the Stoics, some of whom sought to find a solution in a distinction among 'indifferent' things between 'preferred indifferents' such as health and 'unpreferred indifferents' such as sickness. Neither kind of indifferent is better or worse than the other, but nature prompts us to seek the preferred and shun the unpreferred, and goodness consists in making the right choices in accordance with these natural promptings. Critics such as Plutarch (*Stoic Contradictions* 1047–8) claimed that by this manoeuvre the Stoics were attempting to have their cake and eat it, in that they had to claim that the choice of indifferents was both a matter of the utmost concern and a matter of no concern at all. The many fascinating issues which this raises cannot be pursued here.

The dependence in Stoic thought of human goodness on the rational order of the universe presented a special difficulty for their claim to follow Socrates, in that it makes knowledge of nature prior to ethical knowledge, whereas Socrates had famously eschewed interest in natural philosophy and confined himself to ethics (Xen. *Mem*. 1.1.16, Aristotle *Metaphysics* 987^{b}1–2). Yet they could find passages in Xenophon's *Memorabilia* where Socrates draws moral implications from general considerations about nature. In 1.4 Socrates seeks to convert the atheist Aristodemus by arguing for the existence of the gods and their care for humans from the providential design of the human body. In the course of this discussion he argues that human intelligence must be a portion of a larger quantity of intelligence pervading the world, just as the physical elements which compose the human body are portions of the larger totalities of those elements; later he says that the intelligence which is in the universe organizes everything as best pleases it and that the divine sees and hears everything and is everywhere and takes care of everything all at once. This certainly can be read as foreshadowing the Stoic picture of the cosmos as itself a divine, intelligent, self-organizing being, and both Cicero (*De Natura Deorum* 2.6.18) and Sextus (*Adversus Mathematicos* 9.92–104) refer explicitly to this passage of

Xenophon as a source of Stoic argument for cosmic rationality. (A similar argument occurs in *Memorabilia* 4.3, with special reference to the gods' care for humans as evinced in their conferring rationality and language on them.) Another passage of *Memorabilia* which strikingly anticipates Stoic doctrine is 4.4, where Socrates and Hippias agree that there are some universal, unwritten moral laws, for example, that one should worship the gods and honour one's parents, which are not the product of human convention as are the laws of particular communities, but are laid down by the gods for all men, and sanctioned by inevitable punishment. For a detailed Stoic parallel (so close as to raise the possibility of imitation) see Cicero, *Republic* 3.33.

According to the first-century BC Epicurean Philodemus the Stoics wished to be called Socratics, and Socrates remained a paradigm of the sage throughout their history. His acceptance of death was a model of how the wise man should confront death, as is reflected in descriptions of famous Stoic suicides such as that of Seneca. To Epictetus, writing in the first and second centuries AD, he is the sage *par excellence*, whose influence he sums up in the words 'Now that Socrates is dead, the memory of what he did or said when alive is no less or even more beneficial to men' (*Discourses* 4.1.169).

There were two principal traditions of philosophical scepticism in antiquity, the Pyrrhonians and the Academics. The former traced their philosophical ancestry from the fourth-century Pyrrho of Elis, who like Socrates wrote nothing himself and for that reason remains a somewhat elusive figure. There is no firm evidence that adherents of this school regarded Socrates as a sceptic. In the works of Sextus Empiricus, who is our principal source for Pyrrhonian scepticism, Socrates is almost invariably listed among the dogmatists, that is, those who maintained positive doctrines as opposed to suspending judgement on all questions as the sceptics recommended; only once (*Adversus Mathematicos* 7.264) is Socrates cited as suspending judgement, on the strength of his ironical statement at *Phaedrus* 230a that he is so far from self-knowledge that he does not know whether he is a man or a many-headed monster. For the Academics the situation was different. The Academy was Plato's own school, which embraced scepticism under the leadership of Arcesilaus just over a century after its foundation and remained a sceptical school for over two hundred years until it reverted to dogmatism under Antiochus of Ascalon. Arcesilaus claimed that in embracing scepticism he was remaining faithful to the spirit of both Socrates and Plato, whose philosophical practice he claimed to have been sceptical, not dogmatic.

Cicero, our main source, makes it clear that Arcesilaus saw Socrates' argumentative practice as purely negative and *ad hominem*; he maintained no doctrines himself, but merely asked others what they thought and argued against them. In the dialogues we do indeed find many cases where Socrates' interlocutors are brought to an impasse by the revelation of inconsistency in their beliefs; Arcesilaus interpreted this outcome as supporting the general sceptical position that there is nothing which the senses or the mind can grasp as certain (*De Oratore* 3.67; cf. *De Finibus* 2.2, 5.10). He attributed to Socrates the paradoxical claim that he knew nothing except this, that he knew nothing (*Academica* 1.45; cf. 2.74), and criticized him on the ground that he should not have claimed to know even that.

Our previous discussion should have made it clear that while Arcesilaus' reading of Socrates does pick out genuine features of his argumentative practice, it is unduly selective. His profession of ignorance is a denial that he possesses wisdom or expertise, which is compatible with the claims (*a*) that he knows some things in a non-expert way, and (*b*) that others know some things as experts. He neither claims that he knows nothing, nor does he claim that he knows that he knows nothing. He never draws from the negative outcome of his examinations of others the universal thesis that there is nothing which the senses or the mind can grasp as certain. On the contrary, he thinks that knowledge is identical with the good, and takes the negative outcome of his enquiries as a stimulus to the further search for it. Of course, the sceptic is entitled to maintain that the search for knowledge is not incompatible with scepticism. A *skeptikos*

is a searcher, and the sceptic continually searches for knowledge, which constantly eludes him. But despite the claim to be
engaged on an ongoing search for knowledge, the sceptic is
committed to a general pessimism about the human capacity to
achieve it; in Arcesilaus' version 'there is nothing which *can*
[my emphasis] be grasped as certain by the mind or the senses'.
It is not just that any enquiry so far undertaken has failed to
reach certainty. The sceptic believes in advance that that will
be the outcome on any occasion and has some general strat-
egies, such as the appeal to conflicting appearances or arguments, to show that it must. There is no trace of that pessimism
in Plato's portrayal of Socrates.

Not all subsequent philosophers were well disposed towards
Socrates. Some of Aristotle's successors were hostile, notably
Aristoxenus, whose malicious biography was the source of the
story of Socrates' bigamy; it attracted a rejoinder from the Stoic
Panaetius. The most consistent hostility came from the
Epicureans. True to their tradition of abusive comments on
non-Epicurean philosophers, a succession of Epicureans made
rude remarks about Socrates. Typical of these are some remarks
of Colotes which Plutarch cites, describing the story of the
oracle given to Chaerephon as 'a completely cheap and
sophistical tale' (*Against Colotes* 1116e–f), and Socrates' arguments as so much boasting or quackery (*alazonas*) on the
ground that they were discordant with what he actually did
(1117d; presumably Colotes had in mind some instances of
Socrates' ironical professions of admiration of his interlocutors). As both the Stoics and the sceptical Academics were
regarded by the Epicureans as professional rivals, it is plausible
that the Epicureans' hostility to Socrates stemmed in part from
the position which he was accorded by those schools.

The tendency to appropriate Socrates as a precursor was not
restricted to pagan philosophers. Writing in the second century
AD the Christian apologist Justin cited the example of Socrates
in rebuttal of the accusation of atheism levelled at the

Christians. Like them, he claimed, Socrates was accused of atheism because he rejected the fables of the Olympian gods and urged the worship of one true God. Socrates had thus had some partial grasp of the coming revelation through Christ, since, though philosophers are responsible for their own errors and contradictions through their limited grasp of the truth 'whatever has been well said by them belongs to us Christians'.

Medieval and modern philosophy

The Christianization of Socrates so strikingly expressed by Justin was not the beginning of a continuous tradition. Though Augustine was influenced by Plato to the extent of speculating that he might have known the Old Testament scriptures, he does not follow Justin in claiming Socrates for Christianity. While some Christian writers praise Socrates as a good man unjustly put to death, most of those who mention him refer with disapproval to his 'idolatry', citing his divine sign (interpreted by some, including Tertullian, as communications from a demon), his sacrifice to Asclepius, and his oaths 'By the dog', etc. To the extent that the Platonic tradition retained its vitality in the early medieval period it concentrated on later Platonic works, especially *Timaeus*, in which the personality of Socrates plays an insignificant role, and from the twelfth century onwards the influence of Plato was largely eclipsed in the West by that of Aristotle. The major medieval philosophers show little or no interest in Socrates, and it is not until the revival of Platonism in the late fifteenth century that any significant interest in him re-emerges. As part of the neo-Platonist programme of interpreting Platonism as an allegorical expression of Christian truth we find the Florentine Marsilio Ficino drawing detailed parallels between the trials and deaths of Socrates and Jesus, and this tradition was continued by Erasmus (one of whose dialogues contains the expression 'Saint Socrates, pray for us') in a comparison between Christ in the garden of Gethsemane and Socrates in his condemned cell. (The tradition was continued in subsequent centuries, by (among others)

Diderot and Rousseau in the eighteenth and various writers in the nineteenth, all of them adjusting the parallelism to fit their particular religious preconceptions.) As in the ancient world, the figure of Socrates lent itself to appropriation by competing ideologies. For Montaigne in the sixteenth century Socrates was not a Christ-figure but a paradigm of natural virtue and wisdom, and the supernatural elements in the ancient portrayal, particularly the divine sign, were to be explained in naturalistic terms; the sign was perhaps a faculty of instinctive, unreasoned decision, facilitated by his settled habits of wisdom and virtue. The growth of a rationalizing approach to religion in the seventeenth and eighteenth centuries, which rejected revelation and the fanaticism consequent on disputes about its interpretation, allowed Socrates to be seen as a martyr for rational religion, who had met his death at the hands of fanatics. In this vein Voltaire wrote a play on the death of Socrates, and the Deist John Toland composed a liturgy for worship in a 'Socratic Sodality', including a litany in which, following the example of Erasmus, the name of Socrates was invoked.

As in the ancient world, there were dissenting voices. Some writers were critical of Socrates' morals, citing his homosexual tendencies and his neglect of his wife and children. For some, including Voltaire, the divine sign manifested a regrettable streak of superstition. The eighteenth century saw the appearance of the first modern works reviving the claim that the charges against Socrates were political and defending his condemnation on the basis of his hostility to Athenian democracy and his associations with Critias and Alcibiades. (That line of interpretation continues up to the present, the most recent example being I. F. Stone's widely read *The Trial of Socrates*.) And some writers of orthodox Christian views repudiated the parallels between Socrates and Jesus, alleging, in addition to the charges of superstition and immorality already mentioned, that Socrates had in effect committed suicide.

The pattern of appropriation to an alien culture has parallels in the treatment of Socrates in medieval Arabic literature. Apart from Plato and Aristotle, he is the philosopher most frequently referred to by Arabic writers, and the interest in him extended beyond philosophers to poets, theologians, mystics, and other scholars. This interest was not founded on extensive knowledge of the relevant Greek texts. While works dealing with Socrates' death, notably Plato's *Phaedo* and *Crito*, were clearly well known, there is little evidence of wider knowledge of the Platonic dialogues, and none of knowledge of other Socratic literature. There was, however, an extensive tradition of anecdotes recording sayings of Socrates, of the kind recorded in Diogenes Laertius and other biographical and moralizing writers. This tradition represents Socrates as a sage, one of the 'Seven Pillars of Wisdom' (i.e. sages), a moral paragon, an exemplar of all the virtues, and a fount of wisdom on every topic, including man, the world, time, and, above all, God. He is consistently presented as maintaining an elaborate monotheistic theology, neo-Platonist in its details, and his condemnation and death are attributed to his upholding faith in the one true God against the errors of idolators. This allows him to be seen as a forerunner of Islamic sages (as he was seen in the West as a proto-Christian), and to be described in terms which assimilate him to figures venerated in Islam, including Abraham, Jesus, and even the Prophet himself. Some writings represent him as an ascetic, and it is clear that he is conflated with the Cynics, above all with Diogenes, even to the extent of living in a tub and telling Alexander the Great to step out of the light when he was sunbathing. In other writings he is the father of alchemy, in others again a pioneer in logic, mathematics, and physics. Again, as in the West, the generally honorific perception of Socrates was challenged on religious grounds by some orthodox believers (such as the eleventh/twelfth-century theologian al-Ghazali), who represented him as a father of heresies, a threat to Islam, and even as an atheist.[1]

---

[1] For further information see I. Alon, *Socrates in Mediaeval Arabic Literature* (Leiden and Jerusalem, 1991).

The tradition of adapting the figure of Socrates to fit the general preconceptions of the writer is discernible in his treatment by three major philosophers of the nineteenth century, Hegel, Kierkegaard, and Nietzsche. In his *Lectures on the History of Philosophy*, first delivered in 1805–6, Hegel sees the condemnation of Socrates as a tragic clash between two moral standpoints, each of which is justified, and thereby a necessary stage in the dialectical process by which the world-spirit realizes itself in its fullest development. Before Socrates the Athenians had spontaneously and unreflectively followed the dictates of objective morality (*Sittlichkeit*). By critically examining people's moral beliefs Socrates turns morality into something individual and reflective (*Moralität*); it is a requirement of this new morality that its principles stand the test of critical reflection on the part of the individual. Yet, since Socrates was unable to give any determinate account of the good, the effect of this critical reflection is merely to undermine the authority of *Sittlichkeit*. Critical reflection reveals that the exceptionless moral laws which *Sittlichkeit* had proclaimed have exceptions in fact, but the lack of a determinate criterion leaves the individual with no way of determining what is right in particular cases other than inward illumination or conscience, which in Socrates' case takes the form of his divine sign.

Socrates' appeal to his conscience is thus an appeal to an authority higher than that of the collective moral sense of the people, but that is an appeal which the people cannot allow:

The spirit of this people in itself, its constitution, its whole life, rested, however, on a moral ground, on religion, and could not exist without this absolutely secure basis. Thus because Socrates makes the truth rest on the judgement of inward consciousness, he enters upon a struggle with the Athenian people as to what is right and true. His accusation was therefore just . . . (i. 426)[2]

The clash between individual conscience and the state was

---

[2] *Lectures on the History of Philosophy*, tr. E. S. Haldane (London, 1892).

therefore inevitable, in that both necessarily claim supreme moral authority. It is also tragic, in that both sides are right:

In what is truly tragic there must be valid moral powers on both the sides which come into collision; this was so with Socrates. The one power is the divine right, the natural morality whose laws are identical with the will which dwells therein as in its own essence, freely and nobly; we may call it abstractly objective freedom. The other principle, on the contrary, is the right, as really divine, of consciousness or of subjective freedom: this is the fruit of the tree of knowledge of good and evil, i.e. of self-creative reason; and it is the universal principle for all successive times. It is these two principles which we see coming into opposition in the life and philosophy of Socrates. (i. 446–7)

The situation is tragic in that both the collective morality of the people and the individual conscience make demands on the individual which are justified and ineluctable, but conflicting: the only resolution is the development of humanity to a stage in which these demands necessarily coincide. The individual nonconformist such as Socrates is defeated, but that defeat leads to the triumph of what that 'false individuality' imperfectly represented, the critical activity of the world-spirit:

The false form of individuality is taken away, and that, indeed, in a violent way, by punishment, but the principle itself will penetrate later, if in another form, and elevate itself into a form of the world-spirit. This universal mode in which the principle comes forth and permeates the present is the true one; what was wrong was the fact that the principle came forth as the peculiar possession of one individual. (i. 444)

It appears, then, that the condemnation of Socrates arises from the clash between the legitimate demands of collective (*Sittlichkeit*) and individual morality (*Moralität*), which in turn reflects a stage in human development in which the collective and the individual are separate and therefore potentially conflicting. This stage is to be superseded by a higher stage of development in which the individual and the collective are somehow identified, not by the subordination of one to the other, nor by the merging of the individual in the collective, but by the development of a higher form of individuality in which individuality is constituted by its role in the collective.

Kierkegaard discusses Socrates extensively in one of his earliest works, *The Concept of Irony, with Continual Reference to Socrates*. This was his MA thesis, submitted to the University of Copenhagen in 1841, shortly before the major crisis of his life, his breaking off his engagement to Regine Olsen. (The examiners' reports are preserved in the university records, giving an amusing picture of the problems of the academic mind confronted with wayward talent.) His treatment of Socrates is Hegelian: for him as for Hegel Socrates stands at a turning-point in world history, in which the world-spirit advances to a higher stage of development, and for him too that breakthrough demands the sacrifice of the individual. 'An individual may be world-historically justified and yet unauthorized. Insofar as he is the latter he must become a sacrifice; insofar as he is the former he must prevail, that is, he must prevail by becoming a sacrifice' (260).[3] For Kierkegaard as for Hegel the role of Socrates is to lead Greek morality to a higher stage of development; what is original in his treatment is his identification of irony as the means by which this transformation of morality was to be effected. Classical Hellenism had outlived itself, but before a new principle could appear all the false preconceptions of outmoded morality had to be cleared away. That was Socrates' role, and irony was the weapon which he employed:

[I]rony is the glaive, the two-edged sword, that he swung like an avenging angel over Greece ... [I]rony is the very incitement of subjectivity, and in Socrates this is truly a world-historical passion. In Socrates one process ends and with him a new one begins. He is the last classical figure, but he consumes this sterling quality and natural fullness of his in the divine service by which he destroys classicism. (211–12)

[3] *The Concept of Irony, with Continual Reference to Socrates*, tr. H. V. Hong and E. H. Hong (Princeton, NJ, 1989).

By irony Kierkegaard does not mean pretended ignorance or a pose of deference to others. 'Irony' is given a technical sense, taken over from Hegel, of 'infinite, absolute negativity'. What this amounts to is the supersession of the lower stage in a dialectical process in favour of the higher. Kierkegaard gives the example of the supersession of Judaism by Christianity, in which John the Baptist has an 'ironical' role comparable with that of Socrates: '[H]e [i.e. John] let Judaism continue to exist and at the same time developed the seeds of its own downfall within it' (268). But there was a crucial difference between Socrates and John, in that the latter lacked consciousness of his irony:

[F]or the ironic formation to be perfectly developed, it is required that the subject also become conscious of his irony, feel negatively free as he passes judgment on the given actuality and enjoy this negative freedom (ibid.).

This condition was fulfilled by Socrates, who was the first person to exhibit irony as 'a qualification of subjectivity':

If irony is a qualification of subjectivity, it must exhibit itself the first time subjectivity makes its appearance in world history. Irony is, namely, the first and most abstract qualification of subjectivity. This points to the historical turning point where subjectivity made its appearance for the first time, and with this we come to Socrates. (281)

So Socrates' contribution to the development of morality is consciously to reject the authority of all previous moral norms and to be aware of his freedom. The pretended objective authority of these norms is superseded by their subjective acceptance by the individual. So, irony amounts not to moral nihilism, but to moral subjectivism. The connection with irony in the normal sense seems to be twofold: first, that the pretence of ignorance by Socrates was, in Kierkegaard's view, a tactic which he used in his destructive critique of conventional morality, and secondly, that the ironic individual no longer takes morality seriously. He cannot take conventional morality seriously because he has exploded its claims to objectivity. But he cannot take his self-adopted morality seriously either because he looks on it as a task which he has arbitrarily set himself, something perhaps like a hobby which one has just chosen to take up (235). Kierkegaard gives no indication of the answer to the question why the ironist should not simply give up morality altogether; he describes Socrates as arriving 'at the idea of the good, the beautiful, the true only as the boundary, that is com[ing] up to ideal infinity as possibility' (197), which seems to hint at some yet higher level in which moral subjectivism is itself superseded. A comparison earlier in the book (29) between the magnetic effect of Socrates on his acquaintances and Christ's imparting the Holy Spirit to his disciples may point towards the later works in which this higher level is found in the leap of faith, but in this work this remains the merest suggestion.

The suggestion is developed considerably in Kierkegaard's *Concluding Unscientific Postscript* (1846), where the traditional picture of Socrates as a forerunner of Christianity is given a characteristically idiosyncratic turn. The essence of Christianity is now seen as subjectivity. From the objective standpoint of speculative philosophy Christianity is an absurdity, which can be embraced only by the criterionless leap of faith on the part of the individual, a leap which is not the acceptance of an abstract system of propositions, but a personal commitment to a way of life. This subjective commitment transcends objective knowledge, and is held by Kierkegaard to give access to a unique form of truth:

An objective uncertainty held fast in an approximation-process of the most passionate inwardness is the truth, the highest truth attainable for an *existing* individual [Kierkegaard's emphasis] ... [T]he above definition of truth is an equivalent expression for faith. Without risk there is no faith. Faith is precisely the contradiction between the infinite passion of the individual's inwardness and the objective uncertainty. If I am capable of grasping God objectively, I do not believe, but precisely because I cannot do this I must believe. If I wish to preserve myself in faith I must constantly be intent on holding fast the objective uncertainty, so as to remain out upon the deep, over seventy thousand fathoms of water, still preserving my faith. (182)[4]

In his subjective adherence to morality Socrates came as near to this truth as was possible for a pagan:

In the principle that subjectivity, inwardness, is the truth, there is comprehended the Socratic wisdom, whose everlasting merit it was to have become aware of the essential significance of existence, of the fact that the knower is an existing individual. For this reason Socrates was in the truth by virtue of his ignorance, in the highest sense in which this was possible within paganism. (183)

Further, Kierkegaard is prepared to attribute to Socrates not only subjective commitment to morality, but subjective faith in God, a faith which foreshadows indeed the faith of the Christian, while lacking its deeply paradoxical character:

When Socrates believed that there was a God, he held fast to the objective uncertainty with the whole passion of his inwardness, and it is precisely in this contradiction and in this risk, that faith is rooted. Now it is otherwise. Instead of the objective uncertainty, there is here a certainty, that objectively it is absurd; and this absurdity, held fast in the passion of inwardness, is faith. The Socratic ignorance is as a witty jest in comparison with the earnestness of facing the absurd; and the Socratic existential inwardness is as Greek light-mindedness in comparison with the grave strenuosity of faith. (188)

So Socrates combines subjective conviction in the existence of God with the view that objectively the truth of the matter is uncertain. To the extent that that position involves some intellectual discomfort it is a mere approximation to the genuine anguish of the Christian, whose commitment is to truths concerning which it is objectively certain that they are absurd.

For Nietzsche, Socrates was one of a number of figures, including also Christ and Wagner, for whom he had profoundly

---

[4] *Concluding Unscientific Postscript*, tr. D. F. Swenson and W. Lowrie (Princeton, NJ, 1941).

ambivalent feelings: as he said, 'Socrates is so close to me that I am nearly always fighting him.' This ambivalence finds expression in differences of tone, sometimes between different works, sometimes in the same work. His presentation of Socrates in his first published work, *The Birth of Tragedy* (1872), illustrates this. The central thesis of this work is that Greek tragedy arose from the interaction of two opposed aspects of the creativity of the Greeks, which Nietzsche terms the Apollonian and the Dionysian. The Apollonian tendency, which has its purest expression in Homer, is characterized rather obscurely via an analogy with dreaming; it seems to amount to the presentation of an imaginary world, specifically the world of the Homeric gods, in a lucid and delightful form. The Dionysian tendency, whose analogue is intoxication, is the tendency to give expression to ecstatic and excitable impulses, especially sexual impulses and impulses to violence. Religious festivals were the traditional occasions on which these impulses were allowed expression, and it was the unique achievement of the Greeks to develop a form of festival, the dramatic festival, in which the marriage of these two tendencies gave rise to an art form, tragedy, which combines Apollonian illusion and Dionysian excitement in a unique synthesis. The Apollonian element is associated particularly with the episodes of dialogue in Attic tragedy, and the Dionysian with the chorus, but we must not think of the synthesis as simple juxtaposition. Rather (though the obscurity of Nietzsche's writing renders interpretation hazardous), the basic idea is that the world of tragedy is at once as dark and terrible as the Dionysian forces and as lucid and, in a mysterious way, joyful as the sunlit world of the Homeric gods. 'So extraordinary is the power of the epic-Apollonian that before our eyes it transforms the most terrible things by the joy in mere appearance and in redemption through mere appearance' (12).[5]

This synthesis, achieved in the dramas of Aeschylus and Sophocles, disappears in the work of Euripides; Euripidean

---

[5] *The Birth of Tragedy*, tr. W. Kaufmann (New York, 1967).

tragedy is a degenerate form, whose distinctive feature is a realistic depiction of character, closer to the world of New Comedy than to the terrifying yet ideal world of Aeschylus and Sophocles. Nietzsche's term for this is that Euripides

brought the spectator onto the stage. . . . Through him the everyday man forced his way from the spectators' seats onto the stage; the mirror in which formerly only grand and bold traits were represented now showed the painful fidelity that conscientiously reproduces even the botched outlines of nature. (11)

It is this which brings Socrates onto the scene, since Nietzsche, echoing in his idiosyncratic fashion the ancient tradition that Socrates had collaborated with Euripides (DL 2.18), sees him as a decisive influence in the degeneration of tragedy which he saw Euripides as having effected.

Once again, the precise form of this influence is not easy to recover from Nietzsche's prose. He speaks of Euripides as being only a mask through which speaks a new demonic power, neither Dionysus nor Apollo, but Socrates (*Birth of Tragedy* 12). The literal meaning hinted at appears to be this, that Euripidean realism is founded on psychological naturalism. Dramatic characters have to be shown acting on the same psychological principles which we use to explain the actions of actual people in everyday life. This is what Nietzsche calls '*aesthetic Socratism* [author's emphasis], whose supreme law reads roughly as follows "To be beautiful is to be intelligible", as the counterpart of the Socratic dictum "Knowledge is virtue" ' (11). So 'Socratism' seems to be the name for a spirit of naturalistic rationalism, which seeks to tame the terrible forces so gloriously exhibited in Aeschylus and Sophocles by subjecting them to elucidation and criticism.

Socratism condemns existing art as well as existing ethics. Wherever Socratism turns its searching eyes it sees lack of insight and the power of illusion; and from this lack it infers the essential perversity and reprehensibility of what exists. Basing himself on this point, Socrates conceives it to be his duty to correct existence: all alone, with an expression of irreverence and superiority, as the precursor of an altogether different culture, art and morality, he enters a world, to touch whose very hem would give us the greatest happiness. (13)

Aesthetic Socratism seems thus to be the extension to the realm of art of the intellectualism which the Platonic Socrates seeks to apply to conduct. For the Platonic Socrates virtue is knowledge and is sufficient for *eudaimonia*; so the good life is to be achieved through understanding, and all wrongdoing is to be attributed to lack of understanding. Just as the Platonic Socrates gives no positive role to the non-rational elements in the personality, so Socratic art has no room for the mysterious, for what cannot be captured by theory. But it is precisely its resistance to theory which gives tragedy its power and profundity. It explores forces which transcend psychological understanding, and it exhibits dilemmas which it is beyond the power of moral theory to resolve. Socratism thus represents a profound impoverishment of the spirit, which Nietzsche calls (using the French term) *décadence*.

The use of this term brings out the ambivalence in Nietzsche's attitude to Socrates. *The Birth of Tragedy* is pervaded by a sense both of the superhuman quality of the individual person Socrates, 'the human being whom knowledge and reasons have liberated from the fear of death' (15), and of the transcending power of the spirit of enquiry which that person represents. The 'pleasure of Socratic insight' transforms one's whole attitude to the world:

the Platonic Socrates will appear as the teacher of an altogether new form of 'Greek cheerfulness' and blissful affirmation of existence that seeks to discharge itself in actions—most often in maieutic and educational influences on noble youths, with a view to eventually producing a genius. (ibid.)

[W]e cannot fail to see in Socrates the one turning point and vortex of so-called world history (ibid.),

since Socrates is the incarnation of the scientific spirit, which has led to the heights of modern scientific achievement, and without which humanity might not even have survived. But at the same time Nietzsche is convinced that this sense of Socratic optimism, this faith in the power of the intellect to solve all problems of conduct and of nature, is not only a profound delusion, but a symptom of degeneration. Later sections of *The Birth of Tragedy* express this strongly:

From this intrinsically degenerate music [*namely, the New Attic Dithyramb, a musical form developed in the late fifth century* BC] the genuinely musical natures turned away with the same repugnance that they felt for the art-destroying tendency of Socrates. The unerring instinct of Aristophanes was surely right when it included Socrates himself, the tragedy of Euripides, and the music of the New Dithyrambic poets in the same feeling of hatred, recognizing in all three phenomena the signs of a degenerate culture. (17)

One is chained by the Socratic love of knowledge and the delusion of being able thereby to heal the eternal wound of existence. (18)

Later in the same section he speaks of the modern world as entangled in the net of Alexandrian (i.e. uncreative and scholastic) culture, proposing as its ideal the theoretical man labouring in the service of science, whose archetype is Socrates, and of the fruit of Socratic culture as 'optimism, with its delusion of limitless power'. The 'Attempt at a Self-Criticism' added to the second edition of the work fourteen years later returns to this theme: '[T]hat of which tragedy died, the Socratism of morality, the dialectics, frugality and cheerfulness of the theoretical man . . . might not this very Socratism be a sign of decline, of weariness, of infection, of the anarchical dissolution of the instincts?' (1).

In later writings, particularly those written in 1888, shortly before his final mental collapse, the tone is harsher. Nietzsche now identifies himself with the Dionysian forces, and sees Socrates' rejection of them as in effect a personal rejection, to which he responds with extreme emotional violence. In the section of *Ecce Homo* devoted to *The Birth of Tragedy* he says that that work's two decisive novelties are first, the understanding of the Dionysian phenomenon, now seen as 'the sole root of the whole of Hellenic art', and secondly, 'the understanding of Socratism: Socrates for the first time recognized as an agent of Hellenic disintegration, as a typical *décadent*'. 'I was the first to see', he continues,

the real antithesis—the *degenerated* instinct which turns against life with subterranean vengeance ... and a formula of *supreme affirmation* born out of fullness, of superfluity, an affirmation without reservation even of suffering, even of guilt ... This ultimate, joyfullest, boundlessly exuberant Yes to life is not only the highest insight, it is also the *profoundest*, the insight most strictly confirmed and maintained by truth and knowledge.... Recognition, affirmation of reality is for the strong man as great a necessity as is for the weak man, under the inspiration of weakness, cowardice and *flight* in the face of reality—the 'ideal' ... They are not at liberty to know: *décadents need* the lie—it is one of the conditions of their existence.—He who not only understands the word 'dionysian' but understands *himself* in the word 'dionysian' needs no refutation of Plato or of Christianity or of Schopenhauer—*he smells the decomposition.* (80)[6]

The language of sickness and decomposition takes up the theme of the essay on Socrates in *The Twilight of the Idols*, written earlier that year. Nietzsche begins with Socrates' last words, which he interprets as an expression of thanks for release from the sickness of life (see above). But the world-weariness which this expresses is itself the sickness from which Socrates suffers along with all so-called sages who theorize about morality and value.

'Here at any rate there must be something *sick*'—this is *our* retort: one ought to take a closer look at them, those wisest of every age! ... Does wisdom perhaps appear on earth as a raven which is inspired by the smell of carrion? (39)[7]

Socrates and Plato are 'symptoms of decay ... agents of the dissolution of Greece ... pseudo-Greek ... anti-Greek', in that their theorizing involves a negative attitude to life, in

---

[6] *Ecce Homo*, tr. R. J. Hollingdale (Harmondsworth, 1992).
[7] *The Twilight of the Idols*, tr. R. J. Hollingdale (Harmondsworth, 1990).

opposition to the triumphant affirmation of the Dionysian man with whom Nietzsche has identified himself.

But Nietzsche does not stop at the characterization of Socrates as a typical (perhaps the archetypal) *décadent;* in five astonishing sections (3–7) he mounts a ferocious attack on the individual personality of Socrates, in terms expressive of a loathsome snobbishness which even slips into anti-Semitism. Socrates belonged to the lowest social class: he was riff-raff. His ugliness was a symptom of a foul and dissolute temperament. Was he even a Greek at all? Dialectic is a malicious device by which the rabble defeat their betters, people of finer taste and better manners. It is a weapon of last resort in the hands of those who have no other defence. (That is why the Jews were dialecticians.) Socrates was a buffoon who got himself taken seriously.

Reading this stuff with hindsight, in the knowledge of Nietzsche's imminent breakdown, one is inclined to dismiss it as pathological raving. Yet this violence, pathological though it may be, is itself an expression of Nietzsche's deep ambivalence towards Socrates. In section 8 he says that what has gone before indicates the way in which Socrates could repel, which makes it all the more necessary to explain his fascination. So sections 3–7 present an adverse reaction to Socrates, leaving it ambiguous how far Nietzsche himself shares it. In some sense, no doubt, the reaction is his, but then so is what follows. The grotesque caricature of those sections is counterbalanced by a dignified portrait of Socrates as someone who attempted, misguidedly indeed, but seriously and with benevolent intent, to cure the ills of his age by subjecting the dangerous Dionysian impulses to the control of reason. Nietzsche does not withdraw his negative evaluation; Socrates 'seemed to be a physician, a saviour', but his faith in rationality at any cost was error and self-deception: 'Socrates was a misunderstanding: *the entire morality of improvement, the Christian included, has been a misunderstanding.*' Yet the change of voice is most striking, and the return to the theme of Socrates' death in the final section has a genuinely elegiac tone:

Did he himself grasp that [*sc. that so long as life is ascending, happiness and instinct are one*], this shrewdest of all self-deceivers? Did he at last say that to himself in the *wisdom* of his courage for death? . . . Socrates *wanted* to die—it was not Athens, it was he who handed himself the poison cup, who compelled Athens to hand him the poison cup . . . 'Socrates is no physician,' he said softly to himself: 'death alone is a physician here . . . Socrates himself has only been a long time sick . . .'. (44)

Even to the end, it appears, Nietzsche fought against Socrates because he was so close to him.

6 Conclusion

Every age has to recreate its own Socrates. What is his significance for a post-Christian, post-idealist epoch for whom neither
the figure of a precursor of Christ nor that of the embodiment of
the world-spirit in its development of a higher form of consciousness has any meaning? One answer is to view his significance historically, as a pioneer of systematic ethical thought,
as a central influence on Plato, as the focus of Socratic literature, and so on. But the historical importance of Socrates,
unquestionable though it is, does not exhaust his significance,
even for a secular, non-ideological age such as ours. As well as a
historical person and a literary persona, Socrates is in many
ways an exemplary figure, a figure which challenges, encourages, and inspires. To take the most obvious instance, Socrates
still presents a challenge to those whose way into philosophy,
and more generally into systematic critical thinking, is via the
Socratic dialogues. Even in a world where the study of the
ancient classics has lost its cultural pre-eminence, many find
that those dialogues, whose comparative absence of technical-
ity and conversational vividness draw the reader into his or her
own dialogue with the text, provide the best introduction to
philosophy. Again, virtually everyone whose business is teaching finds some affinity with the Socratic method of challenging
the student to examine his or her beliefs, to revise them in the
light of argument, and to arrive at answers through critical
reflection on the information presented. But the critical method
is no mere pedagogical strategy; it is, in real life as much as in
the Socratic dialogues, a method of *self*-criticism. The slogan
'The unexamined life is not worth living for a human being' (Pl.
Apol. 38a) expresses a central human value, partly constitutive

of integrity: namely, the willingness to rethink one's own assumptions, and thereby to reject the standing tendency to complacent dogmatism. Carried to excess self-examination can be paralysing, but Socrates stands as an example of a life in which it is a positive force on a heroic scale, since it produces the confidence to adhere, come what may, to those ideals which have withstood the test of self-criticism. As long as intellectual and moral integrity are human ideals, Socrates will be an appropriate exemplar of them.

Plato

R. M. Hare

Preface

This book is not intended as an addition to the already enormous and growing literature of Platonic scholarship, but as an encouragement and help to ordinary people who wish to make Plato's acquaintance. For this reason I have on the whole concentrated on the easier, which means the earlier and middle, dialogues, though the later ones are not entirely neglected. It is safe to say that no single statement can be made in interpretation of Plato which some scholars will not dispute. I have tried to bring out what I think he is up to, in a way that will be comprehensible; but the limits of a popular book do not allow me to defend my views beyond giving a few references to the text. I do not think that they are all that unorthodox, and where there is a lot of dispute I have tried not to conceal it. Above all, I have aimed to show how relevant Plato's dialogues are to questions which trouble us, or should trouble us, today, including some very practical issues about education and politics. To bring this out I have occasionally mentioned the names of thinkers of the modern period; but nothing of importance in my account of Plato will be missed by a reader to whom these names mean nothing.

In concentrating on what I think is the nucleus of Plato's philosophy, I have had to neglect many interesting and important topics. I should have liked in particular to say more on his views about love and about the arts. I have not thought it necessary to dwell on the superb quality of his dialogues as literature and drama; they are still as fresh and delightful as ever, and need no salesman.

A number of colleagues have been kind enough at my request to look at and criticize my typescript, among them Sir Kenneth Dover, Professors Ackrill and Moravcsik, Jonathan Barnes, Russell Meiggs, Christopher Taylor and Julius Tomin. Although all of these know incomparably more about Plato than I do, I have been stubborn enough not always to agree with them; but all the same my debt to them is very great. I should never have undertaken, let alone completed, this book if I had not been privileged to spend the whole of 1980 at the Center for Advanced Study in the Behavioral

Sciences at Stanford, where I was made so happy and free from worries that this and another larger book flowed from my type-writer without any of the usual interruptions and frustrations. I am enormously grateful to the Director and staff at the Center, and to Oxford University for letting me go there.

To avoid footnotes, the few references have been consigned to the end of the book, except for those to Plato, which are in brackets in the text, giving the pages of Stephanus' edition as used in the margin of nearly all modern editions and translations. References in brackets preceded by 'p.' are to pages in this book. In the very few Greek words I had to quote, and in proper names in the Index, I have indicated the quantity of vowels by putting a bar over all the long ones, and have used a system of transliteration which relates the Greek words closely to modern English words derived from them (for example, *'psychē'*).

R. M. HARE

1 Life and times

Although this is not a work of biography, it is necessary to say something about the environment in which Plato grew up; for without some grasp of this, we cannot understand how he became a philosopher, and became the kind of philosopher that he was. Of the biographical information that has survived much is unreliable, and very little is of relevance to his philosophical development. There are some letters ascribed to him, some of them explicitly autobiographical. Their genuineness is disputed; but even if spurious they are probably close enough in time to their subject to be of use as evidence. The anecdotes of later writers are mostly either doubtful or trivial or both. So we do not need to go into the question of whether, for example, having been named by his parents Aristocles, he got called Platon because of his broad shoulders or his broad forehead, and other such details. But we do know about at least three episodes in his life which must have made a profound impression on him, and which place him in his historical setting.

Plato was born in 427 BC into an upper class Athenian family, and lived to be eighty. He would have been old enough to witness with young and impressionable eyes the last scenes of a tragedy, the decline and fall of the Athenian Empire. And he lived long enough to see the first beginnings of an empire of a very different sort, that of Philip of Macedon, whose son Alexander conquered a large part of the known world. The intervening period was one of constant and inconclusive warfare between the little Greek city states, with first one and then another achieving a brief hegemony, but none managing to bring any unity to Greece. That was left to the Macedonians after Plato's day.

The Athenian Empire started with a moral basis as a league to secure the freedom of the Greek cities, after their wonderful victories which had delivered them from the threat of conquest by Persia at the beginning of the fifth century. Thucydides, whose history of the period should be read by anybody who wants to understand Plato, puts into the mouth of Pericles, the chief architect of the Empire, a speech in honour of the Athenians who had died in the war with Sparta; and it has become famous as an expression of the ideals which excited Athens in the generation before Plato. Plato parodies this speech in his *Menexenus*. The ideals are high, but not exclusively moral according to our way of thinking. Naked imperialism plays a large part in them, and Pericles is more concerned with the fine figure that Athens is cutting than with justice to the allies whom she was turning into subjects. She ruled them in an ever more grasping and tyrannical fashion, and used their tribute to build the temples on the Acropolis which still amaze us, as well as for the navy which was the basis of her power. Recalcitrant cities were punished with increasing severity as the fear of successful rebellion began to bite: Mytilene was threatened with massacre but reprieved at the eleventh hour; Melos actually suffered total extinction.

Reading dialogues like the *Gorgias* with the history of the Athenian Empire in mind, we can see that Plato was reacting with moral revulsion to an attitude of mind current in Greece at the national as well as the personal level; an attitude which valued honour and glory above the virtues which enable people to 'dwell together in unity'. Of the founders of the Empire he says 'Not moderation and uprightness, but harbours, and dock-yards, and walls, and tribute-money, and such nonsense, were what they filled the city with' (519a).

For nearly all the last third of the fifth century, until her defeat in 405 BC, Athens was almost constantly at war with Sparta, which with her allies resisted and in the end brought down the Athenian power. Plato was old enough to have fought in the last part of the war, as all citizens were required to, but we have no reliable record of his military service. A man of his class would naturally have served in the cavalry; and his brothers are said in the *Republic* to have fought well (368a).

The mention of Plato's social position may remind us that there was another dimension to the struggles of the Greek cities during this and the next century. The warfare was not merely between but within the cities. Almost every city was divided politically between the upper class and the rest of the free citizens (the numerous slaves can be left out of this political reckoning). This must not be taken as implying that there were no well-born democrats; indeed patrician Whigs like Pericles played the greatest part in the development of the democracy, and while it prospered, the imperial ideal enjoyed general support from all classes. But increasingly these well-born leaders gave place to self-made men of the people and their sons, who could make themselves congenial to the mass meeting which was their parliament. Plato's class looked on these demagogues with contempt, tinged with fear. The political feelings amid which he would have grown up are those expressed at the beginning of a political pamphlet of the day, the so-called *Polity of the Athenians*: 'The kind of polity the Athenians have chosen is one I do not commend; for by choosing it they have chosen that bad men should come off better than good men.'

Sparta, Athens' enemy, was from inclination and self-interest a supporter of aristocracy or oligarchy; the populist Athenian leaders were always the most violent advocates of the war against her, and the rich, whose wealth and way of life were at risk, showed less enthusiasm for it, as for the Empire. The ambitions that turned young upper-class Englishmen and other Europeans into imperialists in the nineteenth century were indeed there but the prospects were far less attractive; and so, contrary to our way of thinking, it was the poor who were the main beneficiaries and supporters of empire. In most cities the democrats favoured alliance with, or submission to, Athens, and the 'few' sought the support of Sparta.

As the war went on, the internal divisions in the cities became more bitter and more savage; and even after the defeat of Athens the same sort of thing went on throughout the fourth century. Unrestrained personal ambition was a main motive in politicians. In the *Meno* that not untypical young man, asked by Socrates to define 'virtue' or 'excellence', answers that the excellence of a *man* is to be able, while engaging in politics, to do good to one's friends and harm to one's enemies, while taking care not to come to any harm oneself (71e). And in the *Gorgias* another young man holds out as an object of envy Archelaus of Macedon, who by a series of murders of his nearest relatives made himself king (471b).

Athens herself was relatively free of the political murders and massacres which happened elsewhere in Greece; but all the same, if we were to read of events in fifth- and fourth-century Greece in a modern newspaper, we should be glad we did not live there, especially if we had not heard about its cultural achievements—did not know, for example, that the Parthenon was built during this time, or that year by year some of the world's greatest poets and dramatists were bringing out their plays in the festivals. We may note in passing that two moderately sanguinary political leaders, Critias, Plato's cousin, and Dionysius I of Syracuse (both of whom will feature in our story shortly), wrote tragedies which were performed in the Athenian competitions.

Of these two evils in Greece, strife between and strife within cities, Plato says little by way of a remedy for the former (on which his literary rival Isocrates has a better record), and in the *Laws* and elsewhere treats the latter as the principal problem needing solution (628a, b). He thought that civil strife could be ended by a good system of government, and to describe and justify such a system was one of his main aims.

Another more general cause contributed to the moral unsettlement of the Greek cities. This was their increasing intellectual sophistication, the effect, perhaps, of widening cultural horizons. There is a story told in Herodotus' history of the Persian Wars: a Persian ruler confronted some Greeks, who by custom burnt their dead relations, with some Indians, whose practice was to eat them, and concluded from the shocked reactions of both to the others' ways that

> Custom, the king of all,
> Gods and men alike,
> Is their guide.

Plato quotes the same lines of Pindar in the *Gorgias* (484b); they go on

> It justifies the greatest violence;
> Its hand is over all.

The word translated 'custom' also meant 'law'. We can see how the idea got around that law and morality were alike based on mere convention. There was not even a stable religious backing for them. Plato points out in the *Euthyphro* that the gods themselves are, according to tradition, at variance with one another; in heaven as on earth moral differences lead to civil war (7e).

Protagoras, who with Socrates was one of the great thinkers of the preceding generation, articulated this relativism in his doctrine that 'A man is a measure of all things: of what is, that it is, and of what is not, that it is not.' As Plato implies in the *Theaetetus* (152a), where he discusses the doctrine, Protagoras meant 'each man for himself'. We shall come back later to Socrates' and Plato's attempted rebuttal of this relativist view; but it is easy to see how the old moral restraints slipped away, especially in politics.

These factors—unscrupulous political strife and the growth of moral relativism—reinforced each other. Thucydides, in a philosophically penetrating passage, points out that it affected even the language in which thinking had to be done. In his discussion of the effects of political violence he says 'In justifying their actions, they reversed the customary descriptive meanings of words.' He gives examples: what would have been called 'an irresponsible gamble' got to be called 'a brave and comradely venture'. This process, referred to in similar terms in the *Republic* (560d), is the same as that which in recent times has been called 'persuasive definition'. Its immediate result was to turn morality upside down; but indirectly it had the effect of stimulating Socrates and Plato to look instead for a way of finding *secure* definitions of moral words or of the things they connote. That is why we find them asking 'What then *is* courage?'; 'What *is* uprightness?', and in general 'What *is* goodness?'

It is easy to imagine the young Plato, under the influence of Socrates, being inspired by the hope of answering such questions; but in other respects he grew up in an atmosphere of disillusion culminating in disaster. Its effect on him will have been heightened by his upper-class upbringing. As we have seen, the Athenian aristocrats were by no means wholehearted supporters of the Empire; most of them admired Sparta for its orderly and stable system of government, on which Plato's political ideas are in part modelled; and there was at least a suspicion that treachery by members of this class had contributed to the final naval disaster for Athens at Aegospotami.

At any rate when Sparta came to settle the affairs of defeated Athens, although she did not, as some had expected, massacre the democrats, she secured her own interest by installing an oligarchic government, called by its enemies 'The Thirty Tyrants', among whom were two relatives of Plato's: Critias, his mother's first cousin, and Charmides, his maternal uncle. Both receive friendly treatment in his dialogues. The Thirty were indeed tyrannical and arbitrary: Plato records, in the *Apology* (32c), Socrates' courageous refusal to arrest a fellow-citizen, the democrat Leon, whom they had selected for judicial murder. Their government did not last long; it was ousted by a democratic regime, whose record was more moderate. Athens had lost her former glory; she did not, however, sink into complete ignominy, but took her share in the ups and downs of Greek mini-power politics.

We may conceive what effect these events—the collapse of a no longer inspiring imperialist democracy followed by the wretched performance of the opposing party—had on the young Plato. An able man of his class would naturally have sought a place in public life, and there is evidence that he started with this ambition; but since the chief qualification for success in politics was a total lack of scruple, it is not surprising that he was frightened off. He is said to have written poetry when young, and from the evidence of his writings (including a few poems) he would have made a good poet; but he came to see that there was another more lasting way of affecting men's minds, and thus, he hoped, the course of events. Socrates is expressing Plato's own attitude to politics when he says in the *Republic*, 'It would be like a man among wild animals, not willing to join in their crimes, nor able by himself to resist the savagery of all the rest; before he could help the city or his friends he would come to a sticky end without doing any good for himself or anybody else' (496d).

In 399 BC, after the restoration of the democracy, Socrates, Plato's idol, was tried on a charge of disbelief in the gods and corrupting the young, and condemned to death. The effect on Plato was profound and several of his dialogues are related to this event: Socrates' *Apology* or defence at his trial; the *Crito* in which he gives reasons for not making his escape after his condemnation, which would have been easy; and the *Phaedo*, in which he spends his last hours arguing for the immortality of the soul; and there are a number of smaller allusions. Plato seems to have resolved to devote his life to the exposition and development of Socrates' ideas.

Plato's distaste for political action can only have been strengthened by the outcome of his only active intervention in politics. This occurred not in his own city of Athens but at Syracuse in Sicily, at the court of Dionysius I, and of his son and namesake. We do not know why Plato first went to Sicily, when he was about forty; but it may have been as an offshoot of a purely philosophical visit to the neighbouring Italian cities, which boasted some distinguished philosophers, especially the followers of Pythagoras. When he was in Syracuse he formed a deep personal affection for the young Dion, whose sister was married to Dionysius I, and who himself married his own niece, her daughter. Plato later wrote a poem on Dion in which he called the relation 'love', and said that it had driven him out of his mind. According to Greek ideas there was nothing unusual about this, and the second remark seems no great exaggeration if we think of the things that Dion later persuaded Plato to do, against his own better judgement.

Dion became Plato's pupil and absorbed his doctrine. We do not know how long Plato's first visit to Sicily lasted. There is an improbable story that Dionysius caused him to be sold into slavery, whence he was ransomed by friends. He returned to Athens, and there founded a philosophical school called, from its location in the grove dedicated to the hero Academus, the Academy. In it Plato and his fellow-philosophers shared a common table and engaged in mathematics, dialectic (that is, philosophy) and other studies, all seen as relevant to the training of statesmen. It was not the first such institution, but was probably modelled on similar communities of the Pythagoreans in Italy. Aristotle was only one of its distinguished members, and it lasted for centuries.

When Plato was about sixty, Dionysius I died and was succeeded by his son Dionysius II, whose uncle Dion conceived the idea that the young ruler might be moulded by Plato into the philosopher-king of the *Republic*. This was an unpromising scheme from the beginning, and it is likely that Plato accepted the invitation to Syracuse with reluctance and few hopes. But it was hard for him to resist the challenge, in view of what he had said in the *Republic* about such a philosopher-ruler being the only chance of rescuing the human race from its ills (473d). The young Dionysius was clever, but impatient of systematic instruction, and he no doubt had much else to engage his attention. Dion lost favour and was exiled, and Plato soon asked and received permission to return to Athens, where Dion joined him at the Academy. But Dionysius was still friendly to Plato, and there was an understanding that he and Dion should come back when the climate was more propitious.

Four years later Dionysius asked Plato to return, saying that Dion could come back after a year. He professed a continuing zeal for philosophy, and supported this claim with testimonials from eminent philosophers. Plato was pressed from all sides, and in the end consented. But Dionysius was no more tractable; while giving himself airs as a philosopher, he kept Dion in exile and confiscated and sold his property. Plato escaped with some difficulty from Sicily, and wisely refused to lend any support to Dion's attempt to recover his position by force. This attempt was at first successful, but Dion was later assassinated by a supposed friend, a fellow-member of Plato's circle, Callippus (who was not the only student of Plato's to become guilty of the political murder of a fellow-alumnus). Plato, his views about politics amply confirmed, kept out of them and devoted himself to his Academy.

2 *Plato's forebears*

To understand Plato we have also to look at the most significant of the earlier thinkers who may have influenced his ideas. Whether we call them philosophers or not is unimportant; the word has wider and narrower senses. At most a few fragments of their works survive, and nearly all our information comes from much later sources; so the Presocratic philosophers, as they are generically called, have been a happy battleground for scholars. From these disputes little has emerged which can be confidently relied on as true; all we can do here is to pick up a few ideas, attributed to one or other of these great men, which, *if* they were current in Greece by Plato's time, *may* have contributed to his intellectual background. It is on the face of it unlikely that all the ideas we find in his dialogues were newly-minted; and in fact there is quite a lot of evidence that they were not. Originality in philosophy often consists not in having new thoughts, but in making clear what was not clear before.

The earliest natural philosophers, starting with the shadowy figure of Thales in sixth-century Miletus on the eastern shore of the Aegean Sea, made cosmology their main interest. But the fact that the Greek word '*kosmos*', from which 'cosmology' is derived, had also a moral significance ('good order') may make us suspect that their motive was not, any more than that of their successors including Plato, mere scientific curiosity. Plato in the *Phaedo* attributes to Anaxagoras, one of these, the view that 'it is Mind which imposes *order* on all things and disposes each of them as it is *best* for it to be' (97c).

We find in these early thinkers the beginning of the urge to reconcile the 'One' and the 'Many', which is a recurring theme throughout Greek philosophy, above all in Plato. There confronts us a multitude of phenomena in the world as it presents itself to our senses; cannot some unifying principle be found to bring order into this chaos? The early cosmologists sought to find it by claiming that everything in the world was formed out of (or perhaps even *really* consisted of) some single material (Thales suggested water). This kind of solution was later abandoned; but the problem remained of finding some coherent reality which underlay the baffling diversity of the world (the 'manifold' as Immanuel Kant was later to call it). Plato had his own solution to this problem, as we shall see —a solution which depended not on physics but on logic, metaphysics and ethics.

An important step in the direction which Plato afterwards took may have been made by Pythagoras, of Croton in southern Italy (he was born on the island of Samos, not far from Miletus, probably in 570 BC). Since nothing of his work remains, and the stories about him are all suspect, it is even more difficult than usual to sieve out his ideas from those of his later disciples, with whom Plato was acquainted. For our purposes this does not matter; for if an idea which we find developed in Plato could have come from a Pythagorean source, it is less important whether that source was the Master himself. The chief danger to be guarded against is that of supposing that some idea came from the Pythagorean school to Plato, when in fact it went from Plato to the later Pythagoreans.

We may notice at least three suggestions which Plato may have picked up from the Pythagoreans. The first was that of a tightly-organized community of like-minded thinkers who should not only rule their own life together in accordance with strict principles, but provide guidance (even governance) for the polity in which they lived. Plato's political proposals could be said to be a result of the combination of this Pythagorean idea with the Spartan model of orderly government and discipline.

If the stories about Pythagoras are to be believed, he actually for a time came near to making real the dream which Plato was later to dream in his *Republic*—the ideal of the philosopher-ruler. Even if true, it did not last; for Pythagoras had to rely on persuasion, neither having nor seeking the absolute and secure power which Plato demanded for his philosopher-kings. We are told that in about 500 BC, after Pythagoras had been in Croton for some thirty years and in a position of power for some twenty, there was a revolution; many of his followers were killed and he himself had to flee. But twenty years is a long period of stability by Greek standards, if not by Plato's.

The Pythagoreans may also have been the source of the idea, central to Plato's thought, that mathematics, and abstract thinking generally, including logic, can provide a secure basis, not only for philosophy in the modern sense, but also for substantial theses in science and in morals. It is not certain whether either Pythagoras or Plato distinguished clearly enough between the important truth that mathematics and other abstract reasonings are a crucial ingredient in science, and the equally important error of thinking that they can by themselves establish conclusions of substance about the physical world. Aristotle accuses both, in very similar terms, of a related mistake (involving, to put it in his way, the failure to distinguish form from matter): the Pythagoreans, he says, attempt to construct bodies having physical properties like weight out of abstract geometrical or arithmetical entities like points, lines and numbers. It is arguable that in the *Timaeus*, where Plato seeks to found cosmology purely on mathematics (especially geometry), he lays himself open to this criticism.

A simpler illustration of the mistake is to be found in the *Phaedo*, where Plato slides from the logically-established truth that life and death are incompatible to the invalid substantial conclusion that the soul, being the principle of life, cannot perish (105–6). This Pythagorean mistake may have infected Plato's arguments about morality too, which sometimes seem to be conjuring substantial rabbits out of logical hats.

Thirdly, Plato became very Pythagorean in his mystical (or in a broad sense religious) approach to the soul and its place in the material world—although that was not the only source of these views, and both Plato and Pythagoras may have been influenced by ideas from the East and by the 'mystery religions' such as

Orphism which spread through Greece in this period. The early Pythagoreans seem (though this has been disputed) to have been mind-body dualists; that is to say, they thought, as Plato was to think, that the soul or mind (*psȳchē*) was an entity distinct and separable from the body. This was consonant with primitive Greek thinking about the soul, as found, for example, in the earliest Greek poet Homer.

Empedocles of Acragas in Sicily, in the early fifth century, believed in the transmigration of souls, and it is possible that he got the doctrine from Pythagoras; Plato certainly makes use of it. The Platonic teaching about the soul, that before our birth it had acquaintance with objects in an eternal realm, and thus can, through mathematics leading to dialectic (philosophy), regain knowledge of them in this life, has what in ancient times passed for a Pythagorean stamp; and so does his denigration of the body and its base desires (the 'flesh' in St Paul's sense), and his consequent asceticism.

Two great philosophers, very different both from Pythagoras and from each other, but who lived at roughly the same time, also seem to have affected Plato profoundly. They took up opposite points of view on the problem of 'The One and the Many'. The first was Heraclitus, of Ephesus quite near Miletus, with whose more extreme disciple Cratylus Plato associated during his stay in Athens. Perhaps because of Cratylus, Plato treats Heraclitus as emphasizing the diversity and changeability of the Many at the expense of the One; for Plato, Heraclitus is the archetypal believer in universal flux, who thinks that the utterly unstable manifold of phenomena that our senses purvey is all there is. Whether this was actually true of Heraclitus himself we shall never know; his few surviving fragments are extremely cryptic and are used by scholars to support widely varying interpretations.

Parmenides, by contrast, who was born somewhat later at Elea in southern Italy, went to the opposite extreme, denying the reality of appearances altogether. Though things in the world *seem* to be constantly changing and in motion, they logically cannot be. Parmenides' arguments (in verse) are much less clear than the more fragmentary survivals from those of his disciples Melissus and Zeno (not to be confused with Zeno the Stoic). This much is clear, however, that the fundamental premiss of the Eleatics (the name given to this group of philosophers, derived from that of Parmenides' city) was that 'Things which are not are not.' This they regarded as a logically necessary truth, which indeed it must be if there is no equivocation upon 'are not'. Unfortunately the Eleatics seem (committing the same kind of mistake as we have just noticed when discussing Pythagoras) to have meant different things by 'are not' in the subject and predicate of their premiss, taking this logical truth to establish a substantial conclusion, namely that void or empty space cannot exist; and therefore, since any movement requires an empty space for a thing to move into, that movement (and by a related argument change of other kinds) cannot take place. Zeno invented his famous paradoxes with the aim of proving the same point, that the belief in motion and change leads to logical absurdities. So the Eleatics concluded that, in spite of appearances, the universe is really solid throughout and immobile.

The work of Parmenides and his disciples represents the first thoroughgoing attempt to establish a cosmological system on the basis of rigorous logical arguments. Some may hail it as the beginning of metaphysics, others damn it as the first outbreak of metaphysical pseudo-science divorced from the observation of nature; but there is no doubt that it had immense influence. Zeno's paradoxes are still not all solved to everybody's satisfaction; and we find Plato puzzling about the difficulties raised by the Eleatics. He does this in the *Parmenides, Theaetetus* and *Sophist*, although by the third of these the problems have changed into ones about the alleged impossibility of making true negative statements. He shows thereby that he understands (as perhaps the Eleatics themselves did) that their origins lie in logical rather than cosmological difficulties.

In the whole of Plato's philosophy we may think of him as trying, by a more careful examination of the arguments, to find a synthesis between the Heraclitan or Cratylan view, which he accepted, that the world of appearances is a multifarious flux, and the Parmenidean doctrine that reality is one and unchanging. He found it, as we shall see, by postulating two worlds, a world of sense, always in flux, and a unified world of Ideas, not available to our senses but only to thought, which alone are fully knowable. But the two-world view itself can plausibly be attributed to Parmenides, together with the associated distinction, so important to Plato, between knowledge (which is of reality) and mere opinion (which is concerned with appearances).

One other fifth-century cosmologist must be briefly mentioned. Anaxagoras, a natural philosopher of the old school, was born in about 500 BC at Clazomenae not far from Miletus, and lived in Athens as a member of Pericles' circle. He, like Protagoras, another friend of Pericles, and like Socrates later, got into trouble for his philosophy; Anaxagoras and Protagoras escaped with exile, as Socrates could probably have done if his principles had not been so uncompromising, and as Aristotle did later when in similar trouble. We are told in Plato's *Phaedo*, in a passage I have already quoted (97c; see p. 116), that Anaxagoras attracted Socrates' attention with his doctrine that Mind (*nous*) is the cause of all physical processes, but lost it when Socrates discovered that Anaxagoras made no *use* of Mind in explaining what happens, invoking grosser physical causes instead. But all the same he may have put into Socrates' or Plato's head (it is never certain whether the Socrates of the dialogues is the real Socrates) the idea that Mind had a place in explaining how the world works. This idea is prominent in dialogues like the *Timaeus* and the *Laws*, the second at least of which was written late in Plato's life.

It will be best to leave until Chapter 7 a discussion of the thinkers, called collectively the Sophists, against whom Plato was consciously reacting in much of his moral philosophy, and who appear, often but not always in savage caricature, in his dialogues. One of them, Protagoras, has been briefly mentioned already. They belong to the generation before Plato's; that is, they were roughly Socrates' contemporaries.

Of Socrates himself (obviously by far the greatest influence on Plato's thinking) I shall say little, for the reason that his philosophy is so continuous with that of Plato that scholars have found it hard to decide which views belonged to which. We have some, but not much, independent evidence about what Socrates thought, for example from Aristophanes, Xenophon, and Aristotle. However, Aristophanes' portrayal is satirical and popular, and may have had a wider target than Socrates in particular; Xenophon was no philosopher, and therefore not in a position to understand at all deeply what was troubling Socrates; and it is not always clear, when Aristotle attributes a view to Socrates, whether he means the character in the dialogues or the historical person.

My own view, which is fairly orthodox, is that we can with some confidence attribute to Socrates a concern with the difference between opinion which merely happens to be correct and knowledge; with the search for secure definitions to turn the former into the latter; with a certain method of testing such definitions called *elenchos* or scrutiny; with the application of this method to practical decisions about how to live; with the question of whether goodness or excellence of character can be taught, and if so by what educative process; and with the possibility that excellence of character and knowledge of the truth about what was good were somehow inseparable, so that, if one could impart the knowledge, nobody who had it would willingly live badly. To all these doctrines we shall be returning.

On the other hand, I think that it is safer to attribute to Plato himself than to Socrates the cautious approach to moral education we find in the *Republic*, which insists on a thorough indoctrination in right opinions before a select few are introduced to philosophy and put on the path to knowledge; and his later doctrine about the soul, with its three parts and its communion with a world of Ideas separate from things in this world—a communion enjoyed in a former life, and, for those able to undertake philosophic study, in this. This last group of doctrines may well be based on Pythagorean ideas.

The extremely deep and difficult investigations of meta-physical and logical questions which occupy many of the later dialogues are fairly obviously the result of Plato's own perplexities; Socrates and the others who influenced him got him into these, and to some degree he got himself out of them. But their solution did not become clear before the work of Aristotle, if then; though there can be no doubt that the discussions in the Academy, in which he took part, and some of which are reflected in Plato's later dialogues, helped Aristotle on his way. But between the Socratic/early-Platonic caterpillar and the Aristotelian butterfly there intervenes a pupal stage; just what is going on behind the opaque surface of the chrysalis represented by these dialogues, and how much of the development was due to Plato, how much to Aristotle, scholars have not yet succeeded in determining, and probably never will.

3 How Plato became a philosopher

When we find somebody (whether it was Plato or Socrates) troubled by certain important questions for the first time in history, it is worth asking, 'Why *then*?' We have sketched Plato's situation in history and in the history of ideas; but we have so far only hinted at reasons why he, or anybody else, should have asked just the questions he did ask. But this is not hard to understand, especially to us, whose circumstances make the same questions tormenting. Although it may seem to us that the scale and pace of change today are greater than for Plato's contemporaries, they were, subjectively speaking, just as unsettled by it.

Suppose then that we ask what led Plato to put into the mouth of Meno, at the beginning of the dialogue named after him, the question 'Can you tell me, Socrates, whether goodness (virtue, excellence) is a thing that is taught; or is it neither taught nor learnt by practice, but comes to men by nature, or in some other way?' This is the question (also raised earlier in the *Protagoras*) which the whole of Plato's moral philosophy, and thus, indirectly, his other philosophy, is attempting to answer. Although Plato certainly had the philosophical temperament, and could get interested in philosophical questions purely for their own sake, moral philosophy was what set him going, and it started as the philosophy of education.

It is clear from the rest of the *Meno* (perhaps the best dialogue for someone to read first if he wants to understand what made Plato into a philosopher) why Plato asked this question. A lot is made, as in several other dialogues, of the hit-or-miss quality of Athenian moral education: here were admirable citizens like Pericles, who wanted to do the best for their children, and taught them riding and wrestling and music, all very success-fully; but to make them into good men was another matter. Somehow there did not seem to be any way of doing it that offered more than a fifty-fifty chance of success. Could there be a way? How familiar this all sounds!

As we have seen, life in the Greek cities, and especially the political life which engaged so much of their energies, was a pretty dirty game, and becoming more so. It was natural to find one of the causes of these evils in a failure of moral education: in particular, in the emergence of people into public life who were seeking their own good rather than that of the city. The mainspring of Socrates', and through him of Plato's, philo-sophical endeavours was the desire to diagnose the trouble and find a remedy.

The remedy that they were to propose comes out very clearly in the *Meno*. Right at the beginning, Socrates says that he can-not answer Meno's question, whether goodness (or excellence) can be taught, before he knows what it *is*. His point, brought out later, and already made in an earlier dialogue, the *Laches* (190b), is that one is bound to fumble in teaching anything unless one knows what one is trying to teach. But does anybody know this? If somebody had this knowledge, and so was able to teach men to be good men in the kind of way that riding-instructors teach them to be good horsemen or flute-teachers teach them to be good flautists, then by putting him in charge of the education of the young we should ensure a supply of good men in public life, instead of the present inferior crop.

But here Plato makes a very important distinction. It is possible to be a good man, in a manner of speaking, without *knowing* what it is to be a good man. For practical purposes, a man may lead an exemplary life on the basis of what Plato calls 'right opinion' or 'true belief'. This will lead him to do all the right things and give excellent advice to others. But this condi-tion of unreasoned right living is an unstable one. Someone may start with all the best opinions and habits, and then something may happen to upset these (for example, his encountering new ideas propagated by some charismatic intellectual figure).

This, indeed, is exactly why the Athenians sent Socrates to his death: for 'corrupting the young'. They took him as a paradigm of the kind of 'sophist' (as these new intellectual gurus were called) who was leading the young astray. In this witch-hunt they were egged on by Aristophanes, who in his comedy *The Clouds* portrays Socrates as a sophist, turning the young away from their old good habits and putting all kinds of strange new ideas into their heads which undermined their morality; and the play ends with a powerful incitement of his audience to violence. But perhaps Socrates' attackers had got hold of the wrong man. If Plato was right, it was Socrates who was pointing the way to a solution of the problem.

In Plato's reconstruction of Socrates' defence at his trial, he makes him, after he has dismissed Aristophanes' caricature as mixing him up with teachers of a quite different stamp, go on later to narrate a story about himself. The Delphic oracle (a highly respected and authoritative source of religious doctrine and political advice) had said of him that he was the wisest man in Greece. In his efforts to discover what could be meant by this, he had engaged in many conversations with people who were reputed to know about all kinds of things, but who revealed, through their failure to give a satisfactory account of what they claimed to know, that they did not have *knowledge* at all. We may take some of the early dialogues as Plato's versions of encounters of this kind. Socrates concluded that the reason why the oracle called him the wisest man was that he alone knew that he did not know; the others thought they knew but did not.

Near the end of the *Meno* Socrates makes a related point, that although there are few things that he knows, one of these is that there is a difference between knowledge and right opinion (98b). The difference, he says, is that knowledge of anything is 'tied down' by the ability to give a reason for what we know, and this makes it, unlike right opinion, something abiding which will not run away. This demand for a 'reckoning of the reason' or 'account of the explanation' or 'definition of the cause' or 'explicit answer to the question "Why?"' (no one translation is adequate) is Socrates' and Plato's most central and seminal idea.

If we combine this with the point made already, that it is knowledge of what goodness is that enables us to teach it, we can already see the outlines of the proposal which Plato thought he got from Socrates. What we have to do is to find a way of knowing, as opposed to merely having opinions about, what things are, and above all what goodness is. We shall then be able, if we are allowed to, to pass on a stable kind of goodness to future generations. This is the programme of the *Republic*, and there are clear anticipations of it at the very end of the *Meno*.

Let us look more closely at the elements in this programme, in order to understand the task which Plato had set himself, and some of its problems. First of all, there is the idea that the teaching of goodness is somehow like the teaching of riding or flute-playing, which means that goodness itself is some kind of attainment like these. But is it? We use the same word 'good' for a good flautist as for a good man. Does it mean the same in both cases? To answer either 'Yes' or 'No' to this question can be highly misleading, because 'mean the same' is ambiguous. But at any rate Socrates and Plato were irresistibly attracted by the analogy between virtue or good living, and the arts and skills.

Plato, at any rate, saw quite soon that there were difficulties in this assimilation. In the early dialogue called the *Lesser Hippias*, a paradoxical analogy is presented between bad living and, for example, bad wrestling (374a). The wrestler who falls intentionally is a better wrestler than the one who falls because he cannot remain upright; by analogy one should argue that the man who says an untruth intentionally is a better man than one who does it unintentionally. The general point is that, if good living is a skill, then one shows one has it by one's ability to live rightly if *one wants to*. But most of us think that goodness consists in living rightly whether one wants to or not. In the Socratic manner, the paradox is just thrown at us, not resolved; but it clearly needs unravelling.

A related difficulty is presented in the first book of the *Republic* (332-3). If good living is a skill or art, what is it the skill to do? There seems no way of specifying the skill as 'the skill to do *x*' without making it also the skill to do the opposite of *x*. Another difficulty is this: if one has skill in or knowledge of wrestling, then one is a good wrestler. But is knowledge of goodness (that which, as Plato thought, would enable one to teach it) *sufficient* to make one a good man? As it has been put, is knowledge sufficient for virtue? Socrates seems to have thought so; but few people have believed him.

Another problem Plato had to face was that of what it is to know something, a problem closely bound up with the question of what the something is that we know. His Theory of Ideas (which claims that what we know has to be an eternally existing object) is Plato's answer to this question. And along with investigations into the status of the things known, Plato had to face problems about the person who is doing the knowing and about his relation to these things. His account of the soul or mind was to become the framework which held together his entire philosophy. The division of the mind into 'faculties' or 'powers' or even 'parts' enabled him to assign different kinds of mental activity to these different parts and thus, he thought, distinguish them more clearly. The mind was important to him for another reason too: as we have seen, he followed the Pythagoreans in regarding it as a separate entity from the body— an entity which could exist apart and independently. This enabled him, he thought, to solve the problem of how we can obtain knowledge about questions (in mathematics, for example) whose answers cannot be obtained by sense-perception (what later came to be called *a priori* knowledge). His solution was that the mind obtained knowledge of the eternal Ideas before it entered into the body at birth, and only had to recollect it in this life. It also enabled him to claim that after death we are exposed to the rewards and punishments so graphically described in the 'eschatological myths' at the end of several of his dialogues.

If these problems about knowing, the things known, and the knower could be solved, Plato thought that practical philosophy, which was his predominant concern and his incentive for undertaking all the rest of his inquiries, could be put on a secure basis. If it can be established that there are things which we can know for sure, and that the chief among these is the Good, then the gaining and imparting of this knowledge will be the means whereby we can not only lead good lives ourselves, but by education enable others to do the same. There remains the problem of setting up a political framework in which this education can take place; and to this problem Plato devoted his two longest dialogues, the *Republic*, written in middle life and before his disillusion in Sicily, and the *Laws*, written as an old man, as well as great parts of others. His view was that it could be done only by giving absolute power, not only over the educative process but also over the entire machinery of government, to those who had the knowledge.

It may be helpful at this point to give the reader an overview of the scope of Plato's dialogues. Though in the case of various dialogues there is dispute about their relative dating, or even in some cases about whether Plato himself or some disciple wrote them, there is fairly general agreement that they can be divided chronologically into groups having distinctive features. First comes a group of characteristically 'Socratic' dialogues. There are the *Apology* and the *Crito*, already mentioned, and then a group of short dialogues in which Socrates sets up puzzles, especially about particular virtues or good qualities and the relation of these to each other and to knowledge. The puzzles are not resolved in these dialogues; often they are taken up later by Plato, and many are discussed in greater depth by Aristotle.

Puzzle (*aporiā*) or paradox was a recognized method of philosophic inquiry from Zeno onwards, and still is; it can be used either, as by Zeno, to refute a theory by showing that it has unacceptable consequences, or, as most commonly by Socrates, and in modern times by Lewis Carroll, simply to set us thinking about a problem by showing to what apparently absurd results the apparently logical implications of commonly accepted notions or ways of speaking can lead. We may suppose that this method continued in use in Plato's Academy, and that many even of the later dialogues reflect it (though in them Plato is not so chary of positive conclusions); no doubt the puzzles were discussed *ad nauseam* among his students. Aristotle, a participant, produces elegant solutions of some of them. Concentrated examples of such a technique occur in the *Euthydemus*, whose combination of sophistication and *naïveté* has made it hard to date with confidence.

In this first group we may include, besides the dialogues just mentioned, the *Euthyphro*, *Laches*, *Lysis*, *Charmides*, *Theages*, *Greater* and *Lesser Hippias*, *Ion* and *Greater Alcibiades*.

Second in chronological order comes a group of longer dialogues, probably spanning the period of Plato's life immediately before and after his first visit to Sicily. This contains the *Protagoras*, *Meno*, *Gorgias*, *Phaedo*, *Symposium*, and *Phaedrus*, as well as that oddity the *Menexenus* (see p. 108). This was perhaps the most crucial phase in Plato's development; the Socratic puzzles about the virtues are discussed more deeply and connectedly; important positive and substantive doctrines are introduced concerning morality, education and politics; there are two marvellous disquisitions on love; and the 'Theory of Ideas', to be discussed in Chapter 5, makes a gradual appearance, with its insistence that to the moral and other qualities there correspond eternally existing entities, available to inspection by an instructed mind, which either are the models of such qualities, or give them to things by being present in them, or both.

Along with this development comes a strong dose of Pythagoreanism (plausibly connected by scholars with the visit to Italy and Sicily). Plato propounds the view that our souls are immortal and had access to these Ideas in a previous existence.

The *Republic* was probably also written during this time. Since its composition may have taken many years, it is unprofitable to speculate on its dating in relation to this second group (especially the *Phaedrus*). Many scholars think that its first book, which has the characteristics of the earliest group, started life as a separate piece, and that the rest was written much later. The topic of the whole dialogue is 'uprightness' or 'right living', and whether it is to be recommended as good policy for those seeking happiness; this leads Plato into large-scale proposals on how society should be organized (see Chapter 9). It also contains the first full-dress exposition of his views about the nature of knowledge and about philosophical method.

There is no agreement about the date of the *Cratylus*, devoted to the philosophy of language; but it is plausible to put it somewhere in this middle period. The rest of the dialogues, up to Plato's last work the *Laws*, show a trend away from the use of Socrates even as a mouthpiece for Plato's views; often he gets altogether displaced from the discussions, though in the *Philebus*, contrary to this trend, he again plays the chief role. In the *Parmenides* Socrates when young encounters the distinguished Eleatic philosopher of the preceding generation and his disciple Zeno, and, defending in a rather naïve way the Platonic Theory of Ideas, receives something of a trouncing; but he comes back with some telling criticisms of Parmenides' own system. It is natural to take this dialogue as an introduction to the series which includes the *Theaetetus*, *Sophist* and *Politicus* (or *Statesman*). In these, difficulties in the earlier Socratic or Platonic doctrines are penetratingly discussed, and an attempt is made to come to terms with the views of Protagoras, Heraclitus and above all the Eleatics. This leads Plato into very deep waters, into which we shall not be able in this little book to follow him. Plato's chosen philosophical method, called 'dialectic', is further developed, and new moves in it called 'collection' and 'division' (see p. 155) are explained and illustrated at length. The *Politicus'* main object is to expand on Plato's political theory, and it forms a kind of bridge between the *Republic* and the *Laws*.

Scholars disagree on the extent to which Plato modified, or even abandoned, his Theory of Ideas as a result of the criticisms voiced in the *Parmenides* (see p. 143). It is perhaps safest to say that he did not abandon it, but sought to preserve it by more careful exposition and restatement in other words, as he did in the case of the Socratic doctrine about the relation of knowledge to virtue. One of the bones of contention is whether the *Timaeus*, in which the Theory features in something like its earlier form, was written near the end of Plato's life, as used to be generally thought, or whether it belongs to the middle period. There are also passages in the *Politicus* (285d, e) and the *Philebus* (61d, e) which are at any rate couched in the language of the Theory.

The *Timaeus* is a work on cosmology, which has appended to it the *Critias*, an unfinished fragment about the lost island of Atlantis, the conquest of which by an earlier Athenian state governed in Plato's ideal manner was to have been the main subject of the dialogue. The town planning and administrative arrangements of Atlantis are described in engaging detail. The *Philebus*, almost certainly a late dialogue, returns to the subject of the rival merits of pleasure and thought as ingredients in the good life, and in the course of the discussion further pursues the exposition of the dialectical method and the problem of the One and the Many. Lastly the *Laws*, Plato's longest work and probably unrevised, expounds in detail his legislative proposals for his ideal state, somewhat modified from the *Republic*, in the direction (anticipated in the *Politicus*) of greater practicability.

4 *Understanding Plato*

After this necessarily brief survey of Plato's development, we are in a position to look at some of his ideas more closely. But first a warning is necessary. Anybody who takes up one of the early dialogues will have the impression that Plato is a very clear writer; and he certainly writes in a delightfully readable style. That, indeed, is one of the reasons why so many still read him. So the difficulty of really understanding him may not at first be apparent. The trouble is not so much that he writes entirely in dialogue form, so that he might not himself be meaning to endorse the views put into the mouth of one of his characters. Dialogues can be very clear; there is no difficulty, for example, in knowing what is going on in Berkeley's or Hume's. Nor is it that Socrates, the chief character in all the early dialogues, is usually unwilling to state his own views (which, we might assume, Plato would wish us to accept), and likes more to reduce those of others to absurdity. The main difficulty is one about Plato's situation in time: he comes in at the beginning of philosophy as we understand the term (what his predecessors except Socrates had been doing was not quite the same); and therefore he had to invent the method and the terminology as he went along. Not surprisingly, he did not become clear all at once, or sometimes even at all, about the issues he raised.

There is a style of interpretation, practised on Plato by many modern commentators, which goes like this. They first point to some passage in the dialogues whose meaning is not entirely clear. They then suggest various statements in modern English of what he might have meant, and draw consequences from each of them to which they think he would be committed if that were what he meant. If these consequences are absurd or inconsistent, they then, according to their temperaments, either write him off as a bad philosopher, or conclude that, since he was not a bad philosopher, he cannot have meant that.

Although the method has some resemblance to Socrates' treatment of his opponents, it is unfair in that Plato is not here to answer back, and is in any case unsound as a method of getting at what he meant. It is far safer not to attribute to Plato any proposition which cannot be translated into Greek, the language in which he did his thinking. If it cannot be, he cannot have thought that. One is handicapped when writing a short book about Plato in English, and I shall probably find myself committing the fault I have just been condemning, but to be on secure ground, if his own words are unclear or ambiguous, the most we can do is to imagine that we have him with us, put to him questions in Greek, and then speculate as to how he might answer them in Greek. If this method is followed, it will be found that many of the distinctions on which, as modern philosophers, we rightly want to insist, pass him by.

If we want to ask what Plato *would* have said, if he had lived now and had read Hume, Kant, Carnap, Wittgenstein etc., about questions for the posing of which these distinctions are necessary, we can, if we like, imagine additionally that we can teach him modern philosophical English and speculate as to what answers he would then give; but it *will* be speculation (good philosophical training though it is for ourselves), and cannot in any case pose as an interpretation of his views as expressed in the dialogues. What we can do is to look at those views, and then at the subsequent history of philosophy, and see what, in the hands of others, they *turned into*. There are many striking affinities between what Plato said and what later thinkers have said, even some who are not called Platonists; nearly all philosophers are heavily in debt to him. We can therefore, when reading Plato, often find the seed of some later idea. But it is seldom more than a seed.

Later thinkers who acknowledge debts to Plato, or, by contrast, who have reacted against him, often attribute to him views which have been suggested to them by reading him; but this is a dangerous game. Aristotle played it (perhaps with greater right than most, because he knew Plato personally and was taught by him). So did the Neoplatonists in late antiquity, our own Cambridge Platonists in the seventeenth century, and Hegel and other romantic philosophers in the nineteenth. And so do some modern philosophers of mathematics. It is by no means clear that Plato was a 'Platonist' in any of these senses. The problem is compounded by the fact that, although his thought has a remarkable unity, there are different aspects to it which different disciples have seized on.

Let us dramatize the two most prominent of these aspects by imagining that we are speaking not of one person but of two (which is indeed what one *would* imagine, if one compared some commentators with some other commentators). I shall call these two characters Pato and Lato. Pato is an advocate of what Aldous Huxley called 'the perennial philosophy'. He believes in a total difference in kind between the spiritual and the material, the immortal soul and the perishable body, the world of eternal Ideas and 'the world of matter and of sense' as Newman called it; and he endows this difference with a moral significance. The eternal verities are also eternal values, and the soul's task in its thousand-year cyclical journeys is to strive towards these and escape from the contamination of the flesh. These thoughts make Pato into the stern and ascetic moralist portrayed in Raphael's Vatican fresco; he would have been at home in a Zen Buddhist monastery, or even in Egypt with the desert fathers.

Lato seems at first entirely different. He is interested in science, especially in mathematics, and thus in logic and the philosophy of language. He taught Aristotle, and set him on the way to becoming the world's greatest logician and a notable biologist. He has learnt from Socrates to ask searching questions like 'What is justice (or The Just)?'—questions to which the answer would be a definition—and to submit proposed answers to destructive scrutiny, using logical and conceptual and linguistic techniques which he or Socrates invented. He follows Socrates in being an exposer of intellectual pretensions which are not founded on real understanding of what one is saying; but at the same time he encourages us to believe that if we *could* understand, reason would supply us with answers to the questions that trouble us. This intellectual midwifery, the sorting out of genuine from bogus offspring of the mind, makes the name 'Lato' appropriate, because Lato was the Greek goddess of childbirth, and Socrates claims in the *Theaetetus* to have learned the art from his midwife mother (149a).

The two characters are very different; so it is not surprising that the Patonists and the Latonists have given contrasting pictures of Plato. Readers of him will always be tempted to pick out those of his ideas which they find congenial, and forget about the others. In this book I am trying not to do that; but it is very hard. One expedient which I would recommend to anyone who wants to understand Plato is this: sometimes allow him to be unclear. There are many philosophical questions which had not arisen in Plato's time. No doubt, if he were going to be absolutely clear on some issues, he would have had to give a definite answer to such questions. But he did not; and it is historically sounder not to force upon him one answer or another, but rather to leave the questions unanswered, which means leaving his doctrine indeterminate at those points. It goes without saying that Plato was capable of making very clear and precise distinctions, and often does so, for the first time in philosophy, to good effect. But he had not made all that there are to be made; that would be too much to expect of somebody who was creating a whole new branch of inquiry.

We may illustrate this point, at the cost of anticipating questions which will occupy us later, from his treatment of the Socratic search for definitions. When Socrates asked questions like 'What is justice?' or 'What is The Just?', there are at least three things which we might take him as wanting. Does he want a definition of a word or of a thing; and if of a thing, of what *kind* of thing—of something we might come across in this world, or of something which is only available to thought? Let us try constructing a little dialogue to shed light on this question, without making Plato say anything which will not go into Greek.

ENGLISH STRANGER   When Socrates says in the *Theaetetus* (147c) that mud (or clay) is earth mixed with water, is he saying what the *word* 'mud' means?

PLATO   Yes, of course. And *what* the word means, the thing mud, is what one has to be able to define if one is to show that one knows what mud is. As Socrates says, 'Do you think anybody understands the word for anything, if he doesn't know the thing, what it is?' (147b).

E.S.   But what is this mud he has to know? Is it what one gets on one's boots?

P.   How can you expect me to think that? One only gets *particular bits* of mud on one's boots, and one can touch and see them, but not know them in the sense I'm after. I am after what Mud is in itself, not after particular bits of mud. In the *Parmenides* I made Socrates reluctantly aware that, even with so down-to-earth a thing as mud, there is this Mud-in-itself that one has to know if one is to have knowledge what mud is (130c).

E.S.   So when Socrates says mud is earth mixed with water, is he defining a word or a thing?

P.   I don't see the difference. To define the word is to say what the thing is that it means. But this thing isn't what one gets on one's boots; it is what the mind has before it when one thinks of mud.

E.S.   Perhaps we could make the matter clearer if I asked you whether Socrates' definition is the sort of thing that would go into a dictionary. A dictionary is a collection of definitions rather like that first one you or your students compiled and which got into your works under the name *Definitions*. We have very big dictionaries now; the biggest is produced in Oxford and *it* defines 'mud' as 'a mixture of finely comminuted particles of rock with water' (you see, we like to be more exact nowadays). Other definitions in it which are very like those to be found in your *Definitions* are 'even: the latter part or close of the day' (cf. 411b); 'wind: air in motion . . . usually parallel to the surface of the ground' (cf. 411c). And you might find the following familiar: 'circle: a plane figure . . . bounded by a . . . circumference, which is everywhere equally distant from a point within, called the centre';

at least there is something very like this in that famous *Seventh Letter* attributed to you (342b).

P.   Your dictionary does sound as if it were after the same sort of things as I am after, namely statements in words of what other words mean; and of course what they mean are Ideas.

Without prolonging the dialogue, I think we can claim that it is simply not profitable to ask Plato the question 'Are you defining words or things?', because he would not understand what we were asking. In general it is very unclear, and contentious even among philosophers today, whether metaphysics, logic and linguistics are separate disciplines (we would not get a straight answer from either a logical positivist like Rudolf Carnap or an idealist like F. H. Bradley); and therefore it is not surprising that Plato cannot tell us which he is doing. But in what follows we may be able to shed a bit more light on another question, namely why he found the distinction between definitions of words and definitions of things difficult.

5 *Knowing things*

One of Plato's chief incentives to metaphysics was a nest of problems he thought he had encountered about knowledge. To understand his trouble, the first thing to get clear is, What did Plato think was the object of knowledge (that is, *what* somebody knows)? If the first of these expressions does not translate easily into Greek, the second does; and it is all right in Greek, and still quite natural in English, to say things like 'I know something.' 'Does the man who knows know something or nothing?' asks Socrates in the *Republic*; and, having got the obvious answer that he knows something, elicits the further answer that this something is an entity, an existing thing (476e).

As we shall see, Plato did not clearly distinguish between *what exists* and *what is true* (at least not in his earlier work; the distinction is at least hinted at in the *Timaeus* (29c)), and this may have been an extra source of confusion. It is easy to slip from the correct idea that what is known must be true to the mistaken idea that what is known must exist. If we speak in this way of an object of knowledge, we are implying that knowledge is some sort of relation between two things: the knower, that is the person who knows, or his mind or knowing faculty, and an object, that is the thing known, or what he knows. The relation can be thought of as like that between us (or our eyes) and a bird when we see a bird. This way of thinking about knowledge, natural though it is, can lead to a lot of trouble.

If the question 'What is this thing that we know?' is once raised, a modern philosopher is likely to answer 'The truth of a proposition' or, more simply, 'That (for example) five is a prime number', or 'That pigs can't fly.' For those of us who speak in these terms the status of the 'things known' called truths or propositions will be highly obscure, and has troubled many moderns; but it did not trouble Plato, because he did not look at the matter in this way. If he had, he would have been less tempted to (as the professionals say) 'hypostatize', or 'reify', the objects of knowledge (that is, suppose that they are existing things); for, although some philosophers have postulated entities out in the world called propositions, they take a bit of swallowing.

We may note that, even on a propositional view of knowledge, problems arise of a somewhat Platonic sort. Whenever we make a statement, it has to be *about* something (its subject). In the *Sophist* the Eleatic Stranger says 'If it weren't about anything, it wouldn't be a statement at all; for we showed that to be a statement, but one about nothing, is impossible' (263c). This true point is familiar from modern discussions. But it raises difficulties in the case of statements with abstract subjects, such as 'The circle is a plane figure, etc.' This is not a statement about any particular circle or even about any specific kind of circle; but unless we can identify what the person who makes it is talking about, how can we be sure he is talking about anything?

But Plato was not attracted by a propositional view of knowledge. This was partly because of some features of Greek idiom, which, in combination with other traps, led him to posit, as the objects of knowledge, Ideas existing in an eternal realm which are not propositions but *things*. I shall use the word 'Idea', with a capital 'I', to translate Plato's '*ideā*' and '*eidos*' (sometimes also translated 'Form'); but it must be understood that he meant by these a kind of object independent of the mind, with which the mind could become acquainted, and not anything merely mental (i.e. existing only in the mind).

The first feature of Greek idiom which may have misled Plato is this. Greek tends to put what looks like a direct object after verbs of knowing. It says, commonly though not always, 'I know *thee* who thou art'. The dialogues are full of examples of this construction. Given its possibility, it was easy for Plato to think of knowledge as a relation between a knower and a *thing*, the thing being not a proposition but rather the thing denoted by the subject of the 'that'-clause or the indirect question, as in 'I know Meno, who he is', or 'I know Meno, that he is rich' or '. . . whether he is rich'.

There are cases in which it is perfectly natural and indeed correct to use 'know' with a direct object. We can know stories, and know geometry, for example. With some other related verbs it is even easier. 'Understand', but not 'know', is used even in English in a way that could capture the meaning of Plato's Greek in some contexts, as in 'He understands justice (i.e. what it is)'; and the commonest word for 'understand' in Greek is also one of Plato's favourite words for 'know'. Since we can also speak of understanding the *word* 'just', this does something to explain Plato's difficulty, already noticed, in separating definitions of words from definitions of things.

But Plato more commonly uses a different model from these, also natural in English as in Greek: the model of what is now often called 'knowledge by acquaintance'. It is common nowadays to distinguish the kind of knowing expressed by '*savoir*', '*wissen*' and '*scire*' from that expressed by '*connaître*', '*kennen*' and '*cognoscere*' ('I know that pigs can't fly' from 'I know Meno' and 'I know Athens'). Significantly, though Greek has a word cognate with (that is, related etymologically to) the second set of verbs for knowing, it does not use it, any more than English uses 'know', to make this distinction, but allows it indiscriminately to govern direct objects, or 'that'-clauses, or both combined ('I know Meno, that he is rich'), or the equivalent participial construction ('I know Meno, being rich', as Greek puts it); and similarly the verb which is cognate with '*wissen*' is used in all these ways. It is also cognate, like '*ideā*' and '*eidos*', with the Greek and Latin words for 'see', thereby making it even easier for Plato to think of knowing as being, like some kind of mental seeing, a direct acquaintance with an object or thing. So Plato, when he wants to say something about other kinds of knowledge, often recurs to the model of knowledge by acquaintance. I have already given an example from the beginning of the *Meno*; near the end of the dialogue he does the same, illustrating the difference between knowledge and true opinion by the example of knowing the road to Larissa, as opposed to having opinions about it (71b, 97a). Plato is here setting out a theory about knowledge which is supposed to hold for all sorts of knowledge; but he illustrates it by a case of knowledge by acquaintance—acquaintance with a physical thing, namely a road.

It may have been in part this tendency of the Greek language which led Plato to posit a *thing* or *entity* such that knowledge is a relation between us and it, and to think of this entity as being somehow *like* Meno or Athens or the road to Larissa, which we know in the perfectly ordinary sense of being acquainted with them, and yet mysteriously somehow *unlike* them. It had to be unlike them, because knowledge must be of what is true, and moreover (Plato thought) reliably and abidingly true. Because the Greek word for 'true' (like the English) sometimes means 'real' (see p. 145), and because we cannot know what is false, he thought that what we know has to be real. And thinking, as he did, that we could not really know anything unless we had the right to be sure of it, the only candidates he could admit as objects of knowledge in the full sense had to be things which were not merely real, but *necessarily* real, and therefore eternal and indestructible. If we have knowledge of other things (for example, the things we see and touch) it is not of the full-blooded kind.

Plato hankered, in his search for real knowledge, after the kind of certainty which the truths of mathematics have; but because he was after things and not truths, the things had to be necessarily existing things. Looked at in this light, even the road to Larissa does not really qualify (it might be washed away, as roads in Greece sometimes are).

There are other linguistic traps too for Plato. Greek had no separate words for 'word' and 'name'. Thus it was easy for Plato to suppose that the way in which a word like 'man' got its meaning was the same as that in which a proper name like 'Meno' got its meaning—by there being an object of which it is the name (the Idea of Man). This has been called the 'Fido'–Fido theory of meaning: the view that for any word to have meaning is for there to be some entity to which it stands in the same relation as the name 'Fido' does to the dog Fido.

Another trap was the facility with which Greek formed abstract nouns by adding the definite article to the neuter adjective. We still do this (influenced by Plato) when we speak of 'The Right and the Good' (the name of a book on ethics by Sir David Ross); but it is not natural in English. It became extremely common in the political and other rhetoric of Plato's time, as can be seen by reading almost any of the speeches in Thucydides. Where we should speak of knowing what rightness is, or alternatively of what 'right' means, it is easy in Greek, because of the factors already mentioned, to speak of knowing the Right, and thus fail to distinguish between these possibly different things. And from this it is a small step to saying, as Plato was tempted into saying, that the Right which we know is a really and necessarily existing thing, which has to perfection the quality of rightness (for if the Right is not right, what is?).

This view that the Ideas themselves have the properties of which they are the Ideas is known by scholars as the doctrine of *self-predication*, or, alternatively, of *paradigmatic Ideas*. The notion of the Idea as a paradigm or ideal example of the quality in question occurs in Plato as early as the *Euthyphro* (6e), and we can see how seductive it is. And no doubt the temptation offered by this Greek way of expressing abstract nouns was reinforced by a still older way, personification. Aeschylus' avenging Furies mockingly predict that if they gave up their task, people would say 'O Right! O thrones of the Furies!' And of course the goddess Right must always be right, as the lady on top of the Courts of Justice is always just.

Plato, to his credit, came to see that self-predication leads to paradox. In the *Parmenides* (132) he presents the famous 'Third Man' argument. To simplify this a bit: if for something to be a man is for it to resemble the Idea of Man, and if for things to resemble one another is for them to share a common characteristic of which the Idea is the perfect example, then will not there have to be a third man, the Idea by resemblance to which both the first man and the second (the original Idea) are called men; and shall we not need a fourth man to account for the resemblance between these three; and so *ad infinitum*?

It is by no means clear whether this criticism, either in my simplified form or in the various different forms in which it occurs in Plato and Aristotle, is valid and unavoidable. So Plato is perhaps not to be blamed if he did not abandon his Theory of Ideas in the light of it; but all the same it *is* a mistake to suppose that for words to have meanings is (always at any rate) for there to be entities for which they stand. If we know how to use a word in speaking and thus communicating with one another, it has a meaning; and knowing how to use it is not knowing some solid chunk of eternal verity of which it is the name, but knowing the conventions for its use, and in particular what, according to these conventions, is implied by somebody who uses it in a statement. To know what 'circle' means or what a circle is is to know that if we call anything a circle we are implying that it is a plane figure of a certain sort; and in order to know this we do not have to know any celestial entities.

It is hard (for me at any rate) not to think that another factor contributed to Plato's taking this false trail. Some people have a more vivid mental imagery than others; they think more in pictures. Those who lack this gift often find it hard to understand the thought of those who have it. That Plato had it nobody could doubt who read the similes and myths which enliven his dialogues. When he speaks of 'seeing' one of these entities called Ideas, he is thinking of something very like literal seeing, only done with what he calls in the *Republic* 'the mind's eye' (533d). Elsewhere he speaks of 'grasping' Ideas. We have grown accustomed through the long use of such terms in philosophy and common parlance (along with such technical terms as 'intuition', which means, literally, 'looking') to thinking of them as very weak, threadbare metaphors; and translators often, when Plato says 'look', translate 'investigate' or 'reflect' or the like. But for Plato they were hardly metaphorical at all.

Here is a passage from the *Phaedo*, keeping Plato's visual and tactual language:

The soul, when it uses the body to look at something, by sight or hearing or some other sense ... is dragged by the body among things which never stay the same, and it itself gets lost and disturbed and tipsy, just like a drunk, from contact with such things ... But when it looks by itself, on its own, it goes in the other direction, to the pure, the eternal, the immortal, the unchanging, and, because of its affinity with them, joins their company, whenever it is by itself and can do so; it ceases its wanderings and is with them and ever unchanging like them, from contact with such things. And this condition of the soul is called wisdom. (76c, d)

It is clear from such passages, which are very common in the dialogues, that Plato thought of the difference between ordinary sight and touch on the one hand, and the mind's sight and grasp of the eternal Ideas on the other, as lying in a difference in the objects and in the organs of perception, and not in a difference in the kind of relation between knower and known. Knowledge or wisdom is a kind of mental looking—a vision of the Eternal.

But Plato did not think that *everything* which we see or grasp with our mind gives us knowledge; for believing too (in the sense of having opinions) is a mental activity of the same general kind, and opinions or beliefs can be false. The obvious account, within this framework, of false belief is to say that it is the seeing or grasping with the mind of false objects—things which 'are not'. And here the framework got Plato into great trouble, from which he may never have extracted himself completely.

The trouble arises through thinking of truth and falsity in beliefs as properties of the thing believed. Plato frequently uses the words which we translate 'true' and 'false' as if there were no difference between the sense in which we speak of a true statement and that in which we speak of a true (as opposed to forged or in general spurious) Vermeer. The spurious object of belief 'is not' what it purports to be; and Plato, because he did not initially distinguish between the 'is' which means the same as 'exists' (as in 'The British Empire is no more') and the 'is' which expresses predication (the copula, as in 'He is tall'), gets into difficulties about whether, when we have false beliefs, we are seeing or grasping or saying what 'is not', and therefore whether when we do this we have anything at all before the mind. But if we have nothing before the mind, how can we be believing anything at all? The upshot seems to be the paradoxical one that we cannot have false belief.

Plato inherited these difficulties from the Eleatics. He grapples manfully with them in the *Theaetetus* and the *Sophist*; but the beginnings of them can be seen in the *Republic*, where he says that knowledge is of what is, belief is of what is and is not, and ignorance is of what is not (477a). His conception of knowledge and belief as kinds of mental seeing of genuine or spurious objects led him inevitably into these troubles; and scholars do not agree on the extent to which he eventually got himself out of them.

It is not even clear that he always thought of belief as a kind of *mental* seeing; the 'things believed' in the *Republic* are, typically though not always, objects perceived by the senses; so perhaps he did not distinguish clearly between seeing one of these objects with the eyes and believing it (to exist). By the time of the *Republic* he is distinguishing between knowledge and belief by distinguishing between their objects (478a); but earlier, in the *Meno*, he speaks as if the same thing, the road to Larissa, could be an object either of knowledge or of belief, and finds the difference between them in the greater abidingness of knowledge, secured by a 'reckoning of the reason' for what we know (the reason being, he implies, the Idea, and the reckoning, the defining of it—97a, see p. 152). This suggests a definition of knowledge very similar to one which has been popular, but also controversial, recently: 'true belief which has a rational ground'. Plato later in the *Theaetetus* raises difficulties against such a definition; but it is not clear whether they led him finally to abandon it (201c ff.).

By positing the existence of Ideas as real abiding entities visible to the mind, and therefore qualified to be objects of knowledge in the fullest sense, Plato thought he had resolved the problem of 'The One and the Many' which had been an incentive to philosophy ever since the early cosmologists. Even if the Heracliteans were right about the sensible world—even if, that is to say, it is, considered in itself, a multifarious, unintelligible flux – still we can reason about it if we use not our senses but our minds. As he says in the *Theaetetus*, 'Knowledge lies not in the effects [of the senses] upon us, but in our reasoning about them. For it is, it seems, possible in the case of the latter to lay hold on reality and truth, but not in the case of the former' (186d). This reasoning puts us in touch with the eternal Ideas, which have each of them a unity (the one Man as contrasted with the many particular men or the many different kinds of men—it is not clear always which he means). And they also have jointly a unity among themselves, by all partaking of the Idea of the Good (see p. 154). The Ideas, therefore, have the perfect, eternal, unchanging oneness for lack of which Parmenides denied reality to the objects of sense.

Having got thus far, Plato may have been tempted to find the hallmark of knowledge in the clarity and distinctness of its objects. 'If this very thing becomes clear', he says at one point in the *Phaedo*, 'you won't look any further' (106b). If, he might have said, we can with our mind's eye discern some Idea very clearly, is not that a certificate that it exists and that we have knowledge of it? To his great credit, unlike Descartes, he resisted this temptation. He did not rely on the self-evidence of intuition. Following Socrates, he insisted that we have to establish the credentials of claims to knowledge by submitting them to a rigorous testing procedure; and to this we must now turn.

6 *Definition, dialectic and the good*

As we have seen, it was Socrates' practice to ask people who were thought to have knowledge, 'What is ...?', where the gap is to be filled by a word for something which they claimed to know about (courage, for example, in the case of the gallant soldier Laches). In Plato's early dialogues this happens constantly. What often happens after that is that the victim offers some answer, and this is then submitted to scrutiny (*elenchos*); the Greek word also means 'audit'. This frequently starts with Socrates complaining that he has been given the wrong sort of answer. Usually this is because the respondent has given one or more examples of the thing in question, instead of saying what the feature is which they all have, which makes them examples of it.

Thus in the *Meno*, where goodness is what is being inquired into, Socrates asks for 'a single form, the same in them all, in virtue of which they are goodnesses, to which someone who is answering the question, what goodness may be, can well look and point it out' (72c). The word translated 'form' is '*eidos*', which is the standard word later for Plato's Ideas; but we do not need to ask whether by this stage he is insisting, as Socrates himself probably did not, on the substantial and separate existence of the Ideas. Nor do we need to ask whether Plato has distinguished between the fault of offering *kinds* of goodness in lieu of a definition of goodness, and that of offering *particular instances* of goodness; the former interpretation suits most passages. At least we can say that Socrates is asking for some kind of definition (whether a definition of a word or of a thing, it is, as we have seen, not profitable to ask); and Aristotle gives him, rather than Plato, the credit for introducing this move.

I say 'credit'; but recently Socrates has been attacked for seeking definitions, and has even been accused of committing therein a 'Socratic Fallacy'. There are two lines of attack which must be distinguished. The first of them points out that words have a multiplicity of subtly varying uses, and that it is a mistake to suppose that there will always be some *one* common element, *the* meaning of a word ('game' for example), wherever it occurs. There may be only a 'family resemblance' between different things we call games: think, for example, of roulette, tournament chess and the game of pretending to be an aeroplane, and ask what one feature they have in common with all games which things other than games do not have.

Without going into this criticism in detail, it can be shown that it is not very damaging to Socrates' main enterprise. Granted that it may be the case that no one common element will be found, nevertheless it remains important to seek to understand what we are saying, especially when we are arguing; for if we do not understand what we are saying, we shall not know which steps in an argument are valid and which are invalid. It may be that our understanding cannot be captured in cut-and-dried definitions, a single one for each word, but that was not Socrates' or Plato's main point. They were acquainted with the phenomenon of ambiguity, and if it is more complex than they thought, it still does not diminish the importance of understanding.

The other line of attack would be more damaging if it could be sustained. '*Before* we start trying to define a word', it may be said, 'we have in some sense to know how to use it. We have *either* to be able to point to examples of its correct use, *or* to be able to explain its meaning in words. If we can do neither of these things, we cannot even start. But pointing to examples is a perfectly legitimate way of starting, and Socrates does wrong to ban it. When the word that is being asked about is a moral word, Socrates' move can be very harmful. For instance, we all know how to pick out examples of courage, but many of us find it hard to define the word. If Socrates asks us what courage is, and we cannot provide an answer which satisfies his rigorous standards, we may come to think that we don't know what it is, or wonder whether the acts we thought had it in fact had it, or even whether there is such a thing; and this may be bad for our moral characters. Socrates therefore really is 'corrupting the young'.

Behind this criticism lies a theory about meaning which must now be brought out into the open. The most famous modern statement of this claims that 'if language is to be a means of communication there must be agreement not only in definitions but, queer as this may sound, agreement in judgements also'. You and I cannot be using a word in the same way unless there are some uses of it which we agree to be correct, and this implies that we agree on at least some substantial and not merely verbal questions. Unless, for example, there are some things we agree to be pigs, we cannot be using the word 'pig' in the same way. This may be true of certain classes of words; but that it is true of all words has not been established. In particular, it is highly disputable in regard to value words. Is it not possible for you and me to be in radical disagreement on how one ought to behave, so that we cannot find *any* 'ought'-statement on which we could agree, and yet be using the word 'ought' in the same way? If we did not mean the same by the word, our attempts to voice our disagreements would founder; for when I said 'He ought' and you said 'He ought not', we should merely be at cross purposes.

However, it is not necessary for us to insist on this point in order to defend Socrates. For he could easily grant initially that we do have a 'right opinion', or at least a consensus, right or wrong, that such and such acts are courageous, and that this enables us to get along all right with the word; but go on, first to deny that this right opinion amounts to knowledge (it does not have the necessary certitude or abidingness), and secondly to say that what would give it this more reliable quality would be some sort of deeper understanding of what we say. What is being challenged, in this criticism, is the Socratic-Platonic distinction between knowledge and right opinion. The basis of the attack is that right opinion (in Greek *orthē doxa*, the etymological ancestor of 'orthodoxy') ought to be enough for the upright man.

If the attack were justified, then perhaps philosophy itself ought never to have started. For what above all got philosophy started was Socrates' and Plato's insistence that right opinion is not enough; it is utterly unstable and unreliable unless it is turned into secure knowledge by 'a reckoning of the reason'. 'A reason' is what Socrates is asking for in his 'What is . . . ?' questions. If we could understand the words used in setting out the problems that trouble us, we might then go on to find secure solutions to them. That really is what philosophy is about, and so those who press this attack are revealing themselves as antiphilosophers, like the Athenians who put Socrates to death on substantially the same grounds. As a great modern philosopher of mathematics, Gottlob Frege, put it, echoing Socrates and speaking of people who held that definitions were unnecessary in mathematics: 'The first prerequisite for learning anything is thus utterly lacking—I mean, the knowledge that we do not know.'

In default of this deeper understanding, popular agreement is not enough, and is often (especially at times of moral uncertainty like Plato's and our own) not forthcoming. It is to be noted that Euthyphro, in a dialogue which has been singled out for attack, is in *disagreement* with the rest of his family on whether he would be doing his religious duty if he prosecuted his father for the manslaughter of a servant who had murdered another servant. If it was a real case, there was no doubt dissension about it in the city at large. In such a case there is no orthodoxy to appeal to, and we have, however much we should like the comforts of moral assurance, to think the thing out for ourselves. This is what Socrates and Plato are trying to find a way of doing, and the importance of their endeavour for the theory and practice of moral education is, as we shall see, immense.

We must now ask how Plato thought the Socratic question could be answered—what philosophical method he was proposing. As we have seen, he had rejected the mere clarity of a thought as a certificate of its correctness, and was not going to rely on general assent either. Instead, he demanded what he called 'a reckoning of the reason' for thinking it. And this was to take the form 'The . . . is —', that is, some kind of definition. This is what Plato called 'an account (*logos*) of the being' of something. The phrase was adopted by Aristotle, and is the lineal ancestor of the modern expression 'essential definition'. But it is important when reading Plato to keep in mind that it means no more than an answer to the Socratic question 'What is . . .?' Plato thought that the thing about which the question was asked was an eternally existing entity, an Idea, and that the definition was a description of this entity. It is doubtful whether Socrates thought this, and Aristotle did not. Those who follow William of Occam in thinking that such entities ought not to be multiplied more than we have to will seek to discard Plato's separately existing and eternal Ideas, while salvaging all that they can of his philosophical enterprise. This aim probably motivated Aristotle, and it is indeed remarkable how much can be salvaged.

Socrates' method of 'scrutiny' consists in eliciting from his victims answers to his questions, and then demolishing them by showing them to be inconsistent with other opinions which the victims are not willing to give up. Often these are generally accepted views. An example is the first definition of 'rightness' or 'uprightness' considered in the *Republic*: 'Truthfulness, and the giving back of anything that one receives from anybody' (331c). This is rejected because it would have the consequence that, if one had been lent some weapons by a friend, and he had gone mad, it would be right, or upright, to give them back to him.

Unfortunately there are two ways of taking this argument, which have not been generally distinguished, and were not by Plato. Is he saying that any definition which runs counter to the opinions of its proposer, or to received opinion, is to be rejected? This would invite the objection that the opinions might be wrong, and not the definition. However, Plato is generally thought to be proposing such a method of refutation.

He would be on safer ground if he were saying that any definition which can be shown to run counter to the linguistic usage of native speakers is to be rejected. The argument would then go: 'All of us would call the act of giving back the weapons to the madman "not right"; this universally held opinion, whether or not it is *correct*, is certainly not *self-contradictory*; so the definition, which makes it self-contradictory, must be wrong.' On this way of taking the argument, the method is sound by the usual canons of scientific method: a linguistic hypothesis about the meaning of a word has been advanced, and is refuted by showing that the linguistic facts do not square with it. We have already noticed the difficulty of attributing to Plato a clear distinction (if such exists) between linguistic or logical enquiries into the meanings of words and metaphysical enquiries into the things the words mean. He certainly often speaks in the latter way, and it was therefore difficult for him to distinguish, for example, between people's opinions about the nature of the *thing* called 'rightness' and their native ability to use the *word* 'right' correctly.

What is fairly clear, moreover, is that he failed, as many moderns still fail, to make a further distinction. This is the distinction between on the one hand substantial opinions about questions of morality or even of fact, and on the other questions about what rightness, etc. are (whether these latter are thought of as questions about language or about the nature of things). It is perhaps the greatest fault in Plato's way of putting the questions he was asking, as demands for accounts of the *being* of things, that it can make us confuse substantial questions with verbal ones. To revert to a previous example, there is a substantial question about mud, namely how it is, as a matter of fact, composed (a question that is answered by putting it into a centrifuge; earth and water will be the result). There is also a question, 'What is mud?', which, as we have seen, could be taken *either* for a question about the Idea of Mud *or* for one about the word 'mud'. On neither interpretation is it about the thing mud in the down-to-earth sense of what gets on one's boots or what goes into the centrifuge. But it is easy to take the question about the Idea for a more substantial question than it really is, and Plato probably did so.

In moral questions especially, it is very easy (people still constantly do it) to confuse questions about correct use of words with substantial moral questions. If we ask 'What is uprightness?' we might be asking for a definition of a word, concept or Platonic Idea, and, if so, we ought perhaps to be satisfied with the answer which Plato gives in *Republic* IV, 'Doing one's own duty' (433a). On the other hand, we might be asking for a specification of what our duty is; and in that case we should need to be given the precepts for living which Plato provides in the rest of the *Republic*. Plato was probably not as clear as he should have been about the difference between these two sorts of question. But at least he seems to have seen the need for asking both.

The Socratic method of scrutiny is further developed by Plato, who uses the name 'dialectic' for the developed form of it. It is sometimes said that Plato's method changed but that he used the name 'dialectic' for whatever method he at any one time preferred. This is an exaggeration; his method did develop, but retained a recognizable resemblance to that of Socrates. In the *Republic* he says:

Then do you call 'a dialectician' the man who demands an account of the being of each thing? And the man who does not have that, in so far as he cannot give an account to himself and to another, to that extent will you deny that he has understanding (*nous*) of it? ... And then the same applies to the Good. A man who cannot give a determinate account of the Idea of the Good, separating it from everything else, and battling through all the scrutinies of it, being eager to scrutinize it by reference not to opinion but to its real being, and who cannot in all these scrutinies come through with his account unscathed, will you say that a man like that knows neither the Good nor any other good thing (if he gets hold somehow of some simulacrum, he gets hold of it with his opinion, not with knowledge)? (534b, c)

The relation of this to Socrates' method of scrutiny is obvious. And so is the importance of separating what you are defining from everything else, the method later to be known as 'division', which is insisted on as early as the *Euthyphro* (12d), and is indeed ascribed by Xenophon to Socrates.

In later dialogues the method is developed still further, but not in such a way as to cut it off from its Socratic ancestry, which Aristotle, who took over a lot of this from Plato, also shares. The development is chiefly in the method proposed for setting out in a systematic form the definitions which were the answers to Socrates' questions. This form came later to be called '*definitio per genus et differentiam*'; in order to say what something is, one has first to give its genus, assigning it to the class of things into which one has *collected* everything that resembles it generically, and then *divide* up the genus into species, saying what differentiates each, including the thing in question. This method has been immensely influential in biology, from Aristotle to Linnaeus and beyond. Fully worked-out examples of it are given by Plato in the *Sophist* and the *Politicus*.

Before leaving the subject of definition we must explain why the Good plays such an important part in Plato's scheme. He calls it in the *Republic* 'the greatest thing we have to learn' (505a). The reason is in essence simple, but because it was not explicitly stated in Plato's surviving works, commentators have not always understood it. The Idea of any class of things (for example men) was thought of by Plato as a perfect (that is, supremely good) specimen or paradigm of the class. This is involved in the doctrine of self-predication which has already been mentioned. To know what Man is, is not to know what it is to be any old kind of man, but rather what it is to be a good or perfect man. Similarly, to know what the Circle is, is to know what it is to be a good or perfect circle, not just any circle that a slovenly schoolmaster might draw on the blackboard.

This means that in order fully to know what it is to be a man or a circle, we have to know what it is to be a good man or a perfect circle; and thus that knowledge of the being of anything involves knowledge of the goodness or perfection of a good thing of that kind, and (Plato would have added) vice versa.

Thus knowledge of the Good will comprehend knowledge of the goodnesses or perfections of every kind of thing, and thus of their specific natures. This line of thought involves two confusions. The first is between 'good man' in the sense of 'typical specimen of the class *man*', and 'good man' in the sense of 'man having the good qualities demanded in men'. A typical man is not necessarily a morally good man. The second is that of thinking that what it is to be a good man or a good circle is determined by the meaning of 'good' (by the Idea of the Good, as Plato would have put it); it is in fact determined by the standard for goodness in those two classes of thing, which, as Aristotle saw, is different in the two cases.

Aristotle, however, follows Plato in finding a very close link between the essential nature of a species of thing and the perfection of that thing, the end to which its whole development is striving (in Aristotle's terms, between the formal and the final cause). And Aristotle's notion that we can explain everything by giving its purpose goes back, through Plato, to Anaxagoras, who according to a passage in the *Phaedo* from which I have already quoted (97c) suggested that Mind orders all things as it is for the best that they should be—an idea which, according to Plato, Anaxagoras made no use of, but which Socrates took to heart. Since in the *Phaedo* explanation in terms of purpose (of what is for the best) is put alongside explanation in terms of the Ideas which make things what they are, it is natural for Plato to speak, as he does in the *Republic*, of the Good as the source of all being, and of our knowledge of it (509b).

Plato, because he thought of the objects of knowledge as things, and of our knowledge of them as a kind of mental seeing, goes on to represent the hierarchy of Ideas as a kind of quasi-physical chain with the lower items 'attached' to the Good at the top. By looking at (or grasping) this chain we can see (feel) the connections. The chain contains only Ideas; that is to say, nothing from the world of sense is admitted into it (511b, c). This was Plato's way of putting the correct point, further elaborated by Aristotle, that true, certain knowledge (by which he meant knowledge of necessary truths) cannot be had by observation of nature; it can only be of what we can show to be true by giving the required definitions.

Plato here gets near to the notion, much used by some recent philosophers but also disputed by others, of analytic truth. His most important claim in this area could be put into modern dress as the claim that the truths of logic and mathematics, and philosophical truths generally, do not rest on observation of particular things and events, but on definitions available to thought. But, as we saw, it is usually dangerous to try to put Plato into modern dress; that was not how it looked to him, because he was, he thought, talking not about *propositions* and how they are derived or known, but about things inspected with the mind's eye. Whereas for us a definition is one kind of analytically or necessarily true proposition, for him it was a description of a mentally visible and eternally true object.

7 *Education and the good life*

We saw that Plato's search for an adequate account of knowing was motivated, at least in part, by the belief that only this could discriminate right opinion about how to behave from error, and make it secure from deviance. We have now reached a point at which it can be explained more fully how he hoped to achieve this. But we must first look briefly at the educational scene in Athens. In the *Meno* he purports to record a conversation between Socrates and some others shortly before his trial, which took place when Plato was about 28; and this gives a good picture of the situation as it would have impressed itself on Plato. It is suggested that if goodness were teachable there would be teachers of it, and it is asked who these might be. Socrates, in an ironical spirit, suggests that if we are looking for *professional* teachers of goodness or excellence, we can find them in the people known as *sophists* (91b).

This word is connected with '*sophos*', commonly translated 'wise', but often better rendered as 'clever'. '*Sophos*' covers any kind of skill or dexterity, physical or intellectual, artistic or political, and is often a term of commendation—more so than its near equivalent '*deinos*', which can mean 'clever' in a neutral or even hostile sense, but literally means 'terrible' (as in the French '*enfant terrible*'). As the intellectual life of Greece blossomed there came into being a class of people who can be compared, at any rate in their effect on society, with the intellectual gurus of our own day. To these people the name 'sophists' came to be especially applied; it means that they themselves were clever, and that they could impart this cleverness, especially rhetorical skill, to young men who were prepared to pay them handsomely enough. In the *Protagoras* 'sophist' is defined as 'a master of the art of making people into clever speakers' (312d).

In popular estimation Socrates counted as a sophist, and he suffered for the supposed sins of the whole class; but he differed from them in not claiming to be able to make people clever or impart any other kind of excellence, but only to talk with them and perhaps help to birth any good notions that they might themselves bring forth; and also in not taking any money. The sophists held a variety of doctrines, and no doubt made significant contributions to the thought of that intellectually exciting period. But in one way it is not important what their doctrines were; by making young people think at all about problems to which, in the opinion of their elders, there were right answers such as ought not to be questioned, they were thought to have unsettled an entire generation. In this sense, at least, Socrates was the most sophisticated of the sophists, and by their own lights the Athenians did right to put him to death.

In the *Meno* the suggestion that the sophists can count as teachers of goodness is summarily rejected by the traditionally-minded democrat Anytus (the man principally responsible for the prosecution of Socrates). Even one of the sophists themselves, Gorgias, is quoted as saying that he cannot make men good, only clever. Instead, Anytus suggests that the right person to teach young men goodness would be any decent Athenian gentleman (like himself, we are to understand). Socrates then gives him the usual treatment, pointing out that these decent people do not seem to make much of a go of educating their own sons. The same point is made in the *Protagoras* (324d).

The traditional Greek education which a boy would get from any decent gentleman in any Greek city was probably not unlike that prescribed, in a bowdlerized form, in the earlier part of Plato's *Republic*. Plato has made important alterations: he has censored certain passages in Homer and the other poets; and the emphasis is more on the conscious formation of character and less on the learning of accomplishments like wrestling and music-making for their own sakes. But there cannot have been any radical difference in what the boys would actually have done. There would be variations from city to city: in one the mix would include more 'music' (including the performing arts as well as literature); in another more 'gymnastic' (athletics with an eye to military training). In Sparta the whole thing was highly organized as in the *Republic*; in other cities less so. But it is obvious that in the *Republic*, in his primary education, Plato is consciously taking over, with modifications, the traditional Greek education in 'music and gymnastic' such as any well-born Greek boy could expect to receive, and such as Socrates says in the *Crito* that he himself received when young (50e).

This old education did not mix very well with the new education offered by the sophists. The old education aimed primarily at training the character, the new the intellect. A person who was successfully educated in the old way at its best would have the virtues which had made Athens what she was: the virtues extolled by the 'Right Argument' in Aristophanes' *Clouds*. We must not put it too high; we have only to look again at the *Meno* and find Themistocles, who was actually a wily devil with a far from spotless reputation, being cited as a supremely good man (93b). But Themistocles was very *successful*, and commanded the Greek fleet in its most decisive victory over the Persians, and so his sins (like Nelson's) were forgiven.

The well-born, well-educated Greek was not a paragon of virtue by Christian standards. He often wanted to make a hit in politics, and do something notable for the city; at worst he was ambitious to a degree which we should condemn; he wanted to be able to entertain lavishly (Aristotle rates 'magnificence' as one of the virtues, meaning by it having the wherewithal and the aptitude for living in style); he wanted to put his opponents in their places, and even worse; and generally to have that thing which sounds so weak when translated into English, 'honour'; but not only, it must be added, for achievements which we should call honourable.

The education provided by the sophists still aimed at what was called goodness or excellence, but in a very different way. By training not the character but the intellect it aspired to enable its products to pursue just those ambitions which the traditional upbringing cultivated, but pursue them with far greater hope of success. A principal means to this was a training in rhetoric, giving an ability to persuade courts and assemblies, and thus get one's political way. The new education played on the weaknesses of the old: the old produced ambitious but fundamentally upright people; the new fostered the ambitions, and held out greater hopes of realizing them, but paid less attention to uprightness. Readers who doubt this should look at the *Theages*, and see what that young man, who takes Socrates for a sophist, hopes to get from him (125–6).

There is another side to the question. Intellectual education is not a bad thing. Aristotle puts the matter very well in the course of his mature reflections on this subject. Intellectual ability, cleverness, is morally neutral; it all depends on a man's character. If his character leads him to pursue good ends, intellectual ability will enable him to achieve them more readily; if his ends are wicked, he will also more readily achieve *them*. The situation which Plato faced was one in which a new education and an old education confronted each other, not quite as opponents one of which was good and the other bad, as Aristophanes made out, but rather as two factors which actually worked together for ill but could, if reformed on lines which he was to suggest, work together for good. In the *Gorgias* a contrast is drawn between the right and the wrong kind of rhetorician, and in the *Sophist* between the right and the wrong kind of sophist. The right kind in both cases is the philosopher who, because he *knows* the Good and everything which depends on it, can really educate people instead of just pandering to their desires and ensnaring them.

The basis, therefore, of Plato's educational reforms is Socrates' distinction between knowledge and opinion. This theme runs through the whole, not only of Plato's, but of Aristotle's moral philosophy. In Plato's ideal city the scheme is that character-training should precede intellectual training. This diverges from Socrates' practice even as portrayed by Plato in such dialogues as the *Theages* and the *Charmides*; he shows Socrates having intellectually very educative conversations with young men and offering to do it on a regular basis. In the *Gorgias* Plato puts into the mouth of a critic, and does not deny (how could he?), the accusation that it was Socrates' practice to 'whisper with three or four young men in a corner' (485d); and although Aristophanes is wrong in portraying Socrates as the founder of a 'school' in any institutional sense, he is no doubt right in implying that young people were his disciples.

Plato's developed view was different; we should first implant, by entirely non-intellectual training, right opinion leading to right habits and dispositions, and only then will it be safe, at a much later age, to introduce people to philosophy, in order that they may acquire knowledge of the Good which determines which opinions are right. The only kind of intellectual training that the young get in his Republic is mathematics, a morally safe discipline. And philosophy is not for everybody, but only for those gifted people who are capable of it, and who can safely be entrusted with the running of the educational process, and indeed of the entire state. This they are to do in the light of the knowledge which they attain, in order that the society may be one in which the good life can be lived (see p. 171).

Aristotle took over this distinction between goodness of character and goodness of intellect; and he quotes Plato as saying that people should be brought up from their early years to like and dislike what they ought to like and dislike. Aristotle's view, a development of Plato's, was that if they have acquired the habit of right desire they will be able to recognize *that* such and such actions and characters are good, but they may still not know *why* they are; they will not have 'goodness in the full sense', for which the intellectual quality of wisdom (*phronēsis*) is a necessary condition.

On one point Aristotle corrects Socrates' view in the *Meno* (88c): the intellectual quality is only a necessary condition of goodness in the full sense, and not identical with it; the qualities of character are needed as well. But by the *Republic* Plato himself was implying this. Those who have the 'that' but not the 'why' are in the same position as the good men without knowledge in the *Meno*, and as those in the *Republic* who have had the primary education but have learnt no philosophy. They lack the 'reckoning of the reason' which alone can make knowledge of the Good, and therefore goodness, secure. In the Platonic state this security has to be provided by others, those who do have the knowledge.

We see then that Plato has incorporated reformed versions of both the traditional and the sophistic education into his proposed educational system. A purged system of character-formation will be succeeded, at a safe age and for sound pupils, by a development of the intellect; and each will be supervised by people who, because they know what goodness is, know what they are about, unlike both the good Athenian gentlemen and the clever sophists.

8 *The divided mind*

There is a group of doctrines, usually attributed to Socrates, in taking over which Plato encountered difficulties which caused him to modify his views, in particular his views about the mind. The most basic of these doctrines is one about the relation of the Good to desire. Not all its versions are identical. Aristotle, almost certainly endorsing Platonic views, puts it thus: 'the Good is what everything is after'. In the *Gorgias* Socrates says 'We desire the good things', and adds that whatever else we desire, we desire for the sake of these (468c). In the *Philebus* he says (in this late dialogue certainly expressing Plato's own views) 'Everything that knows [the Good] chases and pursues it, desiring to acquire and possess it' (20d). A version passed into medieval philosophy in the maxim 'Whatever is sought, is sought under the appearance of good.'

The doctrine can be given either a logical interpretation: if you are not disposed to choose something, you cannot really be thinking it the best (to think better *is* to prefer, and to prefer *is* to be disposed to choose, other things being equal); or else a psychological one, in terms of what always, by natural necessity, happens: everything as a matter of inevitable fact does choose what it thinks to be best. Plato had probably not distinguished between those interpretations, and I must confess to a doubt whether the latter, if its obscurities were removed, would turn out to be different from the former.

A related doctrine, which Plato also clung to until the end (it occurs in the *Laws*, 731c and 860d), is that, as it is commonly translated, 'Nobody willingly errs.' A translation which makes the doctrine sound self-evidently true is 'Nobody makes mistakes on purpose'; but unfortunately the *Laws* version cannot be translated in this way, since the words used mean 'Nobody willingly is not upright.' Most probably Socrates was misled by the self-evidence of the doctrine in one version into taking the more substantial version to be self-evident too.

Also related is the doctrine, already mentioned, that goodness is somehow like a craft or skill. We saw that Aristotle rightly rejected the view expressed by Socrates early in the *Meno* that goodness is the same thing as wisdom. Wisdom (which Plato equated with knowledge and with skill, two concepts which even as late as the *Politicus* he did not distinguish) is, says Aristotle, only a *necessary condition* of *goodness in the full sense*. This may also represent Plato's mature view, as we shall see.

Allied to these views is the doctrine known to scholars as 'the unity of the virtues', the view that, properly speaking, if we have any kind of goodness, we have all kinds. This might seem to follow from the premiss that wisdom and goodness or virtue are identical; for if all the virtues are identical with wisdom, they must be identical with each other. But this is too quick; courage and uprightness, for example, might each be identical with a different *kind* of wisdom, namely wisdom concerning the areas in which those virtues are exercised; and then they would not be identical with each other. Plato gives his mature views on the question in the *Laws*; virtue is one, in that it is a genus to which all virtues belong; but the species of it differ. But he still stresses the fundamental importance, for good life, education and government, of understanding the common genus (964ff.). And it is probable that he went on thinking, as Aristotle did, that one cannot have virtue *in the full sense* (cannot be, in the words of the end of the *Meno*, 'the real thing in respect of virtue') without this understanding.

But can one have the understanding without the virtue? Only, Plato came to think, if the understanding somehow failed to be in full control of us. In the *Republic* (435ff.) he gives his considered solution to the difficulty raised by the Socratic doctrine that nobody willingly errs, a doctrine which he had defended in the *Protagoras* as part of the group of doctrines we have been considering. The solution lies in thinking of the mind or soul as divided into parts which do not necessarily see eye to eye (a doctrine also found in the *Phaedrus*). For example, when people are thirsty they still may not drink, because 'there is in their soul that which bids them drink, and also something else which forbids them, and prevails over the other'. He calls the former part desire, and the latter, reason, and he adds a third part called spirit, the seat of anger, which is the natural ally of reason against desire. The good ordering of our lives which is called virtue depends on the right schooling of the two lower parts so that they obey the reason, in the same way as good government depends on the lower orders obeying wise rulers.

The way in which this partition of the mind is supposed to solve the problems raised by the Socratic doctrines is this: We can say that one part of the mind has knowledge of the Good, but may not be fully in control of the other parts. Plato had denied in the *Protagoras* that this was possible (352b). 'Self-mastery' and its opposite are, according to the *Republic*, misnomers: in the strict sense it is absurd to speak of someone being the master of himself, because then he would also be the slave of himself, and he surely cannot be both (430e), even though common parlance, and Plato himself earlier in the *Gorgias*, talks that way (491d). But it does make sense to speak of one part of him being master, or not being master, of other parts. So we can say that self-controlled people are those whose reason is in control of their desires. But not all people are in this sense self-controlled, and of those who are not it will make sense to say that they know (with their reason) the Good, but that their baser desires, which are seeking something else under the misapprehension that it is good, defeat the reason, so that bad action rather than good, vice rather than virtue, results.

Plato did not at first divide up the mind or soul in this way. In the *Phaedo*, the soul is represented as 'most like to that which is homogeneous and indissoluble' (80b); it is natural to take this as an insistence on the unity of the soul, and this unity is indeed used in the proof of immortality. The baser desires which lead us to wrongdoing are in this dialogue assigned in St Paul's fashion to the body or 'flesh'.

But even in the *Phaedo* Plato shows that he is not wholly satisfied with this way of putting the matter, and rightly. For desires are conscious states, and the soul or mind is supposed to be the seat of consciousness. A lump of flesh does not have desires: my throat does not have desires when I am thirsty; *I* have them, as part of my conscious experience. By the time he wrote the *Philebus* Plato was expressing this point very clearly (35c); he proves it from the fact that desire is of something not physically present, which therefore cannot be apprehended by the bodily senses, but only envisaged by the mind. The premiss at least of this argument is stated already in the *Symposium* (200); this is probably near in date to the *Phaedo*.

Plato had therefore, if he was to adopt the 'internal conflict' solution, to divide up the soul. But he did so with reluctance, and at the end of the *Republic* he again, when insisting on the immortality at least of the rational part of the soul, seems to be saying that it is indivisible, only we can hardly see whether it is or not because of the impurities, the mutilations and the accretions which cling to it like barnacles owing to its association with the body (611). Since both these ways of drawing up the lines of battle between the good and the evil in us are metaphors, it is perhaps not fair to Plato to insist that he decide between them.

But the solution of dividing up the self (which has continued to attract psychologists all the way to Freud) runs into more serious difficulties than this. First of all, does it leave the self enough of a unity to match our commonsense conviction that it is a single 'I' that has both the conflicting motives? If 'it is no more I, but sin that dwelleth in me', am I sinning at all? Even more seriously, what is supposed to be the role of reason (or of conscience if that is different)? Is it its function to know the Good, or to desire it? Plato is very insistent that each part of the soul, like each part of the city, has its own function; but there seem to be two different functions here.

Aristotle was aware of this difficulty, of which David Hume

in the eighteenth century was to make much. Aristotle divided up the mind or soul in a somewhat Platonic but more complicated way; but he put all the motivative faculties into one part and all the cognitive and in general intellectual faculties into another; and he said of the intellect or reason that 'by itself it moves nothing; it is only when it is in pursuit of an end, and is concerned in action, that it moves anything'. Aristotle wrestled with this problem, inherited from Plato, of how the cognitive and motivative functions can somehow *combine* to produce action; he was driven a long way towards Hume's position that 'Reason is perfectly inert', while struggling, like Plato, to avoid Hume's conclusion that it 'both is and ought only to be the slave of the passions, and can never pretend to any other office than to serve and obey them'.

If Plato had been consistent in separating off the cognitive part of the mind, he would have given it no motivative function. But then, as Hume saw, it would have been totally powerless to make us do anything, except in the service of some desire which had its origin in one of the other parts of the mind. The result would be that in his effort to explain how we could be weak-willed and follow desire in despite of reason, Plato would have made it impossible for us to follow reason in despite of desire. In the *Phaedrus* he uses the simile of reason, the charioteer, controlling two horses, spirit and appetite (246, 253ff.). Even in that simile it is the horses that do the pulling; and Plato has left it unclear what, in reality, correspond to the bridle and the spur. Perhaps all that reason can do is show the horses how to get where *they* want to go.

Actually he is not fully consistent, and so escapes this conclusion. Sometimes he escapes it by making the spirit, if well conducted, the ally of reason, providing the motive force which reason, strictly understood, could not provide. More typically he gives to reason itself a motivative power, claiming, as in a passage already quoted, that merely to know the Good is automatically to be attracted by it, so that the same faculty of reason fulfils both the cognitive and the motivative roles. In the same way, in the *Politicus*, the body of the king has small strength; he manages to govern because of the understanding and power of his soul or mind (259c).

Whether this is a possible solution depends on whether there could be such a thing as Plato thought the Good to be. To fulfil its dual role of object of knowledge and object of desire it would have to be such that, once discovered, it automatically excited desire. If anybody did not desire it once discovered, it would not be the same thing which he had discovered. Two people logically could not both discover this same thing, and one desire it, one not. 'We needs must love the highest when we see it' would then become a logically or metaphysically necessary truth—and that not because 'highest' is a value word, so that to call something 'the highest' is already to express love for it. For if that were so, before we thought of something as the Good, we should have to be already being attracted by it; desire as well as cognition would have to be involved in the 'discovery' of it; and that is ruled out by a consistent separation of reason from motivation. Rather, the Good has to be something determined independently of our wills: propositions describing it have to be factually descriptive. And yet our wills have somehow to be automatically engaged in its pursuit once discovered; propositions about it have therefore to be prescriptive as well.

Whether we can follow Plato in believing in the existence of such a thing will depend on how seriously we take the objections of some modern thinkers to the existence, or even the coherence, of the notion of 'objective prescriptions'—that is to say, of propositions which can somehow at one and the same time both be objectively established as true, independently of how anybody is motivated or disposed, *and* carry a prescriptive force. Whatever side we may take in modern disputes on this issue, it is clear that Plato, in his doctrine of the Good as an eternally existing entity, beyond being but at the same time the source of being, as he says in the *Republic* (509b), did believe in something very like what is now called objective prescriptivity; but, perhaps fortunately for him, he did not have such unwieldy words with which to express it.

9   The authoritarian State

Given Plato's views about knowledge of the Good, and about the role of education in making possible a good life, it is easy to see how he came by his highly authoritarian political doctrines. We can become good men and lead a good life by one of two means. Either we acquire right opinions about the best way to live, or we acquire knowledge. Both, as he says in the *Meno* (98), will serve the limited purpose of living a good life; but right opinion can never be reliably imparted, and will never be secure against corrupting influences, unless somebody—either a man himself or those who teach and subsequently rule him—has not merely right opinion but knowledge: knowledge of the Ideas, which are the explanations of why things are as they are, and are also, because of the dependence of the other Ideas on the Good, explanations of how it is best that they should be. The possessors of this knowledge are the only people who can determine what kind of life is good, and thus the only people who can provide the education (even the primary education which imparts only right opinion) and the governance which are the necessary conditions of the good life.

Given these premises it seems obvious that, if the good life is to be lived in a particular society or state, its institutions will have to be framed in such a way as to further this education, and that this will come about only if those who have the knowledge are put firmly in charge of the machinery of government. Anybody who objects to Plato's authoritarian views will have to find some flaw in this argument; and the best way to understand the strengths and weaknesses of the argument is to look for the flaws. We shall see that the argument is more secure than it looks at first sight, and that to reject it involves rejecting some views which are still widely held.

Let us first look at the political institutions which Plato actually recommends, and then see what justifications he can find for their adoption. The *Republic* contains his first full-scale design for an ideal state, though it is concerned with much else besides, and is, on this as on other questions, a bit sketchy and programmatic. The citizens are to be divided into two classes, and the higher of these subdivided again into two, making three in all. They correspond to the three 'parts' into which man's mind is divided, reason, spirit and appetite; to each class those people are assigned in whom these mental characteristics respectively predominate. It is presumed that heredity will do most of the work of assignment between classes; but Plato makes a point of saying that, if there are any misfits, promotion or demotion is to take place.

The small class of rational people is to rule the state with the support of the 'spirited' or soldier class, from whom the rulers themselves, called 'guardians', are selected during the common process of education which both classes initially share. The masses in the lowest of the three classes are excluded from any part in government; their role is to obey, and to supply the community's needs by engaging in useful trades. Scholars dispute whether Plato intends them to share in the education provided for the guardians and soldiers, but his silence on the question seems to imply that he does not.

The first stage in this education, as we have seen, comprises training in the arts and in athletics with a view to the formation of good character and right opinions, firmly implanted. Intellectual education, the cultivation of the reason as a qualification for ruling, will not otherwise be safe. Mathematics, an essential preliminary to philosophy, is offered to the children but not forced on them. They are also taken as spectators to see battles, mounted on horses for their safety, so that when they come to fight they may do so bravely. By the age of thirty a select few, who have proved themselves in all the branches of the earlier education, are judged fit for the study of philosophy for five years, after which they serve in the lower offices of state, civil and military, for fifteen years. At fifty, 'the survivors, the best of them,' are 'compelled to turn their mind's eye' to the Idea of the Good, and then take their turns for what remains of their lives ordering the city, and the individual citizens, and themselves, using the Good as their model. When not thus occupied, they can indulge in the pleasures of philosophy (540).

The innovation which Plato thinks will seem most startling is that women are to share all this, both the education (including athletics) and the responsibility of government, on equal terms with men. It must be remembered that the Greeks in Plato's time engaged in athletics naked. The picture of Californian beaches which this may suggest is quickly dispelled; we learn that the sex life of all is to be strictly regulated, mating being forbidden except at special festivals and between selected partners at the discretion of the rulers, with a eugenic purpose. Children are to be held in common, as in a strict kibbutz, treating all grown-ups as equally their parents.

The life of the two higher classes is as austere as in Sparta; Plato is insistent here and elsewhere that ruling as such is a disagreeable activity, to be undertaken not for personal advantage but for the good of society as a whole. This was perhaps Plato's greatest contribution to political theory; a much commoner view was that political power is desirable not only for its own sake but also for the material advantages that the powerful can obtain. Plato, by contrast, envisages the rulers ruling unwillingly, and only for fear of being ruled by somebody worse than themselves (347c). Being neither pleasure-seeking nor ambitious, the true philosopher, alone qualified to rule through his knowledge of the Good, can leave the pursuit of material pleasures to the lower orders.

Hardly any detail is given in the *Republic* of how the government of the ideal state is actually to be carried on. In particular, the relation of the rulers to the laws remains somewhat obscure. In the *Crito*, an early work, Socrates is made to enjoin and himself exemplify a highly reverential attitude to law;

although he has been unjustly condemned to death, it would be wrong for him to break the laws by fleeing into exile, because the laws could then accuse him of going back on a compact with them from which he had benefited in the past (50). Did Plato in the *Republic* intend that his rulers should have this same attitude of implicit obedience to the laws? The question is discussed and clarified in a later dialogue, the *Politicus*, to which Aristotle's discussion owes much (293ff.). In an ideal state with ideal rulers, Plato thinks, the rulers ought not themselves to be bound by the laws, but should be able to alter them *ad hoc* to fit individual cases, just as a doctor fits his treatment to the condition of each patient. Any attempt to lay down laws by which the rulers themselves were to be bound would lead to an inability to suit measures to particular cases and to a ban on all innovation however beneficial. *Provided that the ruler possesses the art of ruling*, he should be free to adapt the laws to his knowledge of the Good.

Only in inferior imitations of the ideal state, which lack rulers with this knowledge (and such are indeed hard to find), is universal obedience to the laws, even by the rulers, insisted on. Those who do not have knowledge of the Good have to be controlled by laws. This includes the lower classes even in the best of states; for them the absolute obedience commended in the *Crito* is still appropriate. The judges are to be subordinate to the government: Belloc's 'Lord Chief Justice of Liberia / And Minister of the Interior' held a combined office which would have had a counterpart in Plato's city, in which the judiciary is 'the guardian of the laws and the servant of the kingly power' (305c).

By the time Plato wrote the *Laws* his pessimism had gone further, no doubt increased by his experiences in Sicily and the lack of progress, by Platonic standards, in the politics of the Greek cities. The main speaker plays the role of a lawgiver, of a type which was in demand when new Greek colonies were founded, and to which the Academy provided some recruits, as we have seen. By his mouth Plato sets out a lengthy, elaborate and detailed set of laws, which must have appeared extremely severe and rigid even to a Greek reactionary. They are not to be departed from, although at the end there seems to be provision for amendment by the supreme Nocturnal Council in the light of the Idea of Virtue.

In this second-best city, as Plato recognizes it to be (875), the rulers are 'servants of the law' (715d). But in an ideal city it would not be so. The ideals of the *Republic* remain in another respect too; although in both works great inequality of power is prescribed, the distribution of wealth, though not actually inverted as in the *Republic* so that the rulers are poorer, remains moderately egalitarian; and it does not depend on one's income-group whether one becomes a ruler, but only on one's merit as judged by the existing rulers. The philosopher-king ideal survives (711).

A modern liberal will certainly find these suggested institutions extremely repellent. Let us then ask how he might seek to undermine Plato's argument. He might, first of all, attack the more picturesque features of the Platonic metaphysics. He might dismiss as mythological the view that there is a celestial world of eternally existing Ideas, visible to the eye of the mind provided that it has been suitably schooled. The claim that only those with this superior mental vision are competent to guide others by education and firm government might thus be defeated. Unfortunately matters are not so easy for the liberal. We can show this by restating the Platonic authoritarian argument without the mythology. In order to establish it, it is not necessary for Plato to adopt a mental-vision-of-eternal-objects theory of knowledge. Of the two alternative caricatures of Plato invented in Chapter 4, Pato clearly believed in such a theory, and he was a political authoritarian. What will be more interesting to the liberal is to see whether the more modern-seeming Lato would have to have the same political views. Lato is a linguistic philosopher. Are there views about language, especially evaluative language, which can have such extreme political implications?

It would not be unfair to attribute to Lato a view about evaluative and in particular about moral language which is still widely accepted: the view that moral and other evaluative statements state objective facts about the world, which are capable of being known. This extremely respectable position is variously known as ethical objectivism, cognitivism or descriptivism—terms which do not mean the same as each other, but whose differences in meaning need not concern us here. Lato certainly believed in the 'objectivity of values'; but he could allow us, if we wanted, to dismiss as mythological the metaphysical scaffolding wherewith Pato sought to support it. It is enough for Lato to claim that, when I say that a certain way of life is good, I am claiming to state an objective fact.

If this were granted, the question then arises of how such claims are to be assessed for truth or falsity. How do we settle whether the way of life *is* good? Various sorts of objectivist give different answers to this question; but whatever method of settling these evaluative questions is proposed, the next question will be whether everybody is equally able to operate it, or whether some are better than others at determining questions about value. For if some are better than others, will not the Platonic authoritarian conclusion follow that these superior people should be given the say in all important political decisions? If what we are after is the good life, must we not leave the ordering of our lives to those who *know* what it is?

The crucial fact here, when we ask whether all are equally good at answering questions about values, is that people *differ* about such questions. This point was discussed in Plato's school, and indeed, if the *Greater Alcibiades* is a genuine work of Plato's, as it probably is, discussed by Plato himself. The same views as are there expressed are in any case implicit in the *Theaetetus* (170d), the *Phaedrus* (263a) and elsewhere. The argument is closely bound up with the analogy between the good life and arts and skills. In the *Alcibiades* Socrates is made to point out that, whereas 'the many' are all in agreement about how to speak Greek (for example, they do not disagree about how to apply the words 'stone', 'stick', 'man' and 'horse', and therefore all qualify as competent teachers of the use of these words), when it comes to assessing the merits of men or horses, or in general making value judgements, they do differ, and therefore we cannot say that they are all competent teachers about such evaluative matters. There is, rather, a select class of people who know (that is, who have the appropriate skill) and are therefore competent teachers. This conclusion is applied to questions about what is right or wrong, on which Alcibiades has pretended to instruct the Athenians in their Assembly (111).

If it is once agreed that only some, not all, people are qualified to pronounce on questions of value, then the Platonic authoritarian argument is well under way. And it seems that this argument requires only two premisses: that values are objective, and that people differ about them. It looks as if the second premiss is obviously true, and as if, therefore, anybody who wishes to avoid the authoritarian conclusion will have to reject the first. Unless, that is, we take the pessimistic view that *nobody* knows the objective answers, though these do exist. Short of divine guidance, there would then be no hope of getting our politics right; but although in the *Meno* Plato rather playfully attributed to divine guidance such successes as had been achieved hitherto, he hoped for something more reliable (99c).

It is possible to think of various ways in which a liberal might seek to escape the authoritarian conclusion while remaining an objectivist. These moves rely on two distinctions, that between means and ends and that between questions of substance and questions about the meanings of words. We shall see that the first distinction does not help the liberal against Plato if he remains an objectivist, but that the second enables us to liberalize Lato, if not Pato, in a way that could conceivably have commended itself to Plato himself if, as was not the case, he had been clear about both distinctions. But it leaves him no longer an unmixed objectivist.

It might be suggested that if we distinguish between the end (the good life) and the political and other means to it, we can say that the knowledgeable élite is indeed more competent than the rest of the population to judge of means, but not of ends. Everybody is, in the last reckoning, the best judge of whether his own life has been a good one for himself; but people can be wildly mistaken about what political, social and economic arrangements are most likely to bring it about that the maximum number of people attain this satisfaction with their own lives. But if this is so, we shall maximize satisfaction by finding out (perhaps by democratic vote, or less crudely by sociological researches) what manner of lives will most satisfy various sorts of people, and then leaving it to the experts to see to it that lives of those kinds are achieved.

To this suggestion there are at least two objections. The first is that it is not likely in practice to lead to a very liberal form of government. At any rate a great many of the vexed questions in politics are questions of means, even if we differ about ends too. And secondly, in any case, questions of means and ends in politics are thoroughly tangled up with one another. To take a simple example: imagine that we are all agreed that it is a desirable end to raise the general standard of living (in the crudest material and measurable terms). It will hardly be a liberal society if, having agreed upon this end, we leave the means to it in the hands of experts. For one thing, if the experts pursue this end single-mindedly, they will find themselves doing things inimical to *other* ends which their subjects hold dear, such as personal liberty; but if they try to meet this objection by securing prior agreement to a comprehensive basket of ends, with a weighting or priority attached to each, the sheer political impracticability of such a procedure will at once become apparent. They are more likely to succeed by submitting themselves to the judgement of their subjects at the end of a given term of office, and asking for re-election if their measures have in the outcome advanced what the subjects think to have been in their interest.

Such an arrangement, however, ought not to commend itself to an objectivist liberal any more than it would to Plato. For the question about ends remains pressing. If values are objective, as both Pato and Lato think, then judgements about the ends which ought to be pursued (that is, about the character of the good life) will be objective too, and will have, on the preceding argument, to be left to experts. So the first liberal escape-route is closed.

A more promising line starts from a distinction which Pato would find difficult, but into which Lato might be coaxed if we had him with us. The question 'What is the Good?' can be taken in at least two ways. It can be taken as an inquiry into the meaning of the *word* 'good', or as an inquiry into the qualifying properties which entitle us to call a thing of a certain kind (or, as perhaps Plato would have thought, of any kind) good. Plato had not had the advantage of reading the sixth chapter of Aristotle's *Nicomachean Ethics* I, and therefore made the mistake of thinking that the qualifying properties which make things of all kinds good are the same; but it is easy to see that the properties that make a good strawberry good are not the same as those which make a good motorcycle good.

However, leaving this difficulty on one side, let us take separately, as Plato does not, the question of the meaning of the word 'good' and that of the qualifying properties which entitle us to call things good. The failure to make this distinction is the source of the view, commonly called descriptivism, which has been almost universal in moral philosophy until recently: the view that the two questions which I say have to be distinguished are really the same question. This is no place to argue that they are not the same question (that two people may mean the same by 'good' but use different qualifying properties for assessing goodness in, for example, cheeses). I shall merely assume for the sake of argument that there is a distinction, and then see how it helps with our present problem.

If the question 'What does the phrase "the good life" *mean*?' is a different question from 'What properties make a life good?', then interesting possibilities open up. We have to ask: If Socrates puts the question 'What is the good life?', which of these questions does he mean us to answer? The first question, about the meaning, looks a good candidate for handling by means of the Socratic method of scrutiny. Various definitions or explanations of the meaning will be proposed, and tested against the understanding we all have of how words are rightly used. If we can find an account of the meaning which satisfies this test, then we can proceed to use the phrase, in full awareness of its meaning and therefore its logical implications, in argument about the other question, the question about the properties which make a life good. Our achievement so far would be a philosophical one, reached by the analysis of concepts, without any assumptions of substance about what *does* constitute a good life. If Plato were simply suggesting that this is a necessary and useful contribution on the part of the philosopher, we could perhaps all agree.

But then we have to ask: What bearing will the philosophical, conceptual inquiry so far outlined have upon the answer to the second question, 'What properties make a life good?' That will depend, obviously, on what account of the meaning of 'good' has stood up to the scrutiny-test. Without launching into a survey of rival theories in moral philosophy, let us at least envisage the possibility that the successful account of the meaning of 'good' and of other such words might put into our possession certain logical weapons—certain canons of argument about the question of what kinds of life are good—which could help us settle that question. In that case, Plato's programme would have been in part vindicated. The philosopher would have made an important contribution, not merely to the question of meaning, but also to moral and political ones.

Unfortunately Plato did not bequeath to us an account of the meaning of 'good'; and his account of other moral concepts or Ideas is not sufficient for us to extract canons of moral argument. We can only speculate about what he would have said if he had given a full explanation of the concepts used in moral argument. It is fairly safe to say that the account would have included certain elements. In the first place he would have insisted on the objectivity of statements about the good life, at least in the sense that fully informed and rational people would not disagree about what it consisted in. But he would also have insisted that statements about the good life were prescriptive, in the sense that to accept that a certain way of life would be good would be already to be motivated towards pursuing it.

It is not obvious that, when 'objectivity' is taken in this minimal sense, the notion of an objective prescription (see p. 169) is incoherent, though it probably is incoherent if it is taken in the more usual sense, in which a statement is said to make an objective claim if it is factual or descriptive. Probably Plato would have claimed it in this stronger sense; but even in the weaker sense it could serve to support his political views. For if there are prescriptions on which all rational and informed people would agree, and if only a certain section of the population are rational and informed, ought we not to crown them as philosopher-kings and let them coerce and indoctrinate the others, for their own good, into obeying these prescriptions?

The conclusion could be avoided if we abandoned objectivity, if not entirely, at any rate as regards judgements made by people about *their own* good. Let us suppose that everybody is the best judge of what is good for *him*, in the sense of what most satisfies *him*. We could then avoid the most illiberal aspects of Plato's paternalism by confining the role of his rational rulers to the tasks, first of determining what outcomes would maximally reconcile the divergent interests of all their subjects, thus ensuring for them the greatest possible satisfaction, and secondly of finding the means most conducive to bringing about these outcomes. And we could allow the subjects to dismiss the rulers by popular vote if they proved unsuccessful in this role, and elect others. Given his background, it is unlikely that Plato would have agreed with this democratic solution, but it is consistent with his main philosophical views as interpreted by Lato, except that the claim that value judgements are objective has to be interpreted in a rather weak sense. Philosophy is left with a crucial role, but it is not allowed to dictate to people what they are to find good in life.

Two further points may be made, the first in Plato's favour, the second not. First, as has often been pointed out by recent writers, we are unlikely to be able to escape being ruled by a ruling class of some kind; 'the iron law of oligarchy' is fairly well established by a study of history. If there are going in any case to be relatively few people who have the power of government and exercise its functions, even in a democracy, then Plato is surely entirely right in holding that it will be best if they receive, before they attain this position of power, an education which will enable them to exercise it wisely. Though Pato may be wrong in requiring a deep study of the eternal verities and values, Lato is on safer ground when he asks that they acquire an understanding of the language they use when they debate the crucial moral and other evaluative questions that confront the statesman. For if they do not understand the questions they are asking, they will hardly be able to answer them rationally. If Lato were to claim that this is all the education that is necessary for rulers, he would be going too far, for they need other qualifications besides philosophy. But in fact even in the *Republic* this claim is not made—only that such understanding is a supremely important part of the equipment of a ruler.

Secondly, we must make more allowance than perhaps Plato does for human fallibility. Even if we grant him that there is a skill of ruling which could in theory equip its possessor to make all the right decisions, it may be a skill which no human being will ever attain, and perhaps a skill by the exercise of which he will be corrupted. Plato is in fact fairly pessimistic about this, as can be seen by reading between the lines of the *Republic*, and by looking at the much less ambitious demands made of his rulers in the *Laws*. But Plato does not recognize, as he should, that if rulers are fallible their claim to absolute power is less strong. As Sir Karl Popper rightly insisted, it may be more important to have institutional means of limiting the harm that unwise rulers can do, and removing them without violence if they fail to secure the good of their subjects.

10 *Plato's achievement*

If the first of Europe's philosophers whose works survive does not have the same towering dominance as its first poet, Homer, that is not any reflection on Plato's genius. His actual achievement in his own field was as great. It is merely that we know a little more about what went before. Despite this, he, like Homer, presents to us the appearance (albeit a misleading one) of arising out of nothing, and also of a certain primitiveness which his marvellously polished style does not altogether conceal. He has a greater claim than anybody else to be called the founder of philosophy as we know it. But what, exactly, did he found? The answer will depend on who 'we' are; it will be different for Patonists and Latonists, and even that crude division does not do justice to the complexity of Plato's make-up, and of his influence on the subsequent history of philosophy.

Of the two Platos that we distinguished, it is difficult to think that the achievement of Pato was as great as that of Lato. The 'perennial philosophy' is perennial just because it is a very natural expression of human thinking about the mind and about values; it has appeared in many places at many times in different forms, and Plato's mind-body dualism, with its associated belief in the immortality of the soul, and his particular treatment of the objectivity of values, are not markedly different from anybody else's. What is unique in him is the progress from these quasi-religious speculations, which could have remained, as they have in others, vapid and evanescent, towards a much tougher, more precise logical and metaphysical theory, a moral philosophy and a philosophy of language; these were not entirely new, but, through discussion and criticism of them, they engendered the lasting achievements of Aristotle in those fields, and thus shaped the entire future of philosophy.

Let us start with Plato's development of the topic of 'The One and the Many'. We have seen how the early cosmologists sought an explanation of the bewildering variety of things in the world by seeking for them some common ground or reason. The search started with the question, 'What were their origins?'; went on to the question 'What are they all made of?'; but then divided. Natural scientists went on asking this second question in ever subtler forms and have been answering it ever since. But by this time problems had arisen which could not be answered by this method, and which demanded an entirely different sort of inquiry, whether we style it metaphysics or logic. For the puzzles generated by Parmenides could not be solved without asking 'What are they all?' in a quite different sense. This new inquiry, whether we call it conceptual or logical or even linguistic, consists in asking about the meanings of the words we use, or, to put it in a way more congenial to Plato, about the natures (in a quite different sense from the physical) of the things we are talking about. The Many are to be understood, not by seeking their physical constituents, nor even the efficient causes of their motions and changes, but by isolating and understanding the Idea to which we are referring when we use a certain word. This is to know in the deepest sense what it *is* to be a thing of a certain kind.

Plato had grasped the truth that conceptual understanding is different from natural science, and just as important. He had succeeded in distinguishing from each other the four different types of explanation (the four different kinds of 'Why?'-questions and their answers) which were duly classified by Aristotle in his doctrine of the 'four causes'. Of these we have just mentioned three:

1 The *material* cause, or explanation of the material constitution of a thing;
2 The *efficient* cause, or cause in the narrower modern sense, which made a thing do what it did;

3   The *formal* cause, or explanation of its form—of what it is to be
    that kind of thing;

and he also, as we shall see in a moment, distinguished

4   The *final* cause, or explanation of the purpose for which some-
    thing comes to be as it is.

Plato was more interested in formal and final causes than in
the other two kinds, and thought that they would both be
understood by getting to know the Idea of the kind of thing in
question. This association of the formal and final causes (having
its origin in Plato's doctrine about the Good, already discussed)
may have been a mistake; but, if so, it was a very momentous
one which was taken over by Aristotle and by many philosophers to this day. The notion that what it *is to be* a thing of a
certain kind (its essence) is logically tied to what a thing of that
kind *ought to be* (its purpose) still has its adherents.

To have distinguished the four kinds of explanation would
have been achievement enough, but Plato went further. He
saw that there was a question about how we could claim to
know the answers to the formal and final 'Why?'-questions.
We may concede that in his theory of knowledge knowing
is treated too much like mental seeing, and the objects of
knowledge too much like objects of ordinary vision, being
different from them only in being seen by the mind and not
the eyes, and in having a perfection and abidingness which the
objects of ordinary vision do not have. But nevertheless the
Theory of Ideas does represent Plato's way of stating some very
important discoveries.

The first of these is that the sort of knowledge we are after
both in science and in mathematics and logic is something universal. A causal law or a mathematical or logical theorem, if it
holds at all, holds for all similar cases. That moral principles too
have to be universal is a feature of them whose importance has
to be acknowledged even by those who do not follow Plato in
his cognitivism—do not, that is, allow themselves to speak of
moral *knowledge*.

The second is that all these disciplines including morality are capable of being structured into systems in which more general concepts or statements form the grounds of more specific ones. For both Plato and Aristotle this truth was expressed in their doctrine that in order to say what a thing is, we have to say to what genus it belongs, and then to say how it is differentiated from the other kinds of things in that genus. This is summed up in the Platonic method of dialectic, employing 'collection' and 'division' (see p. 155). We must never forget that the word Plato used for his Ideas, '*eidos*', is the same word, and with very much the same meaning, as we translate 'species' when we meet it in Aristotle's logic. Plato's description in the *Republic* (511) of the way in which the Ideas are subordinated to one another in a hierarchy may sound too crudely physical to us (it is almost as if he were looking with his mind's eye at a lot of quasi-visible onions strung together in a rope); but this was his way of putting the thought that a discipline has to be logically ordered if its propositions are to be *connected* (the metaphor survives) with each other.

In this and other ways Plato's investigations of the Socratic 'What is . . .?' questions led him a very long way into the disciplines of logic and metaphysics. Aristotle's systematization of logic—above all his theory of the syllogism which dominated logic for many centuries—could never have been achieved without Plato's insights.

Plato also, as we have seen, avoided a trap into which he might easily have fallen, given his assimilation of knowing to mental seeing: that of thinking, as Descartes seems to have thought, that the clarity and distinctness of the vision was a certificate of its correctness. Instead, by recognizing the difference between knowledge and right opinion, he was led to demand, as a qualification for knowledge, the ability to give and defend a reason or explanation for the thing known. This explanation normally took the form of a definition (ideally of the type just described). However, the importance of this distinction transcends Plato's particular theory of definition. Whenever anybody, whether in science or mathematics or moral philosophy, makes some statement on the basis of mere intuition, hoping that we will share the intuition and therefore agree with it, he should be disciplined by means of the Socratic-Platonic demand that he 'give an account' of what he has said. Even now too many philosophical frauds are unwilling to face the auditors in this way.

So far we have not, in this chapter, made much of any distinction between on the one hand science and mathematics, and on the other morals and politics. This is in accordance with Plato's practice; he thinks that all are subject to the same disciplines and methods, although in the application of them to this imperfect world rigour may be lost. But those who now wish to make a sharp distinction between evaluative and factual propositions, and thus between the methods appropriate to morality and science, do not have to part company with Plato completely even here. For one of the most remarkable things about him is how, even though he never wavered in his object-ivism, and constantly assimilated moral to other kinds of knowledge, he also recognized quite early, following Socrates, the special feature of value judgements which distinguishes them from factual ones, their prescriptivity. This comes out above all in his equation of thinking something good with desir-ing and therefore being disposed to choose it, and thus in his acceptance, albeit in a modified form, of the links between knowledge and goodness which had led Socrates into paradox.

Nor did the prescriptivity of value judgements die with Plato. It is implicit in Aristotle's statement that the Good is what everything is after; and also in his doctrine known as the 'prac-tical syllogism'. The conclusion of a piece of practical reason-ing, he saw, can be an action just because its premisses contain a value judgement which is prescriptive. He insists that prac-tical wisdom, our guide in matters of evaluation and action, is 'epitactic' (meaning 'prescriptive')—a word he takes over, with the distinction it implies between active prescription and mere passive judgement, from Plato's *Politicus* (260b). The same intimate connection between value judgements and action became important again in the eighteenth century with the work of Hume, who found in it an obstacle to the founding of morality on reason, and of Kant, who thought he had surmounted the obstacle; and it is still important today.

Plato was also the first person in history to attempt a systematic account of the structure of the mind. His account is no doubt crude compared with Aristotle's, let alone with what a satisfactory explanation of 'mental' phenomena would require. And he did not see the necessity for saying precisely what, in more literal terms, the metaphor of 'parts of the mind' really means. All the same, he started a very important and fruitful line of inquiry, and had much more excuse for his crude partition of the mind than some recent thinkers like Freud. Although it is hard to take seriously, as constituents of 'the mind', entities like 'the intellect' and 'the will' (to use modern descendants of Plato's terms), the distinctions which have been made in this kind of way do nevertheless need making.

They need making, above all, in order to emphasize the importance of disciplined thought, if we are to have a satisfactory way of answering any of the more difficult questions that face us. Although we have to allow credit to Plato's predecessors, and especially to the Sophists, for bringing into emphasis the intellectual side of man's nature, we owe to Plato and Socrates more than to anybody else the idea, which has been current ever since, that man will have more success in almost everything he undertakes if he learns to *think* better.

This brings us to what, I am sure, Plato himself thought of as his most important practical contribution: his educational theory. He believed firmly that there could be a body of knowledge or understanding whose attainment and handing down would make possible the orderly solution of political problems such as had brought Athens and all Greece into chaos. In this he taught the world a valuable lesson. If we could fully understand the problems, which involves understanding first of all the words in terms of which they are posed, and then (even harder) understanding the situations and the people that generate them, we should be on a way to their solution. This, at any rate, is a more hopeful line than attributing them to human wickedness which can never be eradicated. Even the wicked can be coped with if we understand what makes them do what they do. Socrates did not think he had attained this understanding, and even Plato was not all that optimistic; but he saw it as the only way out of the troubles of Greece, and founded an institution, the Academy, which he thought would help towards attaining it.

His bolder plans for political reform are more questionable, and more tentative. If the education of the intellect, preceded by a thorough schooling of the will, is necessary in order to put human society to rights, how can this come about? Plato here took a short cut. If absolute power could come into the hands of good and wise men, would not that do the trick? We have seen how much of good sense can be extracted from this bold suggestion. It is not wholly devoid of merit, but simply ignores the difficulty (indeed the practical impossibility) of finding suitable incumbents, and the further difficulty of reconciling absolute power, however wise its possessor, with the attainment of ends which nearly everybody (and who shall say they are wrong?) will include in their requirements for the good life, above all liberty. When Plato, impressed with the practical difficulties, goes on in the *Laws* to subject human and fallible rulers to a rigid code, he only makes matters worse. In its final form the Platonic proposal shares many features with the Holy Inquisition.

Nevertheless, Plato's political theory presents the liberal with a challenge which he has to face, and in facing which he will find himself having to answer questions which too many liberals ignore. If some ways of organizing society are better than others, in the sense that they do better for the people who live in the society, even on their own reckoning; and if some politicians and others are doing their very best to prevent it being organized, or kept organized, in these better ways, what am I to do about them, if not seek the power to frustrate their malign endeavours? If I think I know how a wise dictator would arrange things, ought I not to try to become a wise dictator? Plato has his answer to this question; what is the answer of the liberals?

Plato did not see his political proposals realized, nor perhaps did he expect to. His only excursion into politics, in Sicily, was a disaster. But a change did come over men's minds as a result of his thought. Greek political morality did not improve, it is true; nor was the Roman much better. But though the practice of politics remained as dirty as before, it is fair to claim that, gradually, through the work of Plato and his successors, the Stoics, Christians and others, ideals of a new and better sort came in the end to be current.

The rhetoric of present-day politics is still mostly nothing but rhetoric; but rhetoric does influence people (even its authors), and cause things to happen which otherwise would not. Our political rhetoric is permeated now by ideals which were simply non-existent in the rhetoric of Plato's day. This can be seen by comparing almost any political speech nowadays with almost any speech reported from the fifth and fourth centuries BC. Politicians do not always do what they commend in their speeches; but sometimes they do, and that has made a difference to the world. Part of this difference we owe to Plato. In the end he made many people see that personal or even national ambition and success are not the most important things in life, and that the good of other people is a worthier aim. For this we can forgive him for being also the father of political paternalism and absolutism.

Aristotle

Jonathan Barnes

For Richard Robinson

1 The man and his work

Aristotle died in the autumn of 322 BC. He was sixty-two and at the height of his powers: a tireless scholar, whose scientific explorations were as wide-ranging as his philosophical speculations were profound; a teacher who inspired—and who continues to inspire—generations of pupils; a controversial public figure who lived a turbulent life in a turbulent world. He bestrode antiquity like an intellectual colossus. No man before him had contributed so much to learning. No man after him could hope to rival his achievements.

Of Aristotle's character and personality little is known. He came from a rich family. He was a bit of a dandy, wearing rings on his fingers and cutting his hair fashionably short. He suffered from poor digestion, and is said to have been spindle-shanked. He was a good speaker, lucid in his lectures, persuasive in conversation; and he had a mordant wit. His enemies, who were numerous, made him out to be arrogant and overbearing. His will, which has survived, is a generous and thoughtful document. His philosophical writings are largely impersonal; but they suggest that he prized both friendship and self-sufficiency, and that, while conscious of his place in an honourable tradition, he was properly proud of his own attainments. As a man, he was, I suspect, admirable rather than amiable.

But that is unprofitable speculation; for we cannot hope to know Aristotle as we may know Albert Einstein or Bertrand Russell—he lived too long ago. One thing, however, can be said with certainty: Aristotle was driven throughout his life by a single overmastering desire—the desire for knowledge. His whole career and his every activity testify to the fact that he was concerned before all else to promote the discovery of truth and to increase the sum of human knowledge.

He did not think himself singular in possessing such a desire, even if he pursued his object with a singular devotion: he believed that 'all men by nature desire to know'; for each of us is, most properly speaking, to be identified with his mind, and 'the activity of the mind is life'. In an early work, the *Protrepticus* or *Exhortation to Philosophy*, Aristotle announced that 'the acquisition of wisdom is pleasant; all men feel at home in philosophy and wish to spend time on it, leaving all other things aside'. (Philosophy for Aristotle is not an abstract discipline engaged in by cloistered academics. It is, quite generally, the search for knowledge.) And in the *Nicomachean Ethics* he argues that 'happiness'—the state in which men realize themselves and flourish best—consists in a life of intellectual activity and contemplation. Is not such a life too godlike for a mere man to sustain? No; for 'we must not listen to those who urge us to think human thoughts since we are human, and mortal thoughts since we are mortal; rather, we should as far as possible immortalize ourselves and do all we can to live by the finest element in us—for if it is small in bulk, it is far greater than anything else in power and worth'.

A man's noblest aim is to immortalize himself or imitate the gods; for in doing so he becomes most fully a man and most fully himself. And such self-realization requires him to act on that desire for knowledge which as a man he naturally possesses. Aristotle's recipe for 'happiness' may be thought a little severe or restricted, and he was perhaps optimistic in ascribing to the generality of mankind his own passionate desire for learning. But his recipe came from the heart: Aristotle counsels us to live our lives as he himself tried to live his own.

One of Aristotle's ancient biographers remarks that 'he wrote a large number of books which I have thought it appropriate to list because of the man's excellence in every field': there follows a list of some 150 items, which, taken together and published in the modern style, would amount to perhaps fifty substantial volumes of print. And that list does not include all of Aristotle's writings—indeed, it fails to mention two of the works, the *Metaphysics* and the *Nicomachean Ethics*, for which he is today most renowned.

That is a vast output; yet it is more remarkable for its scope and variety than for its mere quantity. Aristotle's genius ranged widely. The catalogue of his titles includes *On Justice*, *On the Poets*, *On Wealth*, *On the Soul*, *On Pleasure*, *On the Sciences*, *On Species and Genus*, *Deductions*, *Definitions*, *Lectures on Political Theory* (in eight books), *The Art of Rhetoric*, *On the Pythagoreans*, *On Animals* (in nine books), *Dissections* (in seven books), *On Plants*, *On Motion*, *On Astronomy*, *Homeric Problems* (in six books), *On Magnets*, *Olympic Victors*, *Proverbs*, *On the River Nile*. There are works on logic and on language; on the arts; on ethics and politics and law; on constitutional history and on intellectual history; on psychology and physiology; on natural history—zoology, biology, botany; on chemistry, astronomy, mechanics, mathematics; on the philosophy of science and the nature of motion, space and time; on metaphysics and the theory of knowledge. Choose a field of research, and Aristotle laboured in it; pick an area of human endeavour, and Aristotle discoursed upon it. His range is astonishing.

Of his writings only a fifth has survived. But the surviving fraction contains a representative sample of his studies, and although the major part of his life's work is lost to us, we can still form a rounded idea of his activities. Most of what has survived was never intended to be read; for it is likely that the treatises we possess were in origin Aristotle's own lecture-notes—they were texts which he tinkered with over a period of years and kept for his own use, not for that of a reading public. Moreover, many of the works we now read as continuous treatises were probably not given by Aristotle as continuous lecture-courses. Our *Metaphysics*, for example, consists of a number of separate tracts which were first collected under one cover by Andronicus of Rhodes, who produced an edition of Aristotle's works in the first century BC.

It should not be surprising, then, that the style of Aristotle's treatises is often rugged. Plato's dialogues are polished literary works, the brilliance of their thought matched by the elegance of their language. Aristotle's surviving writings for the most part are terse. His arguments are concise. There are abrupt transitions, inelegant repetitions, careless allusions. Paragraphs of continuous exposition are set among staccato jottings. The language is spare and sinewy. The style is accounted for only in part by the private nature of the treatises; for Aristotle had reflected on the appropriate style for scientific writing, and he favoured simplicity. 'In every form of instruction there is some small need to pay attention to language; for it makes a difference with regard to making things clear whether we speak in this or that way. But it does not make *much* of a difference: all these things are show and directed at the hearer—which is why no one teaches geometry in this way.' Aristotle *could* write finely—his style was praised by ancient critics who read works of his that we cannot—and some parts of the treatises are done with polish and even panache. But fine words butter no parsnips, and fine language yields no scientific profit.

The reader who opens his Aristotle and expects to find a systematic disquisition on some philosophical subject or an orderly textbook of scientific instruction, will be brought up short: Aristotle's treatises are not like that. But reading the treatises is not a dull slog. Aristotle's style has a vigour which on intimate acquaintance proves no less attractive than Plato's lovely prose. And the treatises reveal their author's thoughts in a direct and stark fashion: we can, as it were, overhear Aristotle talking to himself.

Above all, Aristotle is tough. It is best to take up a treatise and imagine that you had to lecture from it yourself. You must expand and illustrate the argument, make the transitions clear, set aside some material for another time and another lecture, add a few jokes, subtract a few *longueurs*. Aristotle can be vexing. What on earth does he mean here? How does this follow from that? Why can't he be a little more explicit? One ancient critic claimed that 'he surrounds the difficulty of his subject with the obscurity of his language, and thus avoids refutation—producing darkness, like a squid, in order to make himself hard to capture'. Every reader will, from time to time, think of Aristotle as a squid. But the moments of vexation are far outnumbered by the moments of excitement and elation. Aristotle's treatises offer a unique challenge to their readers; and once a reader has taken up the challenge, he would not have the treatises in any other form.

2   *A public figure*

Aristotle was no intellectual recluse: the life of contemplation which he commends is not to be spent in an armchair or an ivory tower. Although never a politician, he was a public figure and lived often enough in the public gaze. But he died far from the main centres of Greek life. In the spring of 322 he moved to Chalcis, on the island of Euboea, where his mother's family had property; and in the last months of his life he lamented the fact that he had become isolated and cut off.

The preceding thirteen years he had spent in Athens, the cultural capital of the Greek world where he had taught regularly in the Lyceum. Aristotle believed that knowledge and teaching were inseparable. His own researches were carried out in company, and he communicated his thoughts to his friends and pupils, never thinking to retain them as a private treasure-store. He thought, indeed, that a man could not claim to know a subject unless he was capable of transmitting his knowledge to others, and he regarded teaching as the proper manifestation of knowledge.

The Lyceum is often referred to as Aristotle's 'school'. It is tempting to think of it as a sort of university: we imagine timetables and lecture-courses, the enrolment of students and the granting of degrees, and we surround Aristotle with all the formalities of our own educational system. But the Lyceum was not a private college: it was a sanctuary and a gymnasium—a sort of public leisure centre. An old story tells that Aristotle lectured to his chosen pupils in the mornings and to the general public in the evenings. However that may be, arrangements in the Lyceum were surely less formal than those of a modern university. There were no examinations, no degrees, no set syllabus; probably there were no official enrolments—and no fees.

Aristotle combined teaching and research—his lectures must often have been 'research papers', or talks based on his current research interests. He did not work alone. Various friends and colleagues joined him in his scientific and philosophical enterprises. We know little about Aristotle's research arrangements, but I incline to think that we should picture a group of friends working in concert, rather than a Teutonic professor master-minding the projects of his abler students.

Why did Aristotle suddenly abandon the pleasures of the Lyceum and retire to remote Chalcis? He said that 'he did not want the Athenians to commit a second crime against philosophy'. The first crime had been Socrates' trial and execution. Aristotle feared that he might suffer Socrates' fate, and his fears had a political basis.

During Aristotle's lifetime, Macedonia, under the rule first of Philip II and then of his son, Alexander the Great, expanded its power and came to dominate the Greek world, depriving the small city-states of their liberty and independence. Aristotle had lifelong connections with Macedonia. His father, Nicomachus, had been a physician at the Macedonian court and a friend of Philip's father, Amyntas; and in his will Aristotle named Antipater, Alexander's viceroy in Greece, as his executor. The most celebrated episode in the Macedonian connection began in 343 when Philip invited Aristotle to Mieza as tutor to the young Alexander. A rich romance later surrounded that happy coupling of prince and philosopher; but we can hardly hope to penetrate the veil of legend and discover how far Aristotle influenced his ambitious and unlovely charge. (We do know that he wrote a book entitled *Alexander, or On Colonies*.)

Alexander died in June of 323. The Athenians, ever jealous of their autonomy, rejoiced, and anti-Macedonian feeling became strong and violent. Aristotle was not a Macedonian agent, and the political theory he taught in the Lyceum was, if anything, hostile to the Macedonian interest. None the less, he was associated with Macedonia. (There is no reason to doubt the story that the Athenians had once set up an inscription in his honour, recording that he 'had served the city well ... by all his services to the people of Athens, especially by intervening with King Philip for the purpose of promoting their interests'.) Aristotle had Macedonian friends: that was enough to set democratic Athens against him. He found it prudent to leave the city.

Willy-nilly, Aristotle was a public figure. To us, looking back from the vantage point of history, Aristotle is the Prince of Philosophers. Whether his contemporaries regarded him in that light we do not know; but that he enjoyed a certain renown in Greece can be stated with some assurance. An interesting side-light on his public career is shed by a broken inscription found at Delphi: since 'they drew up a table of those who won victories in both Pythian Games and of those who from the beginning organized the contest, let Aristotle and Callisthenes be praised and crowned; and let the Stewards transcribe the table ... and set it up in the temple'. The inscription was engraved in about 330 BC.

Aristotle allegedly wrote to his friend Antipater in the following vein: 'as for what was voted to me at Delphi, of which I am now deprived, this is my attitude: I am neither greatly concerned by the matter, nor quite unconcerned'. It seems that the honours granted to Aristotle in 330 were later withdrawn. The inscription itself was discovered by archaeologists in a well—it may have been thrown there in 322 BC in a fit of anti-Macedonian pique.

The fact that Aristotle was invited to draw up the victory-lists at Delphi is evidence that by the early 330s he had some reputation as a man of science. For the work demanded serious historical research. Victors in the Pythian Games, which were second in importance only to the Olympics, had their names and achievements preserved in the Delphic archives. Aristotle and Callisthenes (who was his nephew) sifted through a mass of ancient records; from that material they had to determine a correct chronology, and then produce an authoritative list. The list was of interest not only to the sporting man. In Aristotle's day historians could not anchor their narratives to a universally employed chronological system (as modern historians use BC and AD). Chronological accuracy depended on the use of catalogues, whether of state officers or of athletic victors.

The index of Aristotle's writings contains the title *Pythian Victors*. Alongside it are other titles testifying to similar projects of detailed historical scholarship: *Olympic Victors*, *Didaskaliae* (a *catalogue raisonné* of the plays produced at the Athenian festivals), *Dikaiomata* (a collection of legal submissions made by various Greek cities, prepared by Aristotle to enable Philip to settle boundary-disputes). Of Aristotle's historical researches, the most celebrated are the *Constitutions of States*, 158 of them in all. A few fragments of the *Constitutions* have survived, and at the end of the last century a papyrus was discovered which contained almost the complete text of the *Constitution of the Athenians*. The work consists of a brief constitutional history of Athens, together with an account of current Athenian political institutions. Aristotle, who was not himself a citizen of Athens, had burrowed in the Athenian archives and familiarized himself with Athenian politics. His researches produced a compact and well-documented history of one aspect of Athenian life. Judged by modern critical standards, the work is of uneven quality; but the *Constitution of the Athenians*, which represents only a small fraction of Aristotle's historical researches, illustrates well the scope and detail of his scientific studies.

3 Zoological researches

Aristotle began teaching in the Lyceum in 335 BC. The thirteen years from 335 to 322 constituted his second Athenian period. His first period in Athens had lasted for twenty years, from 367 to 347. In 347 he suddenly left the city. No reason for his removal is reliably reported; but in 348 the northern town of Olynthus had fallen to the Macedonian army, and on a wave of hostile reaction Demosthenes and his anti-Macedonian allies had come to power in Athens: it is most probable that political issues exiled Aristotle in 347 as they would again in 322.

However that may be, in 347 Aristotle and a few companions sailed eastwards across the Aegean and settled at Atarneus, a town with which Aristotle had family ties. The ruler of Atarneus was Hermias, a good friend both of philosophy and of Macedonia. Hermias gave Aristotle and his friends 'the city of Assos to live in; and they spent their time there in philosophy, meeting together in a courtyard, and Hermias provided them with all they needed'.

Aristotle stayed in Assos for two or three years. He then migrated to Mytilene in nearby Lesbos, where he met Theophrastus, who was to become his greatest associate and pupil. Shortly after that he returned to his native city of Stagira, where he remained until he answered Philip's royal summons.

Hermias received a bad press in antiquity: he was reviled as a tyrant, a barbarian and a eunuch. But he served Aristotle nobly, and Aristotle admired him in return. When, in 341, Hermias was betrayed and put to death in grisly fashion by the Persians, Callisthenes wrote an encomium on him, and in his memory Aristotle composed a hymn to virtue. Aristotle married Hermias' niece, Pythias, who was the mother of his two children, Pythias and Nicomachus. Whatever the character of Hermias may have been, science is in his debt. For it was during Aristotle's years of travel, between 347 and 335, and in particular during his stay in the eastern Aegean, that he undertook the major part of the work on which his scientific reputation rests.

For if Aristotle's historical researches are impressive, they are nothing compared to his work in the natural sciences. He made and collected observations in astronomy, meteorology, chemistry, physics, psychology; but his fame as a research scientist rests primarily on his work in zoology and biology: his studies on animals laid the foundations of the biological sciences; and they were not superseded until more than two thousand years after his death. The enquiries upon which those great works were based were probably carried out largely in Assos and Lesbos; at all events, the place-names which occur from time to time in the biological treatises serve to localize their observations and point to the eastern Aegean as a main area of research.

The facts which Aristotle so assiduously uncovered were displayed in two large volumes, the *History of Animals* and the *Dissections*. The *Dissections* has not survived. It was concerned, as its name implies, with the internal parts and structure of animals; and there is good reason to believe that it contained—and perhaps largely consisted of—diagrams and drawings. The *History of Animals* has survived. Its title (like the titles of several Aristotelian works) is misleading: the word 'history' transliterates the Greek word '*historia*' which means 'enquiry' or 'research', and a better translation of the title would be *Zoological Researches*.

The *Researches* discuss in detail the parts of animals, both external and internal; the different stuffs—blood, bone, hair and the rest—of which animal bodies are constructed; the various modes of reproduction found among animals; their diet, habitat and behaviour. Aristotle talks of sheep, goats, deer, pigs, lions, hyenas, elephants, camels, mice, mules. He describes swallows, pigeons, quails, woodpeckers, eagles, crows, blackbirds, cuckoos. His researches cover tortoises and lizards, crocodiles and vipers, porpoises and whales. He goes through the kinds of insect. He is particularly informative about marine creatures—fish, crustacea, cephalopods, testacea. The *Researches* range from man to the cheese-mite, from the European bison to the Mediterranean oyster. Every species of animal known to the Greeks is noticed; most species are given detailed descriptions; in some cases Aristotle's accounts are long, precise and astonishingly accurate.

Zoology was a new science: where should Aristotle, confronted with such a copious supply of data, make a start?

First, let us consider the parts of man; for just as people test currency by referring it to the standard most familiar to them, so it is in other cases too—and man is of necessity the animal most familiar to us. Now the parts of man are clear enough to perception; nevertheless, in order that we may not break the proper sequence, and in order that we may rely on reason as well as perception, we must describe his parts—first the organic parts, then the uniform parts. Now the chief parts into which the body as a whole divides are these: head, neck, torso, two arms, two legs.

Aristotle begins with man, because man is most familiar, and can be used as a reference point. Much of what he says will, he is aware, be perfectly well known—it may seem childish or pedantic to record that men have necks between their heads and torsos. But Aristotle wants to give a full and orderly account, even at the cost of apparent *naïveté*; and in any case, the discussion quickly becomes more professional. The following passage will give some flavour of the *Researches*.

The octopus uses its tentacles both as feet and as hands: it draws in food with the two that are placed over its mouth; and the last of its tentacles, which is very pointed and the only one of them which is whitish and bifurcated at the tip (it uncoils towards the *rhachis*—the *rhachis* is the smooth surface on the other side from the suckers)—this it uses for copulation. In front of the sac and above the tentacles it has a hollow tube by which it discharges the sea-water which gets into the sac whenever it takes anything in with its mouth. It moves this tube to right and to left; and it discharges milt through it. It swims obliquely in the direction of the so-called head, stretching out its feet; and when it swims in this way it can see forwards (since its eyes are on top) and has its mouth at the rear. As long as the animal is alive, its head is hard and as it were inflated. It grasps and retains things with the underside of its tentacles, and the membrane between its feet is fully extended. If it gets on to the sand, it can no longer retain its hold.

Aristotle goes on to discuss the size of the tentacles. He compares the octopus to the other cephalopods—cuttlefish, crayfish and the like. He gives a detailed description of the internal organs of the creature, which he has evidently dissected and examined with minute care. In the passage I have quoted he refers to the phenomenon of 'hectocotylization'—the bifurcation in one of the tentacles of the male octopus, by means of which it copulates with the female. Aristotle himself was not entirely certain of the phenomenon (at any rate, elsewhere he denies that the octopus uses its tentacle for copulation); but he was correct, and the facts which he reports were not rediscovered until the middle of the nineteenth century.

It is easy to become starry-eyed over the *Researches*, which are on any account a work of genius and a monument of indefatigable industry. Not surprisingly, sober scholars have felt it incumbent upon them to point out the defects in the work.

First of all, it is said that Aristotle often makes errors of a crude and unscientific kind. A notorious example concerns the copulation of insects. Aristotle asserts more than once that during copulation the female fly inserts a tube or filament upwards into the male—and he says that 'this is plain to anyone who tries to separate copulating flies'. It is not: the assertion is wholly false. Another example concerns the bison. After a true but somewhat vague description of the beast, Aristotle observes that it is regularly hunted for its meat, and that 'it defends itself by kicking, and by excreting and discharging its excrement over a distance of eight yards—it can do this easily and often, and the excrement burns so much that it scalds the hair off the hounds'. A splendid picture, but quite absurd: Aristotle was taken in by some tipsy huntsman's after-dinner stories.

Secondly, Aristotle is accused of failing to use 'the experimental method'. The observations he reports are, most of them, amateur; they were made in the open and not in the laboratory. There is no evidence that Aristotle ever attempted to establish correct experimental conditions or to make controlled observations; there is no evidence that he tried to repeat his observations, to check them or to verify them. His whole procedure seems appallingly slapdash.

Finally, Aristotle is criticized for ignoring the importance of measurement. Real science is essentially quantitative, but Aristotle's descriptions are mostly qualitative. He was no mathematician. He had no notion of applying mathematics to zoology. He did not weigh and measure his specimens. He records a layman's impression of how things look rather than a professional's accurate description of how they are.

Now there is certainly some truth in all those charges—Aristotle was not infallible. But the charges are grossly misplaced. The first charge is unexciting. There are numerous mistakes in the *Researches*, some to be explained by the fact that Aristotle possessed few technical instruments and some to be put down as plain errors of observation or judgement. (His most influential error gave rise to the theory of 'spontaneous generation'. Some insects, Aristotle asserts, 'are generated not from parent creatures but spontaneously: some from the dew that falls on leaves ... some in mud and dung when they putrefy, some in wood (either on plants or in dead wood), some in the hair of animals, some in animals' flesh, some in their excrement'. Aristotle had observed lice on the head and worms in dung; but he had not—for want of care or for want of instruments—observed the phenomena with sufficient accuracy.) But the errors are greatly outnumbered by the insights—and what scientific work has ever been free of error?

The *Researches* contain one passage which is often said to report an experiment. Aristotle is describing the early development of chicks in the egg. He records in considerable detail the stage of growth reached by the embryo on successive days. Evidently, he took a clutch of eggs all laid on the same day, removed one a day from the brooding hen, cracked it open, and chronicled the daily changes he observed. If we are to believe the implications of the text, he did this not only for the domestic hen—the case he describes in detail—but for other birds too.

The description of the chicken embryo is one of the many remarkable passages in the *Researches*; but it is not the report of an experiment (Aristotle, so far as we know, did not control the conditions in which the eggs were incubated). Nor is it typical of the *Researches* as a whole, where such dated and consecutive observations are rare. But that is hardly odd: the fact is that the 'experimental method' is of no particular importance to the sort of research that Aristotle was engaged upon. Aristotle was inaugurating a new science. There was a superabundance of information waiting to be collected, sifted, recorded and systematized. Experimental evidence was not required. Nor, in any case, is experiment appropriate in descriptive zoology. You do not need the 'experimental method' to determine that man has two legs or even to exhibit the hectocotylization of the octopus. Aristotle himself was well aware that different sciences call for different methods. Those who accuse him of failing to experiment are victims of the vulgar error that all the sciences must be approached by the experimental path.

It is sometimes said in reply to the third charge that Aristotle's zoology is non-quantitative because he did not possess the technical devices upon which quantitative science relies: he had no thermometer, no finely calibrated scales, no accurate chronometer. That is all true; but the point should not be exaggerated. Greek shopkeepers regularly weighed and measured dead meat, and there was no technical reason why Aristotle should not have weighed and measured it live. Nor is it relevant to observe that Aristotle was no mathematician. Although he did not himself contribute to mathematical progress, he was well acquainted with the work of his contemporaries (mathematical examples and references are common enough in his writings); and in any case it requires no mathematical expertise to introduce measurement into science.

The *Researches* do, in fact, contain plenty of indeterminately quantitative statements (this animal is larger than that, this creature emits more semen than the other). There are also a few determinately quantitative observations. Of the two main types of squid, Aristotle remarks that 'the so-called *teuthoi* are much larger than the *teuthides*, growing to a length of up to 7½ feet; some cuttlefish have been found three feet long, and the tentacles of the octopus sometimes attain that size or even longer'. Aristotle seems to have measured the cephalopods. He could well have weighed them and given their other vital statistics, but he chose not to do so. And that was not an error but a wise choice. As Aristotle clearly saw, it is form and function rather than weight and size which matter in his kind of zoology. The length of an octopus's tentacles, which varies from specimen to specimen, is of little scientific interest; it is with the structure of the tentacles, and with their functional role in the animal's life, that the scientist is concerned.

The *Researches* are not flawless, but they are a masterpiece. Nowhere else does Aristotle show more vividly his 'desire to know'.

4 Collecting facts

Aristotle was a research scientist, and much of his time was devoted to original and first-hand study: he recorded his own observations, and he carried out dissections himself. But he could not have based all his multifarious descriptions on personal research, and like any other seeker after knowledge he borrowed other men's observations and culled other men's flowers. What, then, were Aristotle's research methods? How did he approach his work?

A pleasant story has it that Alexander the Great, 'inflamed by a desire to know the natures of animals', arranged for 'several thousand men throughout the whole of Greece and Asia Minor to be at Aristotle's disposal—everyone who lived by hunting or falconry or fishing, or who looked after parks, herds, apiaries, fishponds or aviaries—so that no living creature should escape his notice'. It is, alas, unlikely that Alexander ever did anything of the sort; but behind the story lies the fact that in the *Researches* Aristotle makes frequent reference to the reports of bee-keepers and fishermen, of hunters and herdsmen, of all those engaged in agriculture and animal husbandry. Bee-keepers are experienced in the ways of bees, and Aristotle relied on their expertise. Fishermen see things which land-lubbers never observe, and Aristotle sought information from them. He was properly cautious in using their information. Some people, he says, deny that fish copulate; but they are wrong. 'Their error is made easier by the fact that such fish copulate quickly, so that even many fishermen fail to observe it—for none of them observes this sort of thing for the sake of knowledge.' Nevertheless, much of Aristotle's work is based partly on the testimony of such professionals.

In addition, Aristotle had written sources at his disposal. The Greek doctors had made some study of human anatomy, and Aristotle uses their writings in his treatment of the parts of man —his detailed account of the vascular system includes long quotations from three of his predecessors. In general, Aristotle's researches included a comprehensive programme of reading: 'he worked so hard . . . that his house was called the House of the Reader'. And he had a large library: 'he is the first man we know to have collected books, and his example taught the Kings of Egypt how to put together a library'.

Book-learning was of relatively little importance to Aristotle in his zoological researches, for there were few books from which he could learn anything. But in other disciplines there was much to peruse. Aristotle recommends that 'one should make excerpts from written accounts, making lists separately for each subject, e.g. for the good, or for animals', and the index of his books shows that he himself prepared various compilations of that sort. Many of his own discussions begin with a brief history of the question at issue, setting out in summary form the opinions which his predecessors had advanced. When discussing the nature and variety of causes in the *Metaphysics* he observes that

we have given sufficient consideration to this subject in the *Physics*; nevertheless, let us also set down the views of those who have preceded us in the enquiry into existing things and in the philosphical investigation of reality; for it is plain that they too say that there are certain principles and causes. Thus, as we proceed, that will be useful to our present enquiry; for either we shall find some further kind of cause, or else we shall be more firmly convinced of those we have just mentioned.

Aristotle wrote several essays in intellectual history. His early work *On Philosophy* contained a full account of the origins and development of the subject; and there were monographs on Pythagoras, on Democritus, on Alcmaeon, and others. Only fragments of these works have survived; but the summary histories in the treatises no doubt drew upon them.

Judged purely as history those summaries are not beyond criticism; but their specific purpose was not to set out a narrative or to chronicle the story of an idea. They were designed to provide starting-points for Aristotle's own investigations and checks upon his own speculations.

There were not always past enquiries to consult. At the end of one of his logical treatises, Aristotle writes that

in the case of rhetoric there was much old material to hand, but in the case of logic we had absolutely nothing at all until we had spent a long time in laborious investigation. If, when you consider the matter and remember the state from which we began, you think that the subject is now sufficiently advanced compared to those other disciplines which have developed in the course of tradition, then it remains for all of you who have heard our lectures to forgive our omissions and to thank us warmly for our discoveries.

The note of self-satisfaction is not typical of Aristotle; and I cite the passage not to show that Aristotle could on occasion give himself a merited pat on the back, but rather to indicate, by contrast, that his customary procedure was to build upon the work of his predecessors. He could not do that in logic; and he could do it only to a limited extent in biology. In other subjects, 'which have developed in the course of tradition', he gratefully accepted all the tradition offered him.

Reliance on tradition, or the use of past discoveries, is a sensible procedure for any intellectual enquirer. But in Aristotle it goes a little deeper than that. He was highly conscious of his own position at the end of a long line of thinkers; he had a strong sense of intellectual history and of his own place therein.

The point bears upon two characteristic features of Aristotle's thought. First, he insists on the value of what he calls 'reputable opinions'. Something believed by all or most men—at any rate by all or most clever men—is reputable and must, he thinks, have something to be said for it. In the *Topics*, a work primarily concerned with reasoning from and about 'reputable opinions', he advises us to collect such opinions and to use them as starting-points for our enquiries. In the *Nicomachean Ethics* he implies that, in practical philosophy at least, reputable opinions are the end-points as well: 'for if the difficulties are solved and the reputable opinions remain, sufficient proof of the matter will have been given'. The best our investigations can hope to achieve is a winnowing of the reputable opinions, which will blow out the chaff of falsity and leave behind the grains of truth.

Aristotle's advice to attend to reputable opinions is more than the banal suggestion that before beginning research you should see what other men have done. Men desire by nature to discover the truth. Nature would not have given men such a desire and left it impossible of satisfaction. Hence if men generally believe something—if a thing is reputable—that is a sign that it is more likely to be true than false.

Secondly, Aristotle had a clear idea of the importance of tradition in the growth of knowledge.

In all cases of discovery, those things which are taken over from others who have earlier laboured upon them make gradual progress later at the hands of those who have taken them over, whereas what is discovered at the very beginning customarily makes but little advance at first—and yet it is far more useful than the later increase which depends upon it. For the beginning is doubtless the most important thing of all, as they say. And that is why it is hardest; for the greater it is in power, the smaller it is in magnitude and the harder to see. But once it is discovered, it is relatively easy to add to and increase the rest.

Or again:

Investigation of reality is in a way difficult, in a way easy. An indication of this is that no one can attain it in a wholly satisfactory way, and that no one misses it completely: each of us says *something* about nature, and although as individuals we advance the subject little if at all, from all of us taken together something sizeable results—and, as the proverb has it, who can miss a barn-door? . . . And it is fair to thank not only those whose beliefs we share, but also those whose views were more superficial; for they too contributed something—for they prepared things for us. If Timotheus had not existed, we should lack a great deal of lyric poetry; but if Phrynis had not existed, Timotheus would not have done so. It is the same with those who have expressed views on reality. For from some we have taken over certain opinions, and others were the causes of the existence of those men.

The acquisition of knowledge is arduous, and science grows slowly. The first step is the hardest, for we have there nothing to guide our journey. Later, progress is easier; but even so, as individuals we can contribute little to the growing pile of knowledge: it is collectively that the ants amass their anthill.

5 The philosophical background

Aristotle was an indefatigable collector of facts—facts zoo-logical, astronomical, meteorological, historical, sociological. Some of his political researches were carried out during the final period of his life when, from 335 to 322, he taught at the Lyceum in Athens; much of his biological research was done during the years of travel, between 347 and 335. There is reason to believe that his collecting activities were just as brisk during the first period of his adult life, the years between 367 and 347: that period is yet to be described.

So far, we have seen Aristotle as a public figure and as a private researcher; but that is at most half the man. Aristotle, after all, is reputed to have been a philosopher, and there is nothing very philosophical about the jackdaw operations I have so far described. Indeed, one of Aristotle's ancient enemies accused him of being a mere jackdaw:

> why did he turn away from the further exhortation of the young and incur the terrible wrath and enmity both of the followers of Isocrates and of some other sophists? He must surely have implanted a great admiration for his powers, from the moment when he abandoned his proper business and for those reasons was found, together with his pupil, collecting laws and innumerable constitutions and legal pleas about territory and appeals based on circumstances and everything of that sort, choosing . . . to know and teach philosophy and rhetoric and politics and agriculture and cosmetics and mining—and the trades performed by those who are ashamed of what they are doing and say they practise them from necessity.

The accusation is puffed up with rhetoric and contains some absurd falsifications: Aristotle never devoted much study to cosmetics. But it is still worth pondering. Aristotle's studies in 'politics and agriculture' are impressive, the *Constitutions* and the *Researches* are magnificent works; but how are they connected with *philosophy*? It will take a long story to answer that question.

Aristotle was born in 384, in the northern Greek town of Stagira. His father died when Aristotle was still young, and he was brought up by his uncle Proxenus, who had connections with Atarneus. Nothing is recorded about Aristotle's early education; but since he came from a rich and learned family, he no doubt received the sort of literary and gymnastic training which was normal for a well-born Greek. In 367, at the age of seventeen, he left Stagira for Athens, where he joined the brilliant group of men who worked and studied in the Academy under the leadership of Plato. In one of his lost works Aristotle told how a Corinthian farmer had happened to read Plato's *Gorgias* and 'at once gave up his farm and his vines, mortgaged his soul to Plato, and sowed and planted it with Plato's philosophy'. Is that fictionalized autobiography? Perhaps the young Aristotle read Plato's dialogues in Stagira and was seduced by Dame Philosophy. However that may be, the move to Athens and the Academy was the crucial event in Aristotle's career.

The Academy, like the Lyceum, was a public place, and Plato's school was no more a modern university than was Aristotle's. Yet there were some differences between the two establishments. Plato owned a private estate near the Academy. His lectures and discussions were not, as a rule, public. Indeed, Plato's school appears to have been a fairly exclusive club. In 367 Aristotle took out membership.

Plato himself was no polymath. He did not pretend to the range which his most famous pupil was to attain. Rather, he limited his own researches to philosophy in the narrow sense—to metaphysics, epistemology, logic, ethics, political theory; and the Academy was primarily a school of philosophy. But Plato was not blinkered. He encouraged other men's researches in other subjects, and he gathered about him the most talented minds in Greece.

Mathematics was certainly studied in the Academy. Plato, himself no mathematician, was keenly interested in the methods of mathematics; he set his pupils mathematical problems and urged them to study the mathematical sciences. It is probable that natural science too was studied. Plato's *Timaeus* contains speculation of a scientific nature, and a comic dramatist guyed the young Academicians thus: 'In the gymnasium of the Academy I heard some absurd and extraordinary arguments; discussing nature, they were distinguishing sorts of animal, and kinds of tree, and species of vegetable—and then they tried to discover to what species the pumpkin belongs.' Plato was interested in problems of classification; and those problems had some bearing upon Aristotle's later attempts at biological taxonomy.

Again, the Academy found a place for rhetoric. It was in that subject that Aristotle first made a name for himself. In about 360 he wrote a dialogue, the *Gryllus*, on the subject of rhetoric, in which he attacked the views of Isocrates, a leading orator of the day, an educator and professional pundit. One of Isocrates' pupils, Cephisodorus, replied with a long counterblast—the first of many polemics to be directed against Aristotle. (Cephisodorus accused Aristotle of wasting his time in collecting proverbs—evidence that by 360 Aristotle had already begun his compilatory activities.) Some years later, in his *Protrepticus*, Aristotle defended the ideals of the Academy against the more pragmatic notions of Isocrates' school, and Isocrates himself replied in his *Antidosis*. Despite this deep division, Aristotle was able later to praise Isocrates' style of writing.

Rhetoric continued to interest Aristotle. The first drafts of his treatise on *Rhetoric*, which, unlike the *Gryllus* and the *Protrepticus*, still survives intact, may well go back to those early years in the Academy; and the final touches were not put to the work until the latest period of Aristotle's life. Rhetoric and the study of literature are closely connected: Aristotle wrote a historico-critical book *On the Poets* and a collection of *Homeric Problems*. Those studies too may have been undertaken in the Academy. They showed Aristotle to be a serious student of philology and literary criticism, and they formed part of the preparatory work for the *Poetics*, in which Aristotle sketched his celebrated account of the nature of tragedy, and for the third book of the *Rhetoric*, which is a treatise on language and style.

Rhetoric is also connected with logic—indeed, one of Aristotle's main claims in the *Gryllus* was that rhetoric should not excite the passions by fine language but should rather persuade the reason by fine argument. Plato himself was greatly interested in logic, or 'dialectic' as it was called; and the Academicians indulged in a sort of intellectual gymnastics in which set theses were to be defended and attacked by means of a variety of stylized arguments. Aristotle's *Topics* were first outlined in his Academic years. The work lists the various argument-forms (*topoi*—hence *Topics*) which the young gymnasts used. The *Sophistical Refutations*, an appendix to the *Topics*, catalogues numerous fallacies which they had to recognize and to solve.

Aristotle remained in Athens as a member of Plato's Academy for twenty years. In 347, the year in which Plato died, he left Athens for Atarneus: he was thirty-seven, a philosopher and a scientist in his own right. What, in those two formative decades, did he learn? What aspects of Academic philosophy influenced him and gave shape to his own later views?

He had a profound love for Plato. On Plato's death he wrote a moving elegy in which he praised him as a man 'whom it is not right for evil men even to praise; who alone or first of mortals proved clearly, by his own life and by the course of his arguments, that a man becomes good and happy at the same time'. But you may love a man while rejecting his beliefs. Aristotle was certainly no thorough-going Platonist. Plato's views are strongly criticized in Aristotle's surviving treatises, and criticisms were made while Plato was still alive. 'Plato used to call Aristotle the Foal. What did he mean by the name? Clearly it was known that foals kick their mothers when they have had enough milk.' Ancient critics accused the Foal of ingratitude, but the criticism is absurd—no teacher requires his pupils to subscribe from a sense of gratitude to his own doctrines. Whether or not Aristotle *believed* Plato's theories he was certainly influenced by them. I shall pick out five points which together determined much of Aristotle's philosophical thought, and turned him into a philosophical scientist rather than a mere collector of agricultural information.

First of all, Plato reflected deeply on the unity of the sciences. He saw human knowledge as a potentially unified system: science, for him, was not the random amassing of facts; it was the organization of facts into a coherent account of the world. Aristotle, too, was a systematic thinker, and he shared wholeheartedly in Plato's vision of a unified theory of science, even if he disagreed with Plato about the way in which that unity was to be achieved and exhibited.

Secondly, Plato was a logician. I have already quoted Aristotle's claim that he was a pioneer in the science of logic, and it is true that Aristotle turned logic into a science and invented the discipline of formal logic. But Plato, both in his dialogues—most notably in the *Parmenides* and the *Sophist*—and in the 'dialectical' exercises he encouraged in the Academy, had prepared the ground for Aristotle. He had investigated the foundations of logic, and he required his pupils to train themselves in the practice of argumentation. Aristotle's study of rhetoric in the Academy, and his closely related interest in 'dialectic', started him on the subject he was to make his own.

Again, Plato was concerned with problems of ontology. ('Ontology' is a grandiose name for a part of general metaphysics: an ontologist attempts to determine what sort of things really exist, what are the fundamental entities of which the world consists.) Plato's ontology was contained in his theory of Ideas or Forms. According to that theory, the ultimate realities —the things on which the reality of everything else is somehow dependent—are abstract universals. It is not individual men and individual horses—Tom, Dick and Harry; Surrey, Barbary and Bucephalus—but the abstract forms of Man or manhood and of Horse or horseness which constitute the basic furniture of the real world. The theory is not easy to understand; what matters here is that Aristotle rejected it, and that he spent much of his philosophical activity in developing an alternative ontology.

Fourthly, Plato thought of scientific knowledge as a search for the causes or explanations of things. In his view, the notions of science and knowledge were intimately tied to that of explanation, and he discussed the types of explanation that might be given and the conditions under which phenomena could and should be explained. Aristotle inherited that concern. He too ties knowledge to explanation. His scientific endeavours were directed not merely to observing and recording, but above all to explaining.

Finally, there is the question of knowledge itself. How can we acquire knowledge in the first place? By what channels do we come to know and understand the world? Why suppose, indeed, that we know anything at all? The part of philosophy which deals with such questions is customarily called epistemology (*'epistēmē'* is the Greek for 'knowledge'). Epistemology matters to any philosopher who is concerned with science and our grasp of reality, and epistemological theories will be determined, in part at least, by issues in ontology. Many passages in Plato's dialogues are given to epistemological discussion. Here, too, Aristotle followed in his master's footsteps.

Knowledge must be systematic and unified. Its structure is given by logic, and its unity rests at bottom on ontology. It is essentially explanatory. It poses deep philosophical problems. All that, and much more, Aristotle learned in the Academy. However profoundly he disagreed with Plato's detailed elaboration of those five issues, he was at one with Plato in principle. In the next few chapters I shall sketch Aristotle's views on these subjects. By the end of the sketch it will be possible to see why Aristotle is much more than a collector of facts—why he is a philosopher-scientist.

6 *The structure of the sciences*

The most developed of Greek sciences was geometry. Euclid's work was done after Aristotle's death, but Euclid himself built on the researches of his predecessors, and those predecessors had given at least some thought to what was to become the distinctive feature of Euclid's own geometrical science. In a word, Euclid's geometry is an axiomatized system: he selects a few simple principles, or axioms, which he posits as the primary truths of his subject; and from those axioms he derives, by a series of logically compelling deductions, all the other truths of geometry. Geometry thus consists of derived truths, or theorems, and primary truths, or axioms. Each theorem follows logically—though often by way of a long and complex chain of reasoning—from one or more of the axioms.

The notion of an axiomatic system is elegant and intellectually attractive. Plato was attracted to it, and he suggested that the whole of human knowledge might somehow be set out as a single axiomatized science. From a small set of primary truths, every other truth might be logically deduced. Knowledge is thus systematic and unitary—it is systematic because it can be presented axiomatically, unitary because all truths can be derived from a single set of axioms.

Aristotle was no less impressed than Plato by the power of axiomatization, but he did not believe Plato's optimistic claim that all knowledge could be founded upon a single set of axioms. For he was equally impressed by the apparent independence of the sciences. Mathematicians and doctors, biologists and physicists, work in different domains, discuss different objects, and follow different methods. Their disciplines rarely overlap. Nevertheless, Aristotle felt the need for system: if human knowledge is not unitary, it is surely not a mere disconnected plurality either. 'The causes and principles of different things are different—in one way; but in another way, if you speak universally and by analogy, they are all the same.' The axioms of geometry and the principles of biology are mutually independent—but they are the same 'by analogy': the conceptual apparatus and the formal structure of all the sciences are the same.

Aristotle divided knowledge into three major classes: 'all thought is either practical or productive or theoretical'. The productive sciences are those concerned with the making of things—cosmetics and farming, art and engineering. Aristotle himself had relatively little to say about productive knowledge. The *Rhetoric* and the *Poetics* are his only surviving exercises in that area. (*Poetics* in Greek is '*poiētikē*', and that is the word translated as 'productive' in the phrase 'the productive sciences'.) The practical sciences are concerned with action, with how men are to act in various circumstances. The *Ethics* and the *Politics* are Aristotle's chief contributions to the practical sciences.

Knowledge is theoretical when its goal is neither production nor action but simply truth. Theoretical knowledge includes all that we now think of as science, and in Aristotle's view it contained by far the greatest part of the sum of human knowledge. It subdivides into three species: 'there are three theoretical philosophies—mathematics, natural science and theology'. Aristotle was intimately acquainted with contemporary mathematics, as any student of Plato's would be, and Books XIII and XIV of the *Metaphysics* are acute essays on the nature of numbers; but he was not a professional mathematician and did not pretend to have advanced the subject.

Natural science includes botany, zoology, psychology, meteorology, chemistry, physics. (The term I translate as 'natural science' is '*phusikē*', often misleadingly transliterated as 'physics'. Aristotle's *Physics* is a treatise about natural science as such.) Aristotle thinks that the objects of natural science are marked off by two characteristics: they are capable of change or motion (unlike the objects of mathematics) and they exist 'separately' or in their own right. (The second point will be examined in a later chapter.) The greater part of Aristotle's life was devoted to the study of such objects.

Nevertheless, natural science is not the best of sciences. 'If there are no substances apart from natural substances, natural science will be the primary science; but if there are changeless substances, the science of them will be prior and will be the primary philosophy'. There are such substances, and they are divine. Theology is thus prior to natural science: 'the theoretical sciences are preferable to the rest, and this to the other theoretical sciences'. The term 'theology' should be used cautiously here. Primary philosophy 'must be the theoretical study of the primary principles and causes of things', and Aristotle follows a long Greek tradition in calling those primary substances 'divine'. I shall say a little about Aristotle's divinities in a later chapter; here it is enough to observe that he usually identifies them with parts of the heavens, so that 'theology' might well seem to be a branch of astronomy.

Two things for which Aristotle cared greatly appear to have escaped the net: metaphysics and logic. Where are they to be placed in the system of the sciences? Both seem to be theoretical, and both are treated by Aristotle as in some way identical with theology.

According to Aristotle, 'there is a science which studies being *qua* being and the things that belong to this in its own right'. (We call the science 'metaphysics', and Aristotle studies it in his *Metaphysics*. But Aristotle never uses the term 'metaphysics', and the title '*Metaphysics*' means literally 'What comes after natural science'.) The phrase 'being *qua* being' has a pleasantly esoteric ring to it, and some scholars have turned it into an abstruse and abstract item. In fact Aristotle means something neither abstract nor abstruse. 'Being *qua* being' is not a special kind of being; indeed, there is no such thing as being-*qua*-being at all. When Aristotle says that there is a science which studies being *qua* being, he means that there is a science which studies beings, and studies them *qua* being; that is, a science which studies things that exist (not some abstract thing called 'being'), and studies them *qua* existing.

The little word '*qua*' plays an important role in Aristotle's philosophy. There is nothing mysterious about it. Pooh-Bah, in *The Mikado*, is, among other things, Chancellor of the Exchequer and Private Secretary to Ko-Ko. He has different attitudes in his different capacities. As Chancellor, he urges a frugal wedding-ceremony for Ko-Ko and his bride; as Secretary, he recommends a splurge. He does one thing *qua* Chancellor or under his Chancellor's hat, another *qua* Secretary or under his Secretarial hat. In the former case the cares of State are relevant to his advice, in the latter his recommendation is determined by different considerations. Similarly, to study something *qua* existent is to study just those features of the thing which are relevant to its *existing*—and not any of the many other features of the thing; it is to study it under its existential hat. Everyone who does not study fictions studies 'beings', things that exist; the student of being *qua* being studies just those aspects of existent things which belong to them in virtue of the fact that they exist.

The study of being *qua* being is thus supremely general: everything that exists falls within its purview (contrast entomology or phonology, which are restricted to insects and to linguistic sounds), and the properties it investigates are those which absolutely everything must have. (Thus Book X of the *Metaphysics* discusses what it is to be *one* thing. *Everything* is *one* thing; by contrast, only some things are monopterous or consonantal.) Aristotle engages in this highly general study in various books of the *Metaphysics*. Several of his logical writings, both extant and lost, were also devoted to it.

Metaphysics, in Aristotle's view, is the primary philosophy, and hence it is identified with theology. But how, we may wonder, can a science which studies absolutely everything be the same as a science which studies only a special and highly privileged class of things? Aristotle anticipated the question. He suggested that theology 'is universal because it is primary'; and he appears to mean that if you study the primary substances on which all other entities are dependent, then you will implicitly be studying *all* existents *qua* existent. Not everyone has found that suggestion compelling, and Aristotle's primary philosophy is sometimes thought to consist of two quite distinct parts, a general metaphysics which studies beings *qua* being, and a special metaphysics which studies the principles and causes of things.

As to logic, Aristotle's successors were unsure of its status. Some later philosophers held that logic was a 'part' of philosophy—a discipline to be set alongside mathematics and natural science. Others, including Aristotle's own followers, stated that logic was a 'tool' of philosophy something used by philosophers and scientists, not an object of their studies. (The Greek for 'tool' is '*organon*': that is why later Aristotelians gave the collective title *Organon* to Aristotle's logical writings.) It seems clear that logic is *both* a part *and* a tool of philosophy. The old dispute rested on the false belief that logic could not be both things at once.

Aristotle himself did not discuss the position of logic in his scheme of things. He argues that the student of being *qua* being will study 'the things called axioms in mathematics' or 'the first principles of deduction'; 'for they belong to everything that exists, and not to some particular kind of thing separately from the others'. And he holds that the logician 'assumes the same shape as the philosopher' or discusses the same range of things as the student of primary philosophy. Logic, being an entirely *general* science, should thus be subsumed under metaphysics or theology. But there are passages in which Aristotle seems to imply that logic is not to be so categorized; and indeed, having said that the logician 'assumes the same shape as the philosopher', he immediately adds that his is for all that a distinct profession.

The structure of human knowledge, according to Aristotle, can be exhibited in a diagram, thus:

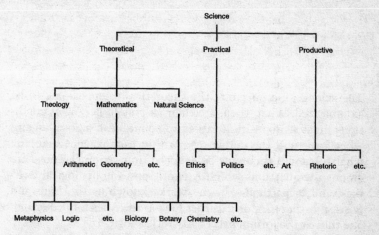

The scheme exhibits the structure and arrangement of the sciences, and shows its author to have been a self-conscious systematizer.

7 Logic

The sciences—at any rate the theoretical sciences—are to be axiomatized. What, then, are their axioms to be? What conditions must a proposition satisfy to count as an axiom? Again, what form will the derivations within each science take? By what rules will theorems be deduced from axioms? Those are among the questions which Aristotle poses in his logical writings, and in particular in the works known as the *Prior* and *Posterior Analytics.* Let us first look at the rules for deduction, and thus at the formal part of Aristotle's logic.

'All sentences are meaningful . . . but not all make statements only those in which truth and falsity are found do.' 'Of statements, some are simple, that is, those which affirm or deny something of something, and others are composed of these, and are thereby compound sentences.' As a logician, Aristotle is interested only in sentences that are true and false (commands, questions, exhortations and the like are the concern of the student of rhetoric or linguistics). He holds that such sentences are all either simple or compounded from simple sentences, and that simple sentences affirm or deny something of something— some *one* thing of some *one* thing, as he later insists.

That much Aristotle adopted from Plato's *Sophist.* In his *Prior Analytics* he goes beyond Plato in several ways. Simple sentences of the sort logic deals with are called 'propositions', and propositions are analysed into 'terms. If a proposition says or denies P of S, then S and P are its terms—P the predicate term, S the subject term. Propositions are either universal or particular: they affirm or deny P either of every S or of some S. Thus 'Every viviparous animal is vertebrate' affirms *being ver-tebrate* of all viviparous animals; and 'Some oviparous animals are not sanguineous' denies *being sanguineous* of some oviparous animals. Thus we have four types of simple proposition: universal affirmatives, affirming P of every S; universal negatives, denying P of every S; particular affirmatives, affirming P of some S; and particular negatives, denying P of some S.

Furthermore, propositions come in a variety of moods: 'every proposition expresses either that something applies or that it necessarily applies or that it possibly applies'. Thus 'Some calamaries grow to a length of three feet' expresses the thought that *being a yard long* actually holds true of some calamaries. 'Every man is necessarily constituted of flesh, bones etc.' says that *being corporeal* holds necessarily of every man—that a thing *could not be* a man without being made of flesh, bones etc. 'It is possible that no horses are asleep' states that *being asleep* possibly belongs to no horses—that every horse *may* be awake. These three moods or 'modalities' are called (though not by Aristotle) 'assertoric', 'apodeictic' and 'problematic'.

That, in brief, is Aristotle's doctrine of the proposition, as it is found in the *Analytics*. All propositions are simple or compounded of simples. Every simple proposition contains two terms, predicate and subject. Every simple proposition is either affirmative or negative. Every simple proposition is either universal or particular. Every simple proposition is either assertoric or apodeictic or problematic.

The doctrine of the *Analytics* is not quite the same as that of the short essay *On Interpretation*, a work in which Aristotle reflects at greater length on the nature and structure of simple propositions. And as a doctrine it is open to various objections. Are *all* propositions either simple or compounded from simples? 'It is now recognized that the octopus's last tentacle is bifurcated' is surely a compound proposition—it contains as a part of itself the proposition 'the octopus's last tentacle is bifurcated'. But it is not compounded *from* simples. It consists of a simple proposition prefixed by 'It is now recognized that', and 'It is now recognized that' is not a complete proposition at all. Again, do all simple propositions contain just *two* terms? 'It is raining' seems pretty simple. But does it contain *two* terms?

Does it affirm *raining* of 'it'? Or what of the sentence 'Socrates is a man'? That surely contains a predicate and a subject. But it is neither universal nor particular—it does not predicate *man* of 'all' or of 'some' Socrates; for the term *Socrates* is not a general term, so that (as Aristotle himself observed) the phrases 'all' and 'some' do not apply to it.

Consider, finally, such sentences as 'Cows have four stomachs', 'Humans produce one offspring at a time', 'Stags shed their antlers annually'—sentences of the sort that Aristotle asserts in his biological writings. It is not true that *every* cow has four stomachs—there are deformed specimens with three or five apiece. Yet the biologist does not want to say merely that *some* cows happen to have four stomachs, or even that *most* cows do. Rather, he claims, correctly, that every cow *by nature* has four stomachs (even if in fact some do not). Aristotle stresses that in nature many things hold 'for the most part', and he believes that most of the truths of the natural sciences will be expressible by way of sentences of the form 'By nature, every S is P', sentences which are true if for the most part Ss are P. But what exactly is the structure of sentences of that form? Aristotle wrestled with the question, but he was obliged to leave it unanswered—and it cannot be answered within his doctrine of the proposition.

The logical system which Aristotle develops in the *Prior Analytics* is based upon his doctrine of the proposition. The arguments he considers all consist of two premisses and a single conclusion, each of their three components being a simple proposition. Logic is a general discipline, and Aristotle wanted to deal generally with *all* possible arguments. But there are indefinitely many arguments, and no treatise could possibly deal individually with all of them. In order to treat generally that indefinitely immense multiplicity, Aristotle introduced a simple device. Instead of employing particular terms—'man', 'horse', 'swan'—in his discussions, he used letters—A, B, C. Instead of such sentences as 'Every octopus has eight tentacles' we find quasi-sentences or sentence-schemata such as 'Every A is B.' That use of letters and schemata allows Aristotle to speak with full generality; for what holds true of a schema, holds true of every particular instance of that schema. If, for example, Aristotle shows that when 'Some A is B' is true so also is 'Some B is A', then he has implicitly shown that every particular affirmative proposition 'converts' in this way: if some sea-creatures are mammals, some mammals are sea-creatures; if some men are Greeks, some Greeks are men; if some democracies are illiberal, some illiberal regimes are democratic; and so on, for all the indefinitely many sentences of the form 'Some A is B.'

Aristotle invented the use of schematic letters. Logicians are now so familiar with his invention, and employ it so unthinkingly, that they may forget how crucial a device it was: without the use of such letters logic cannot become a general science of argument. The *Prior Analytics* makes constant use of schematic letters. Thus the very first argument-pattern which Aristotle discusses runs like this: 'If A is predicated of every B, and B of every C, necessarily A is predicated of every C.' In arguments of this form, all three propositions are universal, affirmative and assertoric. An instance might be: 'Every animal that breathes possesses lungs; every viviparous animal breathes; therefore every viviparous animal possesses lungs.'

In the course of the first part of the *Prior Analytics* Aristotle considers all possible pairings of simple propositions, and determines from which pairs a third simple proposition may correctly be inferred as conclusion, and from which pairs no conclusion can correctly be inferred. He divides the pairings into three groups or 'figures', and his discussion proceeds in a rigorous and orderly fashion. The pairings are taken according to a fixed pattern, and for each pair Aristotle states, and proves formally, what conclusion, if any, may correctly be inferred. The whole account is recognized as the first essay in the science of formal logic.

The logical theory of the *Prior Analytics* is known as 'Aristotle's syllogistic'. The Greek word '*sullogismos*' is explained by Aristotle as follows: 'A *sullogismos* is an argument in which, certain things being assumed, something different from the things assumed follows from necessity by the fact that they hold'. The theory of the *Prior Analytics* is a theory of the *sullogismos*—a theory, as we might put it, of deductive inference.

Aristotle makes great claims for his theory: 'every proof and every deductive inference (*sullogismos*) must come about through the three figures that we have described'; in other words, every possible deductive inference can be shown to consist of a chain of one or more arguments of the type Aristotle has analysed. Aristotle is, in effect, claiming that he has produced a complete and perfect logic. The claim is audacious, and it is false; for there are in fact innumerably many inferences that Aristotle's theory cannot analyse. The reason is simple: Aristotle's theory of inference is based upon his theory of propositions, and the deficiencies of the latter produce deficiencies in the former. Yet those deficiencies are not readily seen, and later thinkers were so impressed by the power and elegance of Aristotle's syllogistic that for two millennia the *Analytics* were taught as though they constituted the sum of logical truth.

The *Prior Analytics* is indeed a work of outstanding genius. There are internal difficulties within Aristotle's system (notably in his account of deductions involving problematic propositions), and the text contains some errors and obscurities. But those are minor flaws: by and large, the *Analytics* is a paradigm of logical thought. It is elegant and systematic; its arguments are orderly, lucid and rigorous; it achieves a remarkable level of generality. If it can no longer be regarded as a complete logic, it can still be admired as a nearly perfect fragment of logic.

8 *Knowledge*

The logic of the *Prior Analytics* serves to derive the theorems of a science from its axioms. The *Posterior Analytics* is primarily concerned to study the nature of the axioms themselves, and hence the general form of an axiomatized science. To a surprisingly large extent, the *Posterior Analytics* is independent of the particular logical doctrine of the *Prior Analytics:* the deficiencies in Aristotle's theory of inference do not infect the theory of axiomatization, nor do they render the *Posterior Analytics* invalid as an account of scientific form.

Aristotle's account of the axioms is based upon his conception of the nature of knowledge; for a science is meant to systematize our *knowledge* of its subject-matter, and its component axioms and theorems must therefore be propositions which are known and which satisfy the conditions set upon knowledge. According to Aristotle, 'we think we know a thing (in the unqualified sense, and not in the sophistical sense or accidentally) when we think we know both the cause because of which a thing is (and know that it is its cause) and also that it is not possible for it to be otherwise'. A zoologist, then, will *know* that cows have four stomachs if, first, he knows *why* they do (if he knows that they have four stomachs *because* of such-and-such a fact) and, secondly, he knows that cows *must* have four stomachs (that it does not merely *happen* to be the case that they do). Those two conditions set upon knowledge govern Aristotle's whole approach to axiomatic science in the *Posterior Analytics*.

The first condition set upon knowledge is a condition of causality. The word 'cause' must be taken in a broad sense: it translates the Greek '*aitia*', which some people prefer to render by 'explanation'. To *explain* something is to say why it is so; and to say why something is so is to cite its *cause*. There is thus the closest of connections between explanation and cause, in the broad sense.

The condition of causality is linked to a number of other requirements which the axioms of any science must satisfy.

If knowing is what we have laid it down to be, demonstrative knowledge must be based upon things which are true and primary and immediate, and more known than and prior to and causes of the conclusion; for thus the principles will be appropriate to what is being proved. There can be an inference without these conditions, but there cannot be a proof; for it will not yield knowledge.

The principles or starting-points of demonstrative knowledge are the axioms on which the science is based; and Aristotle's general point is that those principles or axioms must satisfy certain requirements if the system they ground is to be a science, a system of *knowledge*.

Clearly, the axioms must be true. Otherwise they could neither be known themselves nor ground our knowledge of the theorems. Equally clearly, they must be 'immediate and primary'. Otherwise there will be truths prior to them from which they can be derived—and thus they will not after all be axioms or first principles. Again, in so far as our knowledge of the theorems depends upon the axioms, it is reasonable to say that the axioms must be 'more known' than the theorems.

It is the final condition in Aristotle's list, that the axioms be 'prior to and causes of the conclusion', which is linked most directly to his account of what knowledge is. Our knowledge of the theorems rests upon the axioms, and knowledge involves a grasp of causes; hence the axioms must state the ultimate causes which account for the facts expressed by the theorems. A man who reads through an axiomatized science, starting from the axioms and proceeding through the successive theorems, will in effect be reading off a list of causally connected facts.

At first glance, the causality condition seems odd. Why should we suppose that knowing something requires knowing its cause? Surely we know large numbers of facts about whose causes we are quite in the dark? (We know *that* inflation occurs; but economists cannot tell us *why* it does. We know *that* the Second World War broke out in 1939; but historians dispute among themselves about the *causes* of the war.) And does not the causality condition threaten an infinite regress? Suppose I know X; then according to Aristotle I know the cause of X. Call that Y. Then it seems to follow that I must know the cause of Y too; and so on *ad infinitum*.

The second of those problems was explicitly discussed by Aristotle. He held that there are some facts which are causally primary, or which have no causes apart from themselves; and he sometimes expresses this by saying that they are self-caused or self-explanatory. Why do cows have horns? Because they are deficient in teeth (so that the matter which would have formed teeth goes to make horns). Why are they deficient in teeth? Because they have four stomachs (and so can digest their food unchewed). Why do they have four stomachs? Because they are ruminants. Why, then, are cows ruminants? Simply because they are *cows*—there is no *further* feature, apart from their being cows, which explains why cows are ruminants; the cause of a cow's being a ruminant is just its being a cow.

That cows are ruminants is self-explanatory. Aristotle usually says that such self-explanatory facts are definitions, or parts of definitions; so that the axioms of the sciences will for the most part consist of definitions. A definition, in Aristotle's sense, is not a statement of what some word means. (It is no part of the meaning of the word 'cow' that cows are ruminants; for we all know what 'cow' means long before we know that cows are ruminants.) Rather, definitions state the essence of a thing, what it is to be that thing. (It is part of the essential nature of a cow that it is a ruminant; what it is to be a cow is to be a ruminant animal of a certain kind.) Some modern philosophers have rejected—and ridiculed—Aristotle's talk of essences. But in fact Aristotle grasped an important part of the scientific endeavour: from the fundamental natures of substances and stuffs—from their essences—the scientist seeks to explain their other, non-essential, properties. Aristotle's axiomatic sciences will start from essences and successively explain derivative properties. The theorems of animal biology, say, will express the derived properties of animals, and the deduction of the theorems from the axioms will show how those properties are dependent upon the relevant essences.

But must *all* knowledge be causal or explanatory in this way? Although Aristotle's official view is that 'we know each thing only when we know its cause', he often uses the word 'know'—just as we do—in cases where the cause escapes us. And indeed Aristotle is surely mistaken in asserting that knowledge is always causal. But it would be wrong simply to lament the mistake and pass on. Aristotle, like Plato before him, was primarily concerned with a special type of knowledge—with what we may call scientific understanding; and it is plausible to claim that scientific understanding involves knowledge of causes. Although we may know quite well that inflation occurs without being able to say why it does, we cannot claim to understand the phenomenon of inflation until we have a grasp of its causes, and the science of economics is imperfect until it can supply that causal understanding. Taken as a piece of lexicography, Aristotle's definition of 'knowledge' is false; construed as a remark about the nature of the scientific enterprise, it expresses an important truth.

So much for the condition of causality. The second condition in Aristotle's account of knowledge is that what is known must be the case of necessity: if you know something, that thing *cannot* be otherwise. In the *Posterior Analytics* Aristotle elaborates the point. He connects it with the thesis that only universal propositions can be known. He infers that 'the conclusion of such a proof must be eternal—therefore there is no proof or knowledge about things which can be destroyed'.

The necessity condition with its two corollaries seems no less strange than the causality condition. Surely we do have knowledge of contingent facts (for example, that the population of the world is increasing), and of particular facts (for example, that Aristotle was born in 384 BC). Moreover, many of the sciences seem to countenance such knowledge. Astronomy, for example, deals with the sun and the moon and the stars; and the case is similar with geography, which Aristotle studied in his *Meteorology*, and, most obviously, with history. Aristotle, it is true, thinks that the objects of astronomy are not perishable but eternal. He also holds that 'poetry is more philosophical and more serious than history—for poetry tends to describe what is universal, history what is particular'. (History, in other words, is not granted full scientific status.) But that does not alter the fact that some sciences deal unequivocally with particulars.

Furthermore, Aristotle believed (as we shall shortly see) that the basic entities of the world are perishable particulars. And it would be absurdly paradoxical if he were driven to the view that there is no scientific knowledge of those fundamental objects. In fact, Aristotle is wrong to infer from the necessity condition that knowledge must be about eternal objects. It is a universal and perhaps a necessary truth that humans have human parents ('a man', as Aristotle puts it, 'generates a man'); and that truth is, in a sense, eternal—at least, it is *always* true. But it is not a truth *about* eternal objects—it is a truth about mortal, perishable men. Aristotle himself concludes, at the end of a tangled argument, that 'to say that all knowledge is universal . . . is in a way true and in a way not true . . . It is clear that knowledge is in a way universal and in a way not.' Thus he allows that there is, 'in a way', knowledge of particulars; and we must dismiss the second corollary of the necessity condition as a mistake.

As for the first corollary I have already remarked that in Aristotle's opinion the theorems of science do not always hold universally and of necessity: some of them hold only 'for the most part', and what holds 'for the most part' is explicitly distinguished from what holds always. 'All knowledge deals either with what holds always or with what holds for the most part (how else could one either learn it or teach it to someone else?); for it must be determined either by what holds always or by what holds for the most par—for example, that honey-water for the most part benefits the feverish.' Aristotle's assertion that scientific propositions must be universal is an exaggeration, on his own admission; and the same must be said for the necessity condition itself.

Science strives for generality; in order to understand particular occurrences we must see them as part of some general pattern. Aristotle's view that knowledge is of what cannot be otherwise is a reflection of that important fact. But it is a distorted reflection, and the necessity condition laid down in the *Posterior Analytics* is too stringent.

9 *Ideal and achievement*

Aristotle has emerged thus far as a profoundly systematic thinker. The various sciences are autonomous but systematically interrelated. Each individual science is to be developed and presented in the form of an axiomatic system—'in the geometrical manner', as later philosophers put it. Moreover, the set of concepts within which Aristotle's notion of science finds its place was itself systematically examined and ordered. Perhaps none of that is surprising. Philosophy, after all, is nothing if not systematic, and Aristotle's system—his 'world picture'—has for centuries been held up for admiration and praise.

Some scholars, however, have disputed that view. They have denied that Aristotle was a system-builder. Themselves distrusting the grandiose claims of systematic philosophy, they find Aristotle's virtues to lie elsewhere. For them, Aristotle's philosophy is essentially 'aporetic': he poses masses of particular problems or *aporiai*, and seeks particular solutions to them. His thought is tentative, flexible, changing. He does not sketch a grand design and then fill in the details, each neatly and elegantly fitting its assigned position; rather, his methods, his modes of argument and his conceptual wardrobe all alter from time to time and from topic to topic, being individually tailored to suit individual problems. Aristotle works piecemeal.

That anti-systematic interpretation of Aristotle's thought is now widely accepted. It has something to be said in its favour. Book III of the *Metaphysics*, for example, consists of a long catalogue of problems or *aporiai*, and much of the remainder of the *Metaphysics* is given over to their solution. Or consider the following passage: 'here, as elsewhere, we must set down the phenomena and first go through the puzzles; then we must prove the reputable opinions about these matters—if possible, all of them, if not, the majority and the most important'. First, set down prevailing views on the matter ('the phenomena', that is 'what seems to be the case', are the reputable opinions on the subject); then go through the puzzles those views raise (because they are obscure, perhaps, or mutually inconsistent); finally, prove all or most of the views to be true. That is hardly a recipe for system-building; yet it is a recipe Aristotle commends and himself sometimes follows.

Moreover, the aporetic interpretation at first sight seems to do justice to an aspect of Aristotle's work which on the traditional interpretation must seem puzzling. Aristotle's scientific treatises are never presented in an axiomatic fashion. The prescriptions of the *Posterior Analytics* are not followed in, say, the *Meteorology* or the *Parts of Animals*. Those treatises do not lay down axioms and then proceed to deduce theorems; rather, they present, and attempt to answer, a connected sequence of problems. On the traditional view, the treatises must seem—to put it paradoxically—wholly un-Aristotelian: the trumpeted system is simply not apparent in their pages. On the aporetic interpretation, the treatises represent the essence of Aristotle's philosophy: his occasional reflections on systematization are not to be taken too seriously—they are ritual gestures towards a Platonic notion of science, evidence of Aristotle's own fundamental convictions.

It is undeniable that many of Aristotle's treatises are, in large part, aporetic in style—they do discuss problems, and discuss them piecemeal. It is also undeniable that the treatises contain little or nothing in the way of axiomatized development. It is right to stress those points. But it is wrong to infer that Aristotle was not at bottom a systematic thinker. The theory expounded in the *Posterior Analytics* cannot be dismissed as an irrelevant archaism, a mere genuflection to Plato's ghost. There are so many hints and intimations of systematization in the treatises that the solution of *aporiai* cannot be regarded as the be-all and end-all of Aristotle's scientific and philosophical enquiries; and—a point worth underlining—even the piecemeal discussions of individual problems are given an intellectual unity by the common conceptual framework within which they are examined and answered. Systematization is not achieved in the treatises; but it is an ideal, ever present in the background.

What, then, are we to say of the unsystematic features of Aristotle's works? First, not all of Aristotle's treatises are works of science: many are works *about* science. The *Posterior Analytics* is a case in point. That treatise is not presented axiomatically; but then it is a treatise *about* the axiomatic method—it is concerned not to develop a science but rather to examine the way in which a science should be developed. Again, many parts of the *Physics* and the *Metaphysics* are essays on what we might call the foundations of science. We should not expect writings about the structure and grounds of science to exhibit themselves the features which they demand of writings within the sciences.

But what of the aporetic aspects of Aristotle's properly scientific works? Why are the *Meteorology* and the *Parts of Animals*, say, not presented axiomatically? The answer is disconcertingly simple. Aristotle's system is a grand design for finished or completed sciences. The *Posterior Analytics* does not describe the activities of the scientific researcher—it determines the form in which the researcher's results are to be systematically organized and displayed. Aristotle had not discovered everything. He may, indeed, have had his optimistic moments: Cicero reports that 'Aristotle, accusing the old philosophers who thought that philosophy had been perfected by their own efforts, says that they were either very stupid or very vain; but that he himself could see that, since great advances had been made in so few years, philosophy would be completely finished in a short time.' We know that such optimism on Aristotle's part would itself have been 'either very stupid or very vain'; and in fact Aristotle does not ever, in his treatises, boast of having completed any branch of knowledge. His achievement, great though it was, inevitably fell short of his ideal; and the Aristotelian system was designed with the ideal in mind.

Aristotle says quite enough to enable us to see how, in a perfect world, he would have presented and organized the scientific knowledge he had industriously amassed. But his systematic plans are plans for a completed science, and he himself did not live long enough to discover everything. Since the treatises are not the final presentations of an achieved science, we should not expect to find in them an orderly succession of axioms and deductions. Since the treatises are intended, in the end, to convey a systematic science, we should expect them to indicate how that system is to be achieved. And that is exactly what we do find: Aristotle was a systematic thinker; his surviving treatises present a partial and unfinished sketch of his system.

10 *Reality*

Science is about real things. That is what makes it knowledge rather than fantasy. But what things are real? What are the fundamental items with which science must concern itself? That is the question of ontology, and a question to which Aristotle devoted much attention. One of his ontological essays, the *Categories*, is relatively clear; but most of his ontological thought is to be found in the *Metaphysics*, and in some of the most obscure parts of that perplexing work.

'Now the question which, both now and in the past, is continually posed and continually puzzled over is this: What is being? That is, what is substance?' Before sketching Aristotle's answer to that question we must ask about the question itself: What is Aristotle after? What does he mean by 'substance'? And *that* question is best approached by a somewhat circuitous route.

The *Categories* is concerned with classifying types of predicate ('*katēgoria*' is Aristotle's word for 'predicate'). Consider a particular subject, say Aristotle himself We can ask various types of question about him: *What* is he?—a man, an animal etc. What are his *qualities*?—he is pale, intelligent etc. *How large* is he?—five feet ten, ten stone eight. How is he *related* to other things?—he is Nicomachus' son, Pythias' husband. *Where* is he?—in the Lyceum. These different types of question are answered appropriately by way of different types of predicate. The question 'How large?' attracts predicates of *quantity*, the question 'How related?' attracts predicates of *relation*, and so on. Aristotle thinks that there are ten such classes of predicate, and that each class can be individually characterized. For example, 'what is really peculiar to quantities is that they can be called equal and unequal'; or 'in respect of qualities alone are things called like and unlike'. Not all of Aristotle's classes are equally clearly delineated, and his discussion of what belongs to what class contains some puzzles. Again it is not clear why Aristotle settles for *ten* classes. (He rarely makes use, outside the *Categories*, of all ten classes; and he was probably not firmly committed to that precise number.) But the general point is plain enough: predicates fall into different classes.

Aristotle's classes of predicates are themselves now called 'categories', the term 'category' having been transferred from the things classified to the things into which they are classified, so that it is normal to talk of 'Aristotle's ten categories'. More importantly, the categories are generally referred to as categories *of being*; and Aristotle himself will sometimes refer to them as 'the classes of the things that exist'. Why the move from classes of predicates to classes of *beings*, of things that are or exist? Suppose that the predicates 'man' and 'healthy' are true of Aristotle: then there must *be* such a thing as man, and there must *be* such a thing as health. In general, there must be something corresponding to every predicate which is true of anything; and the things corresponding in this way to predicates will themselves be classified in a manner corresponding to the classification of the predicates. Indeed, in a sense there is only one classification here. In classifying predicates, we thereby classify things. In saying that the predicate applied to Aristotle in the sentence 'Aristotle is in the Lyceum' is a predicate of place, we are saying that the Lyceum is a place. Things, like predicates, come in different sorts; and if there are ten classes or categories of predicate, there are ten classes or categories of things. The classification of predicates is, as it were, merely a reflection in language of the underlying classification of things.

Predicates which answer the question 'What is so-and-so?' fall into the category which Aristotle calls 'substance', and the things which belong to the category are substances. The class of substances is peculiarly important; for it is *primary*. In order to understand the primacy of substance we must turn briefly to a notion of central significance to Aristotle's whole thought.

Aristotle noticed that certain Greek terms are ambiguous. 'Sharp', for example, in Greek as in English, can be applied to sounds as well as to knives; and it is plain that it is one thing for a sound to be sharp and quite another for a knife to be sharp. Many ambiguities are easily detected, like that of 'sharp'; they may provide material for puns, but they do not cause serious puzzlement. But ambiguity is sometimes more subtle, and it sometimes infects terms of philosophical importance; indeed, Aristotle thought that most of the key terms in philosophy were ambiguous. In the *Sophistical Refutations* he spends some time in expounding and solving sophistical puzzles that are based on ambiguity, and Book V of the *Metaphysics*, sometimes called Aristotle's 'philosophical lexicon', is a set of short essays on the different senses of a number of philosophical terms. 'Something is called a cause in one way if . . ., in another if . . .'; 'something is said to be necessary if . . ., or if . . .'. And so on, for many of the terms central to Aristotle's own philosophical system.

One of the terms which Aristotle recognizes as ambiguous is the term 'being' or 'existent'. Chapter 7 of Book V of the *Metaphysics* is given over to 'being'; and Book VII begins by observing that 'things are said to be in many senses, as we described earlier in our remarks on ambiguity; for being signifies what a thing is, that is, this so-and-so, and quality or quantity or each of the other things predicated in this way'. There are at least as many senses of 'being', then, as there are categories of beings.

Some ambiguities are merely 'chance homonymies'—as with the Greek word '*kleis*', which means both 'bolt' and 'collarbone'. Of course it is not a matter of chance that '*kleis*' was applied to collarbones as well as to bolts: what Aristotle means is that there is no connection of meaning between the two uses of the term—you could be perfectly capable of using the word in one of its senses without having an inkling of the other. But not all ambiguities are like that, and in particular the word 'be' or 'exist' is not an example of chance homonymy: 'things are said to exist in many ways, but with reference to one thing and to some single nature, and not homonymously' ('not homonymously' here means 'not by *chance* homonymy'). Aristotle first illustrates what he has in mind by two non-philosophical examples:

Everything that is healthy is so called with reference to health— some things by preserving it, some by producing it, some by being signs of health, some because they are receptive of it; and things are called medical with reference to the art of medicine—for some things are called medical by possessing the art of medicine, others by being well adapted to it, others by being instruments of the art of medicine. And we shall find other things called in a similar manner to these.

The term 'healthy' is ambiguous. We call men, complexions, resorts, diets and other things healthy. But George V, Bognor Regis and All Bran are not healthy in the same sense. Yet those different senses are all interconnected, and their connection is ensured by the fact that all refer to some one thing, namely health. For George V to be healthy is for him to *possess* health; for Bognor to be healthy is for it to *produce* health; for All Bran to be healthy is for it to *preserve* health; and so on. 'Some single nature' enters into the explanation of what it is for each of these diverse things to be diversely healthy. Healthiness thus possesses unity in diversity.

And so it is with being or existence.

Thus things are said to exist also in many ways, but all with reference to one starting-point. For some are said to exist because they are substances, others because they are affections of substances, others because they are paths to substance or destructions or privations or qualities or producers or creators of substances or of things said to exist by reference to substance, or are negations of these or of substance.

Just as everything called healthy is so called with reference to health, so everything said to be or exist is so said with reference to substance. There exist colours and sizes, changes and destructions, places and times. But for a colour to exist is for some *substance* to be coloured, for a size to exist is for some *substance* to have it, for a movement to exist is for some *substance* to move. Non-substances exist, but they exist only as modifications or affections of substances. For a non-substance to exist is for an existing substance to be modified in some way or other. But the existence of substances is not thus parasitic: substances exist in a primary sense; for a substance to exist is *not* for something else—something non-substantial—to be as it were substantified.

Existence, like healthiness, possesses unity in diversity; and substance is the focal point of existence as health is of healthiness. That is the chief way in which the class of substances is primary in relation to the other categories of being.

Then what is it to be substance? Substance-predicates are those which provide possible answers to the question 'What is it?'; but that question is too vague to give any secure guidance. In Book V of the *Metaphysics* Aristotle offers more precise assistance: 'things are called substances in two ways: whatever is the ultimate subject, which is no longer said of anything else; and whatever, being this so-and-so, is also separable'. The second way in which things are called substances couples two notions frequently employed by Aristotle in his reflections on the question: a substance is 'this so-and-so', and it is also 'separable'.

'This so-and-so' translates the Greek '*tode ti*', an unorthodox phrase which Aristotle nowhere explains. What he seems to have in mind can perhaps be expressed in the following way. Substances are things to which we can refer by use of a demonstrative phrase of the form '*this* so-and-so'; they are things that can be picked out, identified, individuated. Socrates, for instance, is an example of a 'this so-and-so'; for he is *this man*—an individual whom we can pick out and identify.

But what about, say, Socrates' complexion, his paleness? Can we not refer to that by the phrase 'this paleness'? Is this paleness not something which we can identify and reidentify? Aristotle says that 'the particular pale is in a subject, namely the body (for all colour is in a body)', and by 'the particular pale' he appears to mean 'this paleness', an individual instance of the quality of being pale. But if this paleness is an *individual* thing, it does not follow that it is a *substance*: substances are not just cases of 'this so-and-so'; they are also 'separable'. What is separability here?

Plainly, Socrates may exist without his paleness (for he may get a sun-tan and cease to be pallid); but Socrates' paleness cannot exist without Socrates. Socrates is separable from his paleness. Socrates' paleness is not separable from Socrates. That is surely part of what Aristotle means by separability; but it is probably not a complete account. For one thing, Socrates cannot exist devoid of *all* coloration—he may cease to be pale, but he cannot cease to be coloured; he may be separable from this paleness, but he is in danger of being inseparable from colour as such.

We need to refer again to Aristotle's account of the ambiguity of being. Some things, we saw, are parasitic upon others: for them to exist is for some *other* existent to be somehow related to them. We may usefully connect parasitism and separation in the following way: a thing is separable if it is *not* thus parasitic. Socrates, then, will be separable—not merely separable from his paleness, but absolutely separable—because for Socrates to exist is not for his paleness—or anything else whatsoever—to be modified in a certain way; Socrates' paleness is not separable, not merely because it cannot exist unless Socrates does, but because for it to exist is for some *other* thing—Socrates—to be pale.

We can now offer the following account of what it is to be a substance: a thing is a substance if it is *both* an individual (a 'this so and-so', something capable of being designated by a demonstrative phrase), *and also* a separable item (something non-parasitic, a thing whose existence is not a matter of some *other* thing's being modified in some way or other).

We can now at last return to Aristotle's eternal question: What things in fact *are* substances? We should not expect a simple and authoritative answer from Aristotle (after all, he says that the question is perpetually puzzling), and his own attempts at an answer are in fact hesitant and difficult to understand. But one or two things do emerge fairly clearly. Aristotle's predecessors had, he thought, implicitly offered a number of different answers to the question. Some had held that *stuffs*—gold, flesh, earth, water—were substances (he is thinking primarily of the earliest Greek philosophers, who focused their attention on the material constituents of things). Others had held that the ultimate *parts* of ordinary things were substances (Aristotle is thinking of the ancient atomists, whose basic entities were microscopical corpuscles). Yet other thinkers had proposed that *numbers* were substances (the Pythagoreans and certain of Plato's followers fall into this camp). Finally, some had chosen to regard abstract entities or *universals* as substances (Plato's doctrine of Forms is the outstanding example of such a theory).

Aristotle rejected all these views. 'It is plain that of the things that are thought to be substances, most are powers—both the parts of animals . . . and earth and fire and air.' For earth to exist, we might say, is for certain substances to have certain powers (in Aristotle's view, for them to have the power or tendency to move downwards); and for fire to exist is for substances to burn and heat and have a tendency to rise. As for the parts of animals, 'all these are defined by their functions; for each is truly such if it can perform its own function—for example, an eye, if it can see—and what cannot do so is an eye only homonymously (for example, a dead one or one made of stone)'. An eye is something that can see; for eyes to exist is for animals to be capable of seeing.

Numbers are plainly non-substantial. The number three exists just in so far as there are groups of three things. Numbers are essentially numbers of things, and although the number ten is not identical with any or every group of ten items, still the existence of the number ten consists precisely in there being such groups or sets of ten substances.

Aristotle devotes most of his polemical attention to the fourth view of substance. Plato's theory of Forms was by far the most elaborate ontological theory with which Aristotle was acquainted, and it was a theory to which, in his years in the Academy, he was perpetually exposed. Aristotle's arguments against the Platonic theory were first set out in a special treatise *On the Ideas*, which survives only in fragments. He returned to the attack again and again, and produced a vast and varied array of considerations against the theory. In addition, he offered a group of more general arguments against any view that takes universals to be substances.

Aristotle held that for whiteness to exist is for certain substances to be white. Plato, on the contrary, held that for a substance to be white is for it to share in whiteness. In Aristotle's opinion, white *things* are prior to *whiteness*, for the existence of whiteness is simply a matter of there being white things. In Plato's opinion, *whiteness* is prior to white *things*, for the existence of white things is simply a matter of their sharing in whiteness. Aristotle's arguments against Platonism demand close inspection; many of them are powerful, but it is only fair to say that they have not convinced determined Platonists.

If Platonism goes, what remains? What are Aristotelian substances? The answer is a robustly commonsensical one. The first and plainest examples of substances are animals and plants; to those we may add other natural bodies (the sun, the moon and stars, for example), and perhaps also artefacts (tables and chairs, pots and pans). In general, perceptible things—middle-sized material objects—are the primary furniture of Aristotle's world; and it is significant that he often poses his ontological question by asking if there are any substances *apart* from perceptible substances. Such, in Aristotle's view, are the basic realities, and the things with which science principally concerns itself.

11 *Change*

Can we say anything more, in general philosophical terms, about those middle-sized material objects which are the chief substances in Aristotle's world? One of their most important features is that they *change*. Unlike Plato's Forms, which exist for ever and never alter, Aristotle's substances are for the most part temporary things which undergo a variety of alterations. There are, in Aristotle's view, four types of change: a thing can change in respect of substance, of quality, of quantity and of place. Change in respect of substance is coming-into-being and going-out-of-existence, generation and destruction; such a change occurs when a man is born and when he dies, when a statue is made and when it is smashed. Change in respect of quality is alteration: a plant alters when it grows green in the sunlight or pale in the dark; a candle alters when it grows soft in the heat or hardens in the cold. Change in respect of quantity is growth and diminution; and natural objects typically begin by growing and end by diminishing. Finally, change in respect of place is motion.

Most of the *Physics* is devoted to a study of change in its different forms. For the *Physics* studies the philosophical background to natural science; and 'nature is a principle of motion and change', so that 'things have a nature if they possess such a principle'. The subject-matter of natural science consists of moving and changing things. Aristotle's predecessors had been puzzled by the phenomena of change: Heraclitus had thought that change was perpetual and essential to the real world; Parmenides had denied the very possibility of coming-into-being, and hence of any sort of change; Plato had argued that the ordinary changing world could not be a subject of scientific knowledge.

In the first books of the *Physics* Aristotle argues that every change involves three things. There is the state *from* which the change proceeds, the state *to* which the change proceeds, and the *object* which persists through the change. In Book V the account is embellished slightly: 'there is something which initiates the change, and something which is changing, and again something in which the change takes place (the time), and apart from those, something from which and something to which. For all change is from something to something; for the thing changing is different from that *to* which it is changing and from that *from* which—for example, the log, the hot, the cold'. When a log becomes hot, it changes *from* a state of coldness; it changes *to* a state of hotness; and the log itself persists through the change.

That in every change there is an initial state and an end state may be granted; and the states must be distinct, or else no change will have occurred. (An object may change from white to black, and then back to white again. But if its colour is the same *throughout* a given period, then it has not changed colour during that period.) And in the cases of qualitative change, quantitative change and locomotion, it is plain that there must be a subject that persists through the change. 'There is no change apart from the things that change', or 'all change is a change of something'; and for a thing to change it must retain its identity while altering in some aspect—in size, in quality, in position. But what of change in respect of substance? How does that fit Aristotle's analysis?

It is natural to suggest that the two end-states in generation and destruction are non-existence and existence. When Socrates came into being, he changed *from* a state of non-existence *to* a state of existence, and he persisted through the change. (In cases of destruction the two end-states occur in reverse order.) But a moment's reflection shows the absurdity of that idea. Socrates does not *persist through* his generation, nor does he *persist through* his destruction. For these two changes mark the beginning and the ending of Socrates' existence.

At this point Aristotle observes that substances—material

bodies—are in a sense *composite*. A house, for example, consists of bricks and timbers arranged in a certain structure; a statue consists of marble or bronze carved or cast into a certain shape; an animal consists of tissues (flesh, blood and the rest) organized on certain principles. All substances thus consist of two 'parts', stuff and structure, which Aristotle habitually calls 'matter' and 'form'. Matter and form are not physical components of substances: you cannot cut up a bronze statue into two separate bits, its bronze and its shape. Rather, matter and form are *logical* parts of substances: an account of what substances are requires mention both of their stuff and of their structure. Nor should we imagine the matter as the physical aspect of a substance and the form as a sort of non-physical additive: both stuff and structure are aspects of the unitary physical object.

We can now see that 'whatever comes into being must always be divisible, and be part *thus* and part *thus*—I mean part matter and part form'. And

it becomes clear . . . that substances . . . come into being from some underlying subject; for there must always be something that underlies, from which what comes into being comes into being—for example, plants and animals from seed. And the things that come into being do so in some cases by change of shape (for example, statues), in some by addition (for example, growing things), in some by subtraction (for example, a marble Hermes), in some by putting together (for example, a house) . . .

When a statue comes into being or is made, the persisting object is not the statue itself but the matter of the statue, the bronze or the marble; and the end-states are those of being shapeless and being shaped. When a man comes into being, what persists is the stuff, not the man; and the stuff is first (in the seed) non-human and then human.

That account of the nature of change had the great merit of allowing Aristotle to overcome many of the difficulties about change which his predecessors had raised. But it is not wholly compelling. Thomas Aquinas, one of Aristotle's most sympathetic critics, observed that the theory rules out the possibility of creation. Aquinas's God had created the world *out of nothing*; the world came into being, and that was a substantial change—but no pre-existing matter had a form imposed upon it, for there was no pre-existing matter there. If you reflect solely on the sublunary world, Aquinas says, you may be inclined to accept Aristotle's analysis of change. But if you look higher you will see that not *all* change will fit the analysis. Whether or not we agree with Aquinas's theology, we may agree with his logic; for we surely do not want to rule out, on purely logical grounds, the very possibility of creation. (The modern cosmologists' theory of the constant creation of particles is not *logically* mistaken.) But if Aristotle's account of change is too restrictive, that is of no great moment for his theory of science; for that theory is primarily concerned with ordinary, sublunary, changing things.

Strictly speaking, what I have described so far is not Aristotle's account of change itself, but rather his account of the pre-conditions for change. At any rate, in Book III of the *Physics* he poses the question 'What is change?', and gives an answer which is meant to complement the discussion of the first book. His answer is this: 'Change is the actuality of the potential *qua* such.' (That sentence is often cited as Aristotle's definition of *motion*. The word 'motion' in English usually means 'change of place', 'locomotion'. Aristotle's word here is *'kinēsis'*: though the word is sometimes restricted to locomotion, it usually means 'change' in general, and in Book III of the *Physics* it has that usual meaning.) Aristotle's critics have pounced upon that sentence as an example of pompous obscurantism. It merits a brief commentary.

The terms 'actuality' and 'potentiality' form a constant refrain in Aristotle's treatises. They serve to mark the difference between something which is actually so-and-so and something which is potentially so-and-so; between, say, a builder who is slapping mortar on bricks, and one who is not doing so but still has the skills and capacities required to do so. It is one thing to have a capacity, another to exercise it; one thing to possess potential, another to actualize it. Aristotle makes a number of claims about the distinction between actuality and potentiality, some of them acute, some dubious. He holds, for example, that 'actuality is in all cases prior to potentiality both in definition and in substance; and in time it is in a way prior and in a way not'. The first point is true: in defining a potentiality we must specify what it is a potentiality *for*, and in doing that we name an actuality. (To be a builder is to be capable *of building*, to be visible is to be able *to be seen*.) Since the reverse is not true (actuality does not in the same way presuppose potentiality), an actuality is prior in definition to its correlative potentiality. But the claim that actuality is prior to potentiality in time is less plausible. Aristotle means that before there can be any potential so-and-sos, there must be actual so-and-sos— before there can be any potential men (that is any stuff that may become human), there must be actual men. For, he says, 'in all cases what is actually so-and-so comes into being from what is potentially so-and-so by the agency of something actually so-and-so—for example, men from men, a musical person by the agency of a musical person—there always being something that initiates the change and what initiates the change being itself actually so-and-so'. The underlying thought seems to be that causing something to be so-and-so is a matter of transmitting a certain character to it—and you can only transmit what you possess yourself. If someone comes to be musical he must have been *made* musical by someone; that agent, since he transmitted musicality, must himself have been actually musical. The argument is ingenious; but in fact causation need not be—and usually is not—a matter of transmission.

Aristotle's account of change calls upon actuality and potentiality. Actuality and potentiality for what? The answer emerges in the course of Aristotle's argument: it is the potentiality *to be changing*. In place of Aristotle's obscure sentence, 'Change is the actuality of the potential *qua* such', we may therefore write 'Change is the actuality of the changeable *qua* changeable.' Now that is supposed to explain what it is for something to be changing: if we replace the abstract nouns 'change' and 'actuality' by verbs, we may paraphrase Aristotle as follows: 'Something is in the process of changing whenever it possesses a capacity to change and is exercising that capacity.' That paraphrase reduces the obscurity of Aristotle's analysis, but it seems to make the analysis platitudinous. Perhaps, however, Aristotle does not intend to give an illuminating definition of change but rather to make an interesting point about the sort of actuality involved in change. For he thinks that some actualities are incompatible with their correlative potentialities. What *is* white cannot *become* white. If a surface is *actually* white, it is not *potentially* white. Before being painted white, a ceiling is potentially but not yet actually white; after being painted, it is actually but no longer potentially white. Other actualities are different: being actually so-and-so is quite compatible with still being potentially so-and-so. When I am actually smoking a pipe, I am still capable of smoking a pipe (otherwise I could not go on). When a steeplechaser is actually galloping over the course, he is still capable of galloping (otherwise he would never reach the end). The point of Aristotle's definition of change is that changes are actualities of the latter sort: while it is actually changing, the object is still capable of changing; for if it ceased to be capable of changing, it would thereby cease to be actually changing.

Aristotle has much more than that to say about change. Change takes place in time and space, and the *Physics* offers intricate theories about the nature of time, of place and of empty space. Since space and time are infinitely divisible, Aristotle analyses the notion of infinity. He also discusses a number of particular problems concerning the relation of motion to time, including a brief treatment of Zeno's celebrated paradoxes of motion.

The different essays which make up the *Physics* are among the more finished of Aristotle's surviving works: although their subject-matter is thorny and sometimes produces difficult passages of argument, their general structure and purport are always clear. The *Physics*, in my own view, is one of the best places to start reading Aristotle.

12 *Causes*

Material objects change, and their changes are caused. The scientist's world is full of causes, and scientific knowledge, as we have already seen, requires the capacity to state causes and to give explanations. We should expect Aristotle's scientific treatises to be filled with causal pronouncements and explanations, and we should want his philosophical essays to include some account of the nature of causation and explanation. Neither expectation is disappointed.

The core of Aristotle's account of explanation is his doctrine of 'the four causes'. Here is his brief exposition of that doctrine:

A thing is called a cause *in one way* if it is a constituent from which something comes to be (for example, bronze of the statue, silver of the goblet, and their genera); *in another way* if it is the form and pattern, that is, the formula of its essence, and the genera of this (for example, 2:1, and in general number, of the octave), and the parts present in the account; *again*, if it is the source of the first principle of change or rest (for example, the man who deliberates is a cause, and the father of the child, and in general the maker of what is being made and the changer of what is changing); *again*, if it is as a goal—that is, that for the sake of which (for example, health of walking—Why is he walking?—we say: 'In order to be healthy', and in so saying we think we have stated the cause); and also those things which, when something else has changed it, stand between the changer and the goal—for example, slimming or purging or drugs or instruments of health; for all these are for the sake of the goal, and they differ from one another in being some instruments and others actions.

Aristotle tells us that things are called 'causes' in four different ways, but his illustrations are brief and enigmatic. Consider the first example: 'bronze of the statue'. Aristotle can hardly mean that bronze explains, or is the cause of, the statue, since that makes no sense at all. But what *does* he mean? The first point to observe is that, in Aristotle's view, to ask for a cause is to seek 'the because-of-which': it is to ask *why* something is the case. A question 'Why?' requires an answer 'Because'; so explanatory sentences which cite causes can always be expressed in the form 'X because Y.'

Secondly, Aristotle says that 'the because-of-which is always sought in this way: Because of what does one thing belong to another? ... for example, Because of what does it thunder? Because of what does noise occur in the clouds? For in this way one thing is being sought of another. Again, Because of what are these things, namely bricks and timbers, a house?' Whenever we seek a cause, we ask why *this is that*, why so-and-so is such-and-such. That is to say, the fact we are trying to explain can be expressed in a simple subject-predicate sentence: S is P. The question we ask is: Why is S P? And the answer can be put in the form S is P because Y. (We can of course ask not only why wading-birds have webbed feet, but why there are any wading-birds at all; and if the former question asks 'Because of what does one thing belong to another?', the latter question seems to be concerned with *one* thing only, namely wading-birds. Aristotle answers that point by appealing to his analysis of substances into matter and form: to ask why there are wading-birds is to ask why animal tissues sometimes have such-and-such a form—and that is to ask 'Because of what does one thing belong to another?')

Finally, Aristotle says that 'the cause is the middle term': to ask why S is P is, as it were, to look for a link joining S to P; and that link will constitute a 'middle term' between S and P. 'Why is S P?'—'Because of M.' More fully: 'S is P, because S is M, and M is P.' Why do cows have several stomachs? Because cows are ruminants and ruminants have several stomachs. Not all explanations need actually have that specific form; but Aristotle holds that all explanations *can* be couched in that form, and that the form exhibits the nature of causal connections most perspicuously.

That account of explanatory sentences enables us to see how Aristotle's notion of explanation is integrated with his logic, and how the causes which are the prime objects of the scientist's search may be expressed within the axiomatic system which presents his finished product. (Every deduction within that system will be, roughly speaking, of the form: S is M; M is P; so S is P. It will thus mirror perfectly the structure of explanatory sentences.) Moreover, we are now better equipped to understand the doctrine of the 'four causes'.

'The constituent from which something comes to be', Aristotle's first type of cause, is usually called 'cause as matter' by him and 'the material cause' by his commentators. The illustration, 'bronze of the statue', is elliptical for something of the form 'The statue is so-and-so because the statue is made of bronze and bronze things are so-and-so.' (Insert 'malleable', 'brown', 'heavy', 'covered in verdigris' etc. in place of 'so-and-so'.) The middle term, 'made of bronze', expresses the cause of the statue's being, for example, malleable; and because bronze is the constituent stuff of the statue the cause here is the 'material' cause.

Aristotle's second sort of cause, 'the form and pattern', is normally referred to as the 'formal' cause. The illustration is again obscure. Consider instead the following example: 'what it is and why it is are the same. What is an eclipse?—Privation of light from the moon by the earth's screening. Why is there an eclipse? or: Why is the moon eclipsed?—Because the light leaves it when the earth screens it.' The moon is eclipsed because the moon is deprived of light by being screened and things deprived of light by being screened are eclipsed. Here the middle term, 'deprived of light by being screened', explains why the eclipse occurs; and it states the form or essence of an eclipse —it says what an eclipse actually is.

We ourselves tend to associate the notion of causation most readily with the action of one thing on another—with pushings and pullings. Modern readers may feel most at home with

Aristotle's third type of cause, which is usually called the 'efficient' or 'motive' cause. At least, Aristotle's illustrations of the efficient cause have features which we now associate closely with the idea of causation. Thus the examples seem to suggest that efficient causes are *distinct* from the objects they operate upon (the father is distinct from the son, whereas the bronze is not distinct from the statue), and that causes *precede* their effects (the man who deliberates does so before he acts, whereas the screening does not occur before the eclipse).

Aristotle, however, does not regard efficient causes as radically different from material and formal causes. Moreover, he holds that efficient causes do not always precede their effects— indeed, he treats simultaneity of cause and effect as the norm. His illustration, 'the father of the child', might be expanded as follows: 'The child is snub-nosed because the child has a snub-nosed father and children with snub-nosed fathers are snub-nosed.' Here the cause, *having a snub-nosed father*, does not precede the effect. Elsewhere we find examples of antecedent causes: 'Why did the Persian War come upon the Athenians? What was the cause of the Athenians' being warred upon?—Because they attacked Sardis with the Eretrians; for that initiated the change.'

Aristotle refers to his fourth cause as 'that for the sake of which' and 'the goal'. It is usually known as the 'final' cause ('*finis*' is the Latin word for 'end' or 'goal'). The normal way of expressing final causes, as Aristotle's example indicates, is by using the connective 'in order to': 'He is walking in order to be healthy.' Final causes are odd, in various ways: first, they are not readily expressed in terms of 'the because-of-which'—'in order to' does not easily translate into 'because'. Secondly, they seem to be appropriate only to a very small number of cases, namely, human intentional actions (for 'in order to' expresses an intention, and only human actions are intentional). Thirdly, they appear to post-date their effects (health, which allegedly causes the walking, comes about *after* the walking). Fourthly, they may be effective without even existing (health may cause the man to walk and yet never exist—he may be too dissipated ever to become healthy, or he may be run over by a bus in the course of his perambulations).

The third and fourth oddities are the least troublesome. Aristotle explicitly recognizes that final causes follow their effects, and he implicitly acknowledges cases in which a final cause is effective but non-existent—neither point struck him as strange. The second oddity is more important. Aristotle does not think that final causes are appropriate only to intentional behaviour; on the contrary, the primary arena within which final causes exert themselves is that of nature—of the animal and vegetable world. I shall return to this in a later chapter. The first oddity demands a comment here.

How do final causes fit Aristotle's account of the structure of explanatory sentences? One favourite example of a final cause is expressed concisely thus: 'Why is there a house?—In order to preserve a man's belongings.' We might expand the explanation as follows: houses are roofed because houses are shelters for belongings and shelters for belongings are roofed. Here 'shelter for belongings' is the middle term, and it expresses the final cause of houses—it states the goal of having a house. But that gloss on Aristotle's illustration takes us some way from his text, and it is very difficult to provide a similar gloss for the example of the man who jogs for the sake of his health.

The fact is that final causes do not fit easily into the tight structure we are using, and we should perhaps relax things somewhat ('Why is S P? Because of M.' In some cases, the relation of M to S and P will be, as before, that S is M and M is P. In other cases it may be more complex. In the case of final causes M will explain why S is P inasmuch as M is both a goal for S and something achievable by way of P. 'Why does he walk?—For health': health is his goal; and health is achievable by walking. 'Why do ducks have webbed feet?—For swimming': swimming is a goal for ducks (that is, it is good for ducks to swim); and swimming is made easier by having webbed feet.

Aristotle's treatment of explanation contains much more than the distinction among four types of cause. I shall mention two further points. 'Since things are called causes in many ways, it happens that the same thing has many causes non-incidentally; for example, both the art of statue-making and the bronze are causes of the statue—not in virtue of something else, but *qua* statue—but not in the same way: one is cause in the sense of matter, the other in the sense of origin of change.' The same thing may have several different causes. It is tempting to construe 'the same thing' in a weak sense: the statue is heavy, say, because it is made of bronze; the statue is life-size because the sculptor made it so. The two causes are causes not of the very same *feature* of the statue, but rather of features of the very same *statue*. But that is not Aristotle's meaning; rather, he holds that one and the same *feature* of the statue may receive two distinct explanations, according to two different modes of causality. Thus he says that thunder occurs 'both because when fire is extinguished it necessarily sizzles and makes a noise and —if things are as the Pythagoreans say—in order to threaten and frighten those in Hell'. And in the biological works he regularly looks for double causes in nature.

That is puzzling. Surely if Y explains X, then there is no room for supposing that, in addition, Z explains X; if Y accounts for X, X is accounted for, and there is no accounting left for Z to do. It hardly makes any difference if Y and Z are different types of cause. If we think we can give an adequate explanation of, say, the behaviour of a dog purely in mechanical terms (by a set of material and efficient causes), then we shall reject any further putative explanation in terms of the animal's goals or ends— such an attempt can explain nothing, since everything is already explained.

It is possible that Aristotle means something a little different from what he says: bronze may, in a way, be a cause of the statue's being heavy; but it is not by itself fully adequate to account for the weight of the statue—we need to add a reference to the sculptor, for he could quite well have fashioned a *light* statue out of bronze. The point, then, is not that X can be adequately explained by Y and also adequately explained by some different Z; but rather that an adequate explanation of X may require mention both of Y and of Z. That is a true observation; but it is not quite the observation Aristotle seems to be making.

Finally, a word about chance. Some of Aristotle's predecessors had ascribed many natural phenomena to chance. Aristotle rejects their view. But did he himself leave any room for chance in nature? He certainly believes that in nature some things happen not invariably but only for the most part; and he identifies 'the accidental' with the exceptions to what happens for the most part. For the most part, men go grey; if Socrates does not go grey, then that is accidental, and may have occurred by chance. 'And that there is no knowledge of the accidental is clear; for all knowledge deals either with what holds always or with what holds for the most part (for how else could one either learn it or teach it to someone else?).'

Thus, in Aristotle's view, there *are* accidental phenomena in nature, but they are not subject to knowledge—that is to say, they cannot form part of any developed science. Does Aristotle infer that the world is to some extent indeterminate, that not all events are bound together by the nexus of causation? He does not do so explicitly; indeed, he tends to say that the exceptions to natural regularities occur because of, and can be explained in terms of, peculiarities in the matter of the thing in question. Thus accidental phenomena do, or at least may, have causes. Aristotle does not, or need not, admit random or causeless events into his world. But he does allow that not all events are amenable to scientific understanding, for not everything exhibits the sort of regularity which science requires.

13 *Empiricism*

How are we to acquire the knowledge which is to be packaged in neat Euclidean sciences? How do we get in touch with the substances which constitute the real world? How do we chart their changes? How do we hit upon their causes and uncover their explanations? Deductive logic is not the means of discovering facts about the world: Aristotle's syllogistic provides a system within which knowledge can be articulated, but logic is not, save incidentally, a device for discovery.

The ultimate source of knowledge is, in Aristotle's view, perception. Aristotle was a thoroughgoing empiricist in two senses of that term. First, he held that the notions or concepts with which we seek to grasp reality are all ultimately derived from perception, 'and for that reason, if we did not perceive anything, we would not learn or understand anything, and whenever we think of anything we must at the same time think of an idea'. Secondly, he thought that the science or knowledge in which our grasp of reality consists is ultimately grounded on perceptual observations. That is hardly surprising: as a biologist, Aristotle's primary research tool was sense-perception, his own or that of others; as an ontologist, Aristotle's primary substances were ordinary perceptible objects. Plato, having given abstract Forms the leading role in his ontology, was led to regard the intellect rather than perception as the searchlight which illuminated reality. Aristotle, placing sensible particulars at the centre of the stage, took sense-perception as his torch.

Perception is the source of knowledge, but it is not knowledge itself. How, then, are the facts given in perception transformed into scientific knowledge? Aristotle describes the process as follows.

All animals ... have an innate capacity to make discriminations, which is called perception; and if perception is present in them, in some animals the percept is retained and in others it is not. Now for those in which it is not retained ... there is no knowledge outside perception. But for some perceivers it is possible to hold the percept in their minds; and when many such things have come about, there is a further difference, and some, from the retention of such things, come to have a general account, while others do not. Thus from perception there comes memory, as we call it; and from memory (when it occurs often in connection with the same thing) experience—for memories that are many in number form a single experience. And from experience, or from the whole universal that has come to rest in the mind ... there comes a principle of skill and of knowledge.

We perceive particular facts—that this thing, here and now, is thus-and-so (that Socrates, say, is now going grey). Many of the facts we perceive are similar—it is not just Socrates, but Callias and Plato and Nicomachus and the rest who are seen to go grey. Those percepts stick in the mind and become memories. When we possess a mass of similar memories we have what Aristotle terms 'experience'; and 'experience' is turned into something close to knowledge when the multitude of particular facts are, as it were, compressed into a single general fact—the fact that, for the most part, all men go grey. (I say 'something close to knowledge': knowledge itself only arrives when we grasp the cause of greying—when we learn that men go grey because, say, the sources of pigmentation dry up.) Knowledge, in sum, is bred by generalization out of perception.

That story may seem open to criticism. First of all, it is quite clear that most of our knowledge is *not* acquired in the way Aristotle suggests. We do not normally require a mass of similar observations before we jump to a universal judgement—I doubt if Aristotle observed hectocotylization in more than one or two octopuses, and he surely dissected very few prawns before giving his general description of their internal parts. The story he tells of the growth of general knowledge from particular observations may be correct at bottom, but its plot must be made considerably more sophisticated if it is to be an adequate account of our actual procedures.

Secondly, Aristotle's story will meet a philosophical challenge. Is sense-perception really reliable? If so, how can we tell that it is? How can we distinguish illusion from genuine perception? Or again, are we really justified in moving from particular observations to general truths? How can we know if we have made enough observations or if our actual observations are a fair sample of the field of possible observations? Questions of that sort have been asked by sceptically-minded philosophers for centuries, and they render dubious Aristotle's reliance on perception and generalization.

Aristotle was well aware of the dangers of hasty generalization; for example, 'the cause of the ignorance of those who take that view is that, while the differences among animals with regard to copulation and procreation are manifold and unobvious, those people observe a few cases and think that things must be the same in all cases'. But Aristotle has nothing to say on a more general level about the problems raised by generalization: those problems—problems of 'induction' as they were later called—did not receive detailed philosophical attention until long after Aristotle's death.

Aristotle has a little more to say about the problems of perception. In his psychological treatise *On the Soul* he remarks in passing that the reliability of the senses varies according to the objects they are directed towards. If our eyes tell us 'That is white' they are most unlikely to be wrong; if they say 'That white thing is a daisy' they have a greater chance of erring. And Book IV of the *Metaphysics* considers and dismisses a number of sceptical positions. But the remarks in *On the Soul* are not backed by argument, and Aristotle's reply to the sceptics is (in the part which concerns us here) little more than a brusque dismissal. He thinks that their views are not seriously held: 'it is evident that no one—neither those who state the thesis nor anyone else—is actually in that condition. For why does anyone walk to Megara rather than stay where he is when he thinks he should walk there? Why doesn't he walk into a well or over a cliff in the morning if there is one about?' And he asks, scorn-fully, if 'they are really puzzled as to whether sizes and colours are such as they seem to those at a distance or to those who are near, to the healthy or to the sick; whether what seems heavy to the weak or to the strong really is heavy; whether what seems to be the case to men awake or to men asleep really is true'.

The fact is that Aristotle did not take sceptical doubts about perception very seriously, and he did not pay any attention to sceptical doubts about generalization. One great service of later Greek philosophy was to make up for Aristotle's omission: epi-stemological questions became the focus of attention for Stoics, Epicureans and Sceptics.

14 *Aristotle's world-picture*

Aristotle was an industrious collector who amassed a prodigious quantity of detailed information on a vast variety of topics. He was also an abstract thinker, whose philosophical ideas ranged wide. Those two parts of his thought were not kept in distinct compartments. On the contrary, Aristotle's scientific work and his philosophical investigations together formed a unified intellectual outlook. Aristotle was a remarkable scientist and a profound philosopher, but it is as a philosopher-scientist that he excels. He was, according to an ancient aphorism, 'a scribe of Nature who dipped his pen in Thought'.

His main philosophico-scientific writings are *On Generation and Destruction, On the Heavens, Meteorology, On the Soul*, the collection of short psychological treatises known collectively as the *Parva Naturalia*, the *Parts of Animals*, and the *Generation of Animals*. All those treatises are scientific, in the sense that they are based on empirical research, and attempt to organize and explain the observed phenomena. They are all philosophical, in the sense that they are acutely self-conscious, reflective and systematically structured attempts to arrive at the truth of things.

Aristotle himself indicates the general plan of his work at the beginning of the *Meteorology*.

I have already dealt with the first causes of nature and with all natural motion [in the *Physics*], and also with the heavenly bodies, arranged in their upper paths [in *On the Heavens*], and with the number and nature of the material elements, with their mutual transformations, and with generation and destruction in general [in *On Generation and Corruption*]. The part of this enquiry remaining to be considered is what all the earlier thinkers called meteorology . . . When we have dealt with these subjects, let us see if we can give some account, on the lines we have laid down, of animals and plants, both in general and in particular; for when we have done that, we shall perhaps have arrived at the completion of the plan we set ourselves at the beginning.

Aristotle offers a clear view of the nature of reality. The basic constituent stuffs of the sublunary world are four: earth, air, fire and water. Each element is defined by its possession of two of the four primary powers or qualities—wetness, dryness, coldness, hotness. The elements have each a natural movement and a natural place. Fire, if left to itself, will move upwards and will find its place at the outermost edges of the universe; earth naturally moves downwards, to the centre of the universe; air and water find their places in between. The elements can act upon and change into one another; such elemental interactions are discussed in *On Generation and Destruction*, and something approximating to chemistry may be found in Book IV of the *Meteorology*.

Earth tends downwards, and our earth is naturally at the centre of the universe. Beyond the earth and its atmosphere come the moon, the sun, the planets and the fixed stars. Aristotle's geocentric astronomy, which attaches the heavenly bodies to a series of concentric spheres, was not his own creation. He was not a professional astronomer but relied upon the work of his contemporaries, Eudoxus and Callippus. The treatise *On the Heavens* is concerned with abstract astronomy. Aristotle's main contention is that the physical universe is spatially finite but temporally infinite—it is a vast but bounded sphere which has existed without beginning and will exist without end.

Around the earth is its atmosphere. The events in the sublunary sphere had occupied much of the attention of the early Greek scientists, and Aristotle follows their lead. The *Meteorology* studies '*ta meteōra*', literally 'the things suspended in mid-air': the phrase referred originally to such phenomena as clouds, thunder, rain, snow, frost, dew—roughly speaking, to the weather; but it was easily extended to include matters which we should classify under astronomy (meteors, comets, the Milky Way, for example) or under geography (rivers, the sea, mountains, etc.). Aristotle's *Meteorology* contains his own explanations of these various phenomena. The work has a strong empirical base, but it is firmly governed by theory. The unity it possesses derives largely from the dominance of one notion, that of 'exhalation'. Aristotle holds that 'exhalations' or evaporations are continuously being given off by the earth. They are of two sorts, wet or steamy, and dry or smoky. Their action can explain, in a uniform fashion, most of the events that take place in the atmosphere.

On the earth itself the most remarkable objects of study are living things and their parts. 'Of the parts in animals, some are incomposite, namely those which divide into uniform pieces (for example, flesh into flesh), others are composite, namely those which divide into non-uniform pieces (for example, a hand does not divide into hands, nor a face into faces) . . . All the non-uniform parts are composed from the uniform parts, for example, hands from flesh and sinews and bones.' There is no sharp boundary between non-living and living things; and although living things can be arranged in a hierarchy—a 'ladder of nature' of ascending worth and complexity—the grades in the hierarchy are not rigorously separated. Plants blend into the lowest of animals; and from those to man, who naturally stands at the top of the scale, there is a continuous progression. Such is the natural world. It continues for ever, exhibiting constant regularity in continuous change.

Circular motion, that is, the motion of the heavens, has been seen . . . to be eternal, because its motions and those determined by it come into being and will exist from necessity. For if that which moves in a circle is always moving something else, the motion of those things too must be circular—for example, since the upper movement is circular, the sun moves in this way; and since this is so, the seasons for that reason come into being in a circle and return upon themselves; and since they come into being in this way, so again do the things governed by them.

And how is the world run? Are there gods to keep it going? Outwardly Aristotle was a conventional polytheist; at least, in his will he ordered statues to be dedicated at Stagira to Zeus and to Athena. But such performances did not mirror his beliefs:

Our remote ancestors have handed down remnants to their posterity in mythical form to the effect that these [sc. the heavenly bodies] are gods and that the divine encompasses the whole of nature. But the rest has been added by way of myth to persuade the vulgar and for the use of the laws and of expediency. For they say that they are anthropomorphic and like some of the other animals— and other things consequent upon and similar to that; but if you were to separate what they say and accept only the first part, that they thought the primary substances to be gods, you would think they had spoken divinely.

Zeus and Athena, the anthropomorphic gods of the Olympian pantheon, are mere myths; but 'our remote ancestors' were not purveyors of unmixed superstition. They rightly saw, or half saw, first that the 'primary substances' are divine ('god seems to everyone to be among the causes and a sort of first principle'), and secondly that the primary substances should be sought in the heavens.

The heavenly bodies, which Aristotle often refers to as 'the divine bodies', are made of a special stuff; a fifth element or 'quintessence'; for 'there is some other body, separate from those here about us, whose nature is more honourable in that it is further removed from the world below'. Now 'it is the function of what is most divine to think and to use its intellect', so that the heavenly bodies, being divine, must therefore be alive and intelligent. For although 'we tend to think of them as though they were simply bodies—units exhibiting order but quite without life—we must suppose that they partake in action and in life ... We must think that the actions of the stars are just like those of animals and plants.'

In Book VIII of the *Physics* Aristotle argues for the existence of a changeless source of change—an 'unmoved mover' as it is normally called. If there is to be any change in the universe, there must, he holds, be some original source which imparts change to other things without changing itself. The unmoved mover is outside the universe: 'must there be something unchanging and at rest outside what is changing and no part of it, or not? And must this be true of the universe too? It would presumably seem absurd if the principle of change were *inside* it.' The external mover 'initiates change as an object of love; and other things initiate change by changing themselves'. The concentric celestial spheres, and the celestial bodies they carry, are all quintessential and divine; but they are moving divinities. Beyond them, incorporeal and outside the universe, is the primary divinity, the changeless originator of all change.

What are we to make of all this? Some scholars take Aristotle's words at what seems to be their face value, and find living gods scattered throughout his writings—he thus becomes a profoundly religious scientist. Other scholars dismiss Aristotle's use of the words 'god' and 'divine' as a mere *façon de parler*: the primary substances are divine only in the sense that other things are dependent upon them—and Aristotle becomes a wholly secular thinker.

Neither of those two views is plausible. There is too much about gods in the treatises to permit us to discount Aristotle's theologizing as empty word-play; and, on the other hand, Aristotle's gods are too abstract, remote and impersonal to be regarded as the objects of a religious man's worship. Rather, we might connect Aristotle's remarks about the divinity of the universe with the sense of wonderment which nature and its works produced in him. 'It is because of wonderment that men, both now and at first, start to study philosophy'; and that study, properly conducted, does not diminish the initial admiration. For Aristotle was impressed by a deep reverence for the value and excellence of the universe about him:

In what way does the nature of the world contain what is good and what is best—as something separate and independent, or as its own orderliness? Rather, in both ways, as an army does. For the excellence of an army resides both in its orderliness and in its general, and especially in the latter. For he does not depend on the orderliness but it does depend on him. And all things—fish and birds and plants—are ordered in a way, yet not in the same way; and it is not the case that there is no connection between one thing and another —there is a connection.

15 *Psychology*

There is a fundamental distinction within the natural world: some natural substances are alive, others are inanimate. What marks off the former from the latter is their possession of *psuchē*. The word '*psuchē*' (from which our word 'psychology' derives) is usually translated as 'soul', and under the heading of *psuchē* Aristotle does indeed include those features of the higher animals which later thinkers tend to associate with the soul. But 'soul' is a misleading translation. It is a truism that all living things—prawns and pansies no less than men and gods—possess a *psuchē*; but it sounds bizarre to suggest that a prawn has a soul. Since a *psuchē* is what animates, or gives life to, a living thing, the word 'animator' (despite its overtones of Disneyland) might be used. (I shall generally keep to the conventional 'soul', but I shall also occasionally use 'animator'.)

Souls or animators come in varying degrees of complexity.

Some things possess all the powers of the soul, others some of them, others one only. The powers we mentioned were those of nutrition, of perception, of appetition, of change in place, of thought. Plants possess only the nutritive power. Other things possess both that and the power of perception. And if the power of perception, then that of appetition too. For appetition consists of desire, inclination and wish; all animals possess at least one of the senses, namely touch; everything which has perception also experiences pleasure and pain, the pleasant and the painful; and everything which experiences those also possesses desire (for desire is appetition for the pleasant) . . . Some things possess in addition to these the power of locomotion; and others also possess the power of thought and intelligence.

Thought, in Aristotle's view, requires imagination and hence perception; so that any thinking creature must be capable of perceiving. And perception never exists apart from the first principle of animation, that of nutrition and reproduction. Thus the various powers or faculties of the soul form a hierarchical system.

What is a soul or animator? And how do living creatures acquire one?

In his treatise *On the Soul* Aristotle offers a general account of what a soul is. He first argues to the conclusion that 'if we are to state something common to every type of soul, it will be that it is the first fulfilment of a natural body that has organs'. He later observes that such an account is not particularly illuminating, and suggests, as an improvement, that 'a soul is a principle of the aforesaid powers and is defined by them, namely by nutrition, perception, thought, movement'. Aristotle himself advises us not to spend too much time over these generalities but rather to concentrate on the different functions of the soul.

Yet the generalities contain something of great importance. Aristotle's first general account of the soul amounts to this: for a thing to have a soul is for it to be a natural organic body actually capable of functioning. The second general account simply explains what those functions are. Thus Aristotle's souls are not *pieces* of living things; they are not bits of spiritual stuff placed inside the living body; rather, they are sets of powers, capacities or faculties. Possessing a soul is like possessing a skill. A skilled man's skill is not some part of him, responsible for his skilled acts; similarly, a living creature's animator or life-force is not some part of it, responsible for its living activities.

That view of the soul has certain consequences, which Aristotle was quick to draw. First, 'one should not ask if the soul and the body are one, any more than one should ask of the wax and the shape or in general of the matter of anything and that of which it is the matter'. There is no problem of the 'unity' of soul and body, or of how soul and body can act upon each other. Descartes later wondered how on earth two things so different as body and soul could coexist and work together; for Aristotle such issues do not arise.

Secondly, 'that the soul—or certain parts of it, if it is divisible into parts—is not separable from the body is not unclear'. Fulfilments cannot exist apart from the things that are fulfilled. Souls are fulfilments of bodies. Hence souls cannot exist apart from bodies, any more than skills can exist apart from skilled men. Plato had held that souls pre-existed the birth and survived the death of those bodies they animated. Aristotle thought that that was impossible. A soul is simply not the *sort* of thing that could survive. How could my skills, my temper or my character survive me?

Aristotle's general view of the nature of souls is elaborated in his detailed accounts of the different life-functions: nutrition, reproduction, perception, movement, thought. Such functions or faculties are functions or faculties *of the body*, and Aristotle's psychological investigations can take a biological turn without, as it were, changing the subject. Thus imagination, for example, is described as 'a motion coming about by the agency of an act of perception': an act of perception is a physiological change, and it may cause a further physiological change, which constitutes an imagination. Some may object that Aristotle ignores the psychological aspect of imagination by concentrating on its physiological manifestations. But Aristotle holds that the physiology *is* the psychology, that souls and their parts are *physical* capacities.

On the Soul and the *Parva Naturalia* are governed by that biological attitude towards animation. In the *Generation of Animals* Aristotle asks where the soul or animator comes from: how do creatures begin to live? A popular view, accepted by Plato, had it that life begins when the soul enters the body. Aristotle comments: 'clearly, those principles whose actuality is corporeal cannot exist without a body—for example, walking without feet; hence they cannot come in from outside—for they can come in neither alone (for they are inseparable), nor in some body (for the semen is a residue of food that is undergoing change).' The 'principles' or powers of the soul are corporeal principles—to be animated is to be a body with certain capacities. Hence to suppose that those capacities could exist outside any body is as absurd as to imagine that walking could take place apart from any legs. The soul cannot simply drift into the foetus from outside. (In principle, it could arrive 'in some body', that is, in the semen; but in fact the semen is the wrong sort of stuff to carry or transmit those capacities.)

Aristotle's accounts of nutrition, reproduction, perception, desire and movement are all consistently biological. But consistency is threatened when he turns to the highest psychological faculty, that of thought. In the *Generation of Animals*, immediately after the sentences just quoted, Aristotle continues: 'Hence it remains that thought alone comes in from outside, and that it alone is divine; for corporeal actuality has no connection at all with the actuality of thought.' Thought, it seems, *can* exist apart from body. The treatise *On the Soul* speaks of thought with special caution, hinting that it *may* be separable from body. In what is perhaps the most perplexing paragraph he ever wrote, Aristotle distinguishes between two sorts of thought (later known as 'active intellect' and 'passive intellect'). Of the first of these he says: 'this thought is separable and impassive and unmixed, being essentially actuality . . . And when separated it is just what it is, and it alone is immortal and eternal.'

The special status of thought depends upon the view that thinking does not involve any corporeal activity. But how can Aristotle hold that view? His general account of the soul makes it plain that thinking is something done by 'natural organic bodies', and his particular analysis of the nature of thought makes thinking dependent upon imagination and hence upon perception. Even if thinking is not itself a corporeal activity, it requires other corporeal activities in order to take place.

Aristotle's treatment of thought is both obscure in itself and hard to reconcile with the rest of his psychology. But neither that fact, nor the various errors and inexactitudes in his physiology, should dim the light of his work on psychology: it rests on a subtle insight into the nature of souls or animators, and it is persistently scientific in its approach to psychological questions.

16 Evidence and theory

Aristotle's general account of the world is wholly exploded. Most of his explanations are now seen to be false. Many of the concepts he operated with appear crude and inadequate. Some of his ideas seem quite absurd. The chief reason for Aristotle's downfall is simple: in the sixteenth and seventeenth centuries, scientists applied quantitative methods to the study of inanimate nature, and chemistry and physics came to assume a dominating role. Those two sciences seemed to be fundamental in a way in which biology was not: they examined the same stuffs as biology, but from a closer, and a mathematical, viewpoint—a biology unsupported by physics and chemistry lacked all foundation. Aristotle's physics and chemistry are hopelessly inadequate when compared to the work of the new scientists. A new 'world picture', based on the new sciences, replaced the Aristotelian view, and if Aristotle's biology survived for a further century or so, it survived as a limb torn from the body, as a fragment of a colossal statue.

Why did Aristotle not develop a decent chemistry or an adequate physics? His failing must be set down in large part to a certain conceptual poverty. He did not have our concepts of mass, force, velocity, temperature, and he thus lacked the most powerful tools of the physical sciences. In some cases he had a rough and primitive form of the concept—after all, he knew what speed was, and he could weigh things. But his notion of speed is in a sense non-quantitative. He did not *measure* velocity; he had no notion of miles per hour. Or again, consider temperature. Heat is a central notion in Aristotelian science. The hot and the cold are two of the four primary powers, and heat is vital to animal life. Aristotle's predecessors had disagreed among themselves over what objects were hot and what cold. 'If there is so much dispute over the hot and the cold,' Aristotle remarks, 'what must we think about the rest? — for these are the clearest of the things we perceive'. He suspects that the disputes occur 'because the term "hotter" is used in several ways', and he conducts a long analysis of the different criteria we use for calling things hot. The analysis is subtle, but—to our eyes—it suffers from a glaring deficiency: it does not mention *measurement*. For Aristotle, hotness is a matter of degree, but not of *measurable* degree. To that extent he lacked the notion of temperature.

Conceptual poverty is closely tied to technological poverty. Aristotle had no proper clocks, and no thermometers. Measuring devices and a quantitative conceptual apparatus go together. The former are inconceivable without the latter, the latter are useless without the former. Lacking one, Aristotle lacked both. In an earlier chapter I suggested that Aristotle's zoological researches did not suffer from his non-quantitative approach. The case is different with the natural sciences: chemistry without laboratory equipment and physics without mathematics are bad chemistry and bad physics.

It would be absurd to blame Aristotle for his conceptual poverty: poverty is a lack, not a failing. But many students of Aristotle's science are inclined to impute two serious failings to him, one methodological and the other substantial. It is alleged, first, that Aristotle regularly subordinated fact to theory, that he would start from theory, and then twist the facts to fit it; and secondly, that his natural science was permeated by a childlike determination to find plans and purposes in the world of nature. Let us take the methodological accusation first.

Consider the following passage:

we might say that plants belong to earth, aquatic animals to water, land-animals to air . . . The fourth kind must not be looked for in these regions; yet there *should* be a kind corresponding to the position of fire—for this is reckoned the fourth of the bodies . . . But such a kind must be sought on the moon; for that evidently shares in the fourth remove—but that is matter for another treatise.

The passage comes in the middle of a sophisticated and informed discussion of certain questions of generation. It would be charitable to regard it as a joke, but it is not jocular in tone—Aristotle convinces himself, by a feeble analogy, that there are kinds of animals corresponding to three of his elements; he infers that there must be a kind corresponding to the fourth element; and, failing to find such things on the earth, he places them on the moon. What could be more absurd? What less scientific?

Well, the passage *is* absurd; and there are one or two others to match it. But all scientists are capable of idiocy: there are remarkably few idiotic passages in Aristotle's writings, and the judicious reader will not make much of them. Rather, he will find other passages more characteristic of the man. Speaking of the motions of the heavenly bodies, Aristotle writes:

as to how many there are, let us now say what some of the mathematicians say, in order to get some idea of the matter and so that our mind will have some definite number to grasp hold of. As to the future, we must make enquiries ourselves and discuss the matter with other enquirers, and if those who study these matters have views different from those now expressed, we must love both parties but listen to the more accurate.

Again: 'to judge by argument and by the facts which seem to hold about them, the generation of bees takes place in that manner. But we have not yet acquired an adequate grasp of the facts: if we ever do acquire such a grasp, we must then rely on perception rather than on arguments—and on arguments if what they prove is in agreement with the phenomena'. Aristotle has just given a long and careful account of the generation of bees. The account is based primarily on observations, but it is also speculative, relying to some extent on theoretical considerations. Aristotle explicitly recognizes this speculative aspect of his account, and he explicitly holds that speculation is subordinate to observation. Theory is indispensable when the facts are as yet insufficiently known, but observation always has priority over theory.

Aristotle elsewhere makes the same point in more general terms: 'we must first grasp the differences between animals and the facts about them all. After that, we must try to discover their causes. For that is the natural method of procedure, once the research about each of them is done; for from that will become apparent the subjects about which and the principles from which our proofs must be conducted.' Again:

empirical science must pass down the principles—I mean, for example, empirical astronomy must supply those of the science of astronomy; for when the phenomena were sufficiently grasped, the astronomical proofs were discovered. And similarly in every other art and science whatsoever. Thus if the facts in each case are grasped, it will then be our task to give a ready supply of proofs. For if none of the true facts of the case is missing, we shall be able to discover the proof of everything of which there is proof and to construct a proof—and to make plain where proof is not possible.

Aristotle frequently criticizes his predecessors for putting theory before the facts. Thus, of Plato and his school:

speaking of the phenomena, they say things that do not agree with the phenomena ... They are so fond of their first principles that they seem to behave like those who defend these in dialectical arguments; for they accept any consequence, thinking that they have true principles—as though principles should not be judged by their consequences, and especially by their goal. And the goal in productive science is the product, but in natural science it is whatever properly appears to perception.

Nothing could be clearer. Empirical research precedes theory. The facts must be collected before the causes are sought. The construction of an axiomatic science (of 'proofs') depends upon the presence of 'all the true facts of the case'. Of course, Aristotle never had a grasp of *all* the facts; he often thought he had facts when he only had falsehoods; and he sometimes jumped precipitately into theorizing. Moreover, theory should to some extent control the collection of facts: undisciplined amassing of facts is an unscientific exercise; and it may be, as some philosophers both ancient and modern have argued, that there is no such thing as a 'pure' fact uncontaminated by theory. But despite all this, two things are perfectly plain: Aristotle had a clear view of the primacy of observation, and his scientific treatises—in particular, his works on biology—regularly remain true to that view.

In the next chapter I turn to the accusation that Aristotle childishly makes the natural world a stage on which plans and purposes are acted out.

17 *Teleology*

We see more than one kind of cause concerned with natural generation—namely that for the sake of which, and the source of the principle of change. Thus we must determine which of these comes first and which second. It seems that the first is the one we call 'for the sake of something'; for this is the account of the thing, and the account is a principle in the same way both in the products of skill and in those of nature. For, either by thought or by perception, the doctor determines on health and the builder on a house; and then they give accounts and causes of everything they do, and explain why it should be done in this way. Now that for the sake of which, or the good, is more prevalent in the works of nature than in those of skill.

Here, in the introductory chapter of the *Parts of Animals*, Aristotle sets out what is called his teleological view of nature. Final causes occur in the works of nature no less than in the products of human skill, and in order to explain natural phenomena we must appeal to 'that for the sake of which'. Explanation in terms of final causes is explanation in terms of 'the good', for if ducks have webbed feet *for the sake* of swimming, then it is *good*—that is, good for *ducks*—to have webbed feet. Final causes are primary because they are identified with 'the account of the thing': being a swimmer is part of a duck's essence, and a proper account of what it is to be a duck will require reference to swimming. Final causes are not imposed on nature by theoretical considerations; they are observed in nature: '*we see* more than one kind of cause'. (The term 'teleology' is connected with the Greek '*telos*', which is Aristotle's word for 'goal': a teleological explanation is one which appeals to goals or final causes.)

Throughout his biological works Aristotle constantly looks for final causes. Why do teeth, unlike the other hard parts of animal structure, continue to grow?

The cause of that growth in the sense of that for the sake of which is to be found in their function. For they would soon be worn away if there were no accretion to them—as it is, in certain old animals which are gross feeders but possess small teeth, the teeth are completely worn away, for they are destroyed more quickly than they grow. That is why here too nature has produced an excellent contrivance to fit the case; for she makes loss of the teeth coincide with old age and death. If life lasted for ten thousand or one thousand years, the teeth would have had to be enormous at first and to grow up often; for even if they grew continuously, they would nevertheless be smoothed down and so become useless for their work. So much for that for the sake of which they grow.

Why do men have hands?

Anaxagoras says that men are the most intelligent of animals because they possess hands; but it is reasonable to think that they have got hands because they are most intelligent. For hands are a tool, and nature, like an intelligent man, always assigns each thing to something that can use it (it is better to give a flute to someone who is actually a flute-player than to provide a man who owns a flute with the skill of flute-playing); for she has provided the greater and superior thing with that which is less, and not the less with that which is more honourable and greater. Thus if this is better, and if nature does what is the best in the circumstances, man is not most intelligent because of his hands but has hands because he is the most intelligent of animals.

Often final causes are contrasted with 'necessity', and in particular with the constraints imposed by the material nature of the animals or animal parts in question. But even where necessity is invoked to explain the phenomena, there is still room for explanation in terms of final causes. Why do water-birds have webbed feet?

For these causes, they have them from necessity; and because of what is better they have such feet for the sake of life, so that, living in the water where their wings are useless, they may have feet that are useful for swimming. For they are like oars to oarsmen or fins to fish; hence if in fish the fins are destroyed or in water-birds the webbing between the feet, they no longer swim.

Aristotle's teleology is sometimes summed up in the slogan 'Nature does nothing in vain', and he himself frequently uses aphorisms of that tenor. But although Aristotle holds that final causes are to be found throughout the natural world, they are not to be found literally everywhere. 'The bile in the liver is a residue, and is not for the sake of anything—like the sediment in the stomach and in the intestines. Now nature sometimes uses even residues for some advantageous purpose; but that is no reason for seeking a final cause in all cases.' Book V of the *Generation of Animals* is entirely devoted to such non-purposeful parts of animals.

Natural behaviour and natural structure usually have final causes—for nature does nothing in vain. But the final causes are constrained by necessity—nature does the best she can 'in the circumstances'; and sometimes there is no final cause to be discovered at all.

The *Physics* contains a number of arguments in support of natural teleology. Some of them rest upon the characteristically Aristotelian notion that 'art imitates nature' or 'the arts are imitations of nature': if we can see final causes in the products of skill, all the more so can we see them in the products of nature. Another argument enlarges upon the assertion in the *Parts of Animals* that 'we see' final causes in nature.

It is particularly clear in the case of the other animals which act neither by skill nor after enquiry nor after deliberation (hence some people wonder whether spiders, ants and the like perform their tasks by reason or by something else). And if you proceed little by little in this way, it becomes apparent that in plants too there occurs what is conducive to the goal—for example, leaves for the sake of sheltering the fruit. So that if the swallow builds its nest and the spider its web by nature and for the sake of something, and if plants too produce leaves for the sake of the fruit and grow their roots downwards rather than upwards for the sake of nutrition, it is plain that there are causes of this sort in the things that come to be and are by nature.

But *do* we 'see' final causes in nature? And what exactly are we supposed to see? The phrases 'in order to' and 'for the sake of' seem to be primarily of service in explaining the intentional actions of conscious agents. Then is Aristotle ascribing agency and intentionality to natural phenomena? He is surely not attributing intentions to animals and plants or saying that the final causes of their activities are what *they* purpose; for it is evident that ducks do not plan to have webbed feet or plants contrive their leaves. Aristotle's teleology does not consist in a puerile ascription of intentions to vegetables.

Is Aristotle attributing intentions not to natural creatures but to Nature herself? There are several passages in which Aristotle does speak of Nature as the intelligent artificer of the natural world. 'Like a good housekeeper, Nature does not waste anything which might be put to good use.' Such passages should not be lightly dismissed. But Nature the Artificer cannot be all that there is to Aristotle's teleology; for in the detailed teleological explanations which fill his biological writings he rarely adverts to the plans of Nature or the purposes of a grand Designer.

But if we are not to interpret Aristotle's teleology in terms of intentional planning, how are to interpret it? Consider the following passage.

Snakes copulate by twining around one another; and they have no testicles and no penis, as I have already observed—no penis because they have no legs, no testicles ... because of their length. For because they are naturally elongated, if there were further delay in the region of the testicles, the semen would grow cool because of its slow passage. (This happens in the case of men who have large penises: they are less fertile than those with moderate penises because cold semen is not fertile and semen that is carried a long way cools.)

If the snake's semen had to wind its way through a pair of testicles after travelling the length of the snake's body, it would become cold and infertile—and *that* is why snakes have no testicles. (They have no penis because the penis is naturally located between the legs, and snakes have no legs.) In order to procreate successfully, snakes must lack testicles: they would not survive if they did not procreate, and they could not procreate if they had testicles. That explains their lack of testicles. The explanation is fantastical in its content, but it is an explanation of a perfectly respectable type.

In general, most structural features and behavioural traits of animals and plants have a function. That is to say, they serve the performance of some activity which is essential, or at least useful, to the organism—if the organism did not perform that activity it would not survive at all, or would only survive with difficulty. If we are seeking an understanding of animal life, we must grasp the functions associated with the creature's parts and behaviour. If you know that ducks have webbed feet and also know that they swim, you are not yet in possession of full understanding—you need to grasp in addition that the webbing *helps* ducks to swim, and that swimming is an essential part of the duck's life.

Aristotle expresses this by saying that one answer to the question 'Why do ducks have webbed feet?' is 'In order to swim.' His 'in order to' sounds odd to us only because *we* associate 'in order to' primarily with intentional action. Aristotle associates it primarily with function, and he sees function in nature. He is surely right. Natural objects do contain functional parts and do exhibit functional behaviour; the scientist who is unaware of such functions is ignorant of a major part of his subject-matter.

'Nature does nothing in vain' is a regulative principle for scientific enquiry. Aristotle knows that some aspects of nature are functionless. But he recognizes that a grasp of function is crucial to an understanding of nature. His slogans about the prudence of Nature are not pieces of childish superstition, but reminders of a central task of the natural scientist.

18 *Practical philosophy*

The preceding chapters have been concerned with the theoretical sciences. Aristotle himself devoted most of his time to that great branch of knowledge, but he did not ignore the practical sciences. Indeed, two of his most celebrated treatises, the *Politics* and the *Nicomachean Ethics*, belong to the practical branch of philosophy. Those works are not practical in the sense of being manuals. On the contrary, they are full of analysis and argument, and they rest upon much historical and scientific research. They are works of practical *philosophy*, practical in the sense that their purpose or aim is not merely to purvey truth but also to affect action: 'the present treatise is not, like the others, undertaken for the sake of understanding—for we are conducting the enquiry not in order to know what goodness is but in order to become good men.'

Aristotle wrote two *Ethics*, the *Nicomachean* and the *Eudemian*. The title '*Ethics*' is slightly misleading, and so too are the standard English translations of two key terms in Aristotle's practical philosophy—'*aretē*', normally rendered 'virtue', and '*eudaimonia*', normally rendered 'happiness'. A few remarks on these words are in order.

Aristotle himself refers to his treatises as the '*ēthika*', and the transliteration of that Greek word gives us the title '*Ethics*'. But the Greek term means 'matters to do with character', and a better title would be *On Matters of Character*. As for '*aretē*', the word means something like 'goodness' or 'excellence'. Aristotle can talk of the *aretē* of an argument or of an axe as well as of a man. Human *aretē* is human excellence—what it is to be a good human being—and it has only an indirect connection with what we think of as virtue. Finally, '*eudaimonia*' does not refer to a mental state of euphoria, as 'happiness' tends to in English: to be *eudaimōn* is to flourish, to make a success of life, and the connection between *eudaimonia* and happiness is again indirect.

What, then, is Aristotle's 'ethical' philosophy? 'It seems no doubt uncontroversial to say that *eudaimonia* is the best thing, but we need to say more clearly what it is.' Each of us wants to flourish or do well, and all our actions, in so far as they are rational, are directed to that ultimate goal. The primary question for practical philosophy, then, is this: How are we to achieve *eudaimonia*? In what does flourishing consist? What is it to be a successful human being? Aristotle is not asking what makes us happy, and he is not concerned with the question of how we *ought* to lead our lives, if that question is construed as a moral one. He wants to instruct us in how to make a success of our lives.

Aristotle's answer depends upon a philosophical analysis of the nature of *eudaimonia*. *Eudaimonia*, he argues, is 'an activity of the soul in accordance with excellence'. To say that *eudaimonia* is an 'activity' is to say that to flourish involves *doing* things as opposed to being in a certain state. (Being happy —like, say, being in love—is a state of mind: flourishing is not a state but an activity or set of activities.) To say that *eudaimonia* concerns the soul (or the animator) is to say that human flourishing requires the exercise of certain of the faculties by which life is defined; in particular, a person cannot be said to flourish as a human being unless he is exercising distinctively human faculties. Finally, *eudaimonia* is an activity 'in accordance with excellence'. To flourish is to do certain things excellently or well. A man who exercises his faculties but does so inefficiently or badly cannot be said to be making a success of his life.

Then what are the excellences in accordance with which we should act? Aristotle distinguishes between excellences of character and excellences of intellect. The former include both what we think of as moral virtues—courage, generosity, fair-mindedness and so on—and also such dispositions as a proper self-respect, an appropriate degree of ostentation, and wit; the latter include such things as knowledge, good judgement, 'practical wisdom'. In addition, Aristotle spends some time in discussing the quasi-excellence of friendship.

Men are marked off from other animals by possessing reason and the power of thought. Men 'contain something divine—what we call the intellect is divine', and our intellect is 'the divine within us'. Indeed, 'each of us actually *is* intellect, since that is our sovereign and best element'. The excellences most properly human, then, are the intellectual excellences, and *eudaimonia* consists primarily in activity in accordance with those excellences—it is a form of intellectual activity. 'Thus any choice or possession of the natural goods—of the body, wealth, friends or any other good—which will best produce contemplation by the god [that is, by our intellect, the god within us], is best and is the finest standard; and any which, either because of deficiency or because of excess, prevents us from cultivating the god and from contemplating, is bad.' To flourish, to make a success of life, requires engagement in intellectual pursuits. Aristotle thought that such pursuits were immensely enjoyable, and that the intellectual life offered an unparalleled happiness; but his main thesis in the *Ethics* is not that happiness consists in intellectual activity, but that excellent intellectual activity constitutes success or flourishing for men. The intellectual giants of history may not all have been happy men, but they were all successful men—they all flourished and achieved *eudaimonia*.

Intellectual activity is not enough. Men are not isolated individuals, and the human excellences cannot be practised by solitary hermits. 'Man', Aristotle says, 'is by nature a social animal' (the word I translate as 'social' is usually rendered by 'political'). That remark is no casual aphorism, but a piece of biological theory. 'Social animals are those which have some single activity common to them all (which is not true of all gregarious animals); such are men, bees, wasps, ants, cranes.' 'What is peculiar to men, compared to the other animals, is that they alone can perceive the good and the bad, the just and the unjust, and the rest—and it is partnership in these things which makes a household and a State.' Society and the State are not artificial trappings imposed upon natural man: they are manifestations of human nature itself.

Societies appear in different forms. The first thing to be stressed in connection with Aristotle's idea of a State is its size. 'A State cannot be made from ten men—and from 100,000 it is no longer a State.' The Greek city-states whose histories formed the factual background to Aristotle's political theory were, most of them, of pygmy proportions. They were frequently torn by faction, and their independence was ultimately destroyed by the advance of Macedonian power. Aristotle was familiar with the evils of faction (Book V of the *Politics* is given over to an analysis of the causes of civil strife), and he was intimate with the Macedonian court; yet he never lost his conviction that the small city-state was the right—the natural—form of civil society.

A State is a collection of citizens, and a citizen, in Aristotle's view, 'is defined by nothing else so well as by participation in judicial functions and in political office'. The affairs of a State are run directly by its citizens. Each citizen will be a member of the assembly or deliberative body of the nation, he will be eligible for the various offices of State, which include financial and military appointments, and he will be a part of the judiciary (for under Greek legal procedure the functions of judge and jury were not distinguished).

How much political power a citizen possessed would depend on the type of constitution which his State enjoyed, different constitutions entrusting to different persons or institutions the authority to pass legislation and to determine public policy. Aristotle produced a complex taxonomy of constitutions, the three main types of which are monarchy, aristocracy and democracy. In certain circumstances Aristotle favoured monarchy. 'When either a whole family or an individual is so remarkable in point of excellence that his excellence exceeds that of everyone else, then it is just that that family or that individual should be king and sovereign over all matters.' But such circumstances are rare, and in practice Aristotle preferred democracy. 'The view that the multitude, rather than a few good men, should be sovereign . . . would seem perhaps to be true. For although each member of the multitude is not a good man, still it is possible that, when they come together, they should be better—not as individuals but collectively, just as communal dinners are better than those supplied at one man's expense.'

A State, however constituted, must be self-sufficient, and it must achieve the goal or end for which States exist.

It is evident that a State is not a sharing of locality for the purpose of preventing mutual harm and promoting trade. Those things must necessarily be present if a State is to exist; but even if they are all present a State does not thereby exist. Rather, a State is a sharing by households and families in a good life, for the purpose of a complete and self-sufficient life.

The 'good life', which is the goal of the State, is identified with *eudaimonia*, which is the goal of individuals. States are natural entities, and like other natural objects they have a goal or end. Teleology is a feature of Aristotle's political theory no less than of his biology.

That notion of the goal of the State is linked to another high ideal. 'A fundamental principle of democratic constitutions is liberty . . . One form of liberty is to rule and be ruled turn and turn about . . . Another form is to live as one wishes; for men say that that is the aim of liberty, since to live not as one wishes is the mark of a slave.' Liberty at home is complemented by a pacific external policy; for Aristotelian States, although armed for defence, will have no imperialist ambitions. (But Aristotle is said to have urged Alexander the Great to 'deal with Greeks in the manner of a leader, with foreigners in that of a master, caring for the former as friends and relatives, treating the latter as animals or plants'.)

But liberty is severely restricted in Aristotle's State. It is the prerogative of citizens, and a large majority of the population does not possess citizenship. Women have no liberty. And there are slaves. Some men, according to Aristotle, are slaves by nature, and it is therefore permissible to make them slaves in fact. 'Someone who, being a man, belongs by nature not to himself but to someone else, is a slave by nature. He belongs to someone else if, being a man, he is an article of property—and an article of property is an instrument which aids the actions of and is separable from its owner.' Slaves may enjoy a good life—they may have kind masters. But they have no liberty and no rights.

The citizens own slaves, and they own other forms of property too. Aristotle argues at length against communism. 'Evidently', he concludes, 'it is better that property should be private, but that men should make it common in use.' But he immediately adds that 'it is the task of the legislator to see that the citizens become like that'. Aristotle's State will not own the means of production, nor will it direct the economy; but the legislature will ensure that the citizens' economic behaviour is properly governed.

The voice of the State, muted in economic affairs, is strident in social matters. The State intervenes before birth: 'since the legislator must from the start consider how the children who are reared are to have the best physique, he must first pay attention to sexual union, determining when and between what sort of people marital relations may exist'. Interference continues during childhood, especially in connection with education:

No one would dispute that the legislator must busy himself especially about the education of the young . . . Since the whole city has one goal, it is evident that there must also be one and the same education for everyone, and that the superintendence of this should be public and not private . . . Public matters should be publicly managed; and we should not think that each of the citizens belongs to himself, but that they all belong to the State.

Aristotle describes in considerable detail the various ways in which the State should regulate the lives of its citizens. Each regulation, however benevolent in purpose, is a curtailment of liberty—and in Aristotle's claim that the citizens 'all belong to the State' the reader may detect the infant voice of totalitarianism. If Aristotle loved liberty, he did not love it enough. His State is highly authoritarian.

What has gone wrong? Some may suspect that Aristotle erred at the very first step. He confidently assigns a positive function to the State, supposing that its goal is the promotion of the good life. Given that, it is easy to imagine that the State, eager to ameliorate the human condition, may properly intervene in any aspect of human life and may compel its subjects to do whatever will make them happy. Those who see the State as a promoter of Good often end up as advocates of repression. Lovers of liberty will prefer to assign a negative function to the State and to regard it rather as a defence and protection against Evil.

19 The arts

Aristotle is often accused of presenting a narrowly intellectual view of the good life: Homer and Phidias—or Rembrandt and Bach—will not, in his opinion, serve as examples of success or as illustrations of *eudaimonia*. That accusation may well be unjust, for the ideal of 'contemplation' advanced in the *Ethics* is perhaps large enough to encompass a life of artistic or literary genius. But however that may be, Aristotle did in practice have the greatest veneration for such genius: that is apparent from every page of his treatise on the arts, the *Poetics*.

The *Poetics* is short, and it survives only in a curtailed form. It contains an interesting essay on language and linguistics, which may be supplemented by the treatment of style in Book III of the *Rhetoric*. It says a little about the emotions, on which Aristotle writes at length and with great subtlety in Book II of the *Rhetoric*. But it consists largely of what most commentators have seen as literary theory or literary criticism. That, however, is not how Aristotle saw his tract: the *Poetics* is a contribution to 'productive' science—its aim is to tell us not how to judge a work of art, but how to produce one.

Art, Aristotle thinks, is a matter of representation or imitation 'Epics, and tragic poetry, and also comedy and dithyrambs and most flute- and harp-music, are all by and large imitations.' Art imitates or represents human life, and in particular human actions. Human actions differ in character, 'and it is this difference which distinguishes tragedy from comedy; for the latter is supposed to imitate men who are worse, the former men who are better, than those of today'. Much of the *Poetics* is devoted to tragedy. The discussion starts from a celebrated definition. 'Tragedy is an imitation of an action which is serious and complete, and which has a certain magnitude. Its language is well seasoned, with each of the kinds of seasoning used separately in its different parts. It is in dramatic, not narrative, form. And through pity and fear it accomplishes a purgation of emotions of that sort'.

Of the six elements of tragedy which Aristotle distinguishes—plot, character, language, thought, spectacle, song—the plot is the most important. It is in virtue of its plot that a tragedy will be 'complete' or unitary, and it is through its plot that a tragedy will perform its purgative function: 'the chief means by which a tragedy works on the emotions are parts of the plot, namely discoveries and reversals'. The plot revolves about a central figure, the 'tragic hero' as he was later called, who must be a man 'neither pre-eminent in excellence and goodness nor falling into misfortune through badness and villainy, but rather through some mistake—a man of high reputation and good fortune, like Oedipus or Thyestes or famous men from such families'. The protagonist of a tragedy enjoys great success (Oedipus was King of Thebes). He has made some 'mistake' (Oedipus unwittingly killed his father and married his mother). The mistake is discovered, and a 'reversal' occurs (Oedipus' mother commits suicide, he blinds himself and is banished from Thebes). By its organic unity, and its implicit universality, the story works upon the feelings of the audience.

Aristotle's conception of tragedy, which had a profound effect upon the later history of European drama, may seem blinkered. His definition hardly fits the great tragedies of Shakespeare, not to mention the works of modern playwrights whose heroes, or antiheroes, possess neither the social standing nor the grand history of an Oedipus. But Aristotle was not attempting to produce a 'theory' of tragedy which would hold good for all time. He was telling his contemporaries, who worked within the conventions of the Greek stage, how to write a play. (His advice is based upon a mass of empirical research into the history of Greek drama.)

Again, Aristotle's notion of the goal of tragedy may appear odd. He stresses the effect which tragedy has on the feelings and passions of an audience. But do tragedies always purge an audience of pity and fear? And if they do, is it plausible to regard emotional purgation as the primary function of tragedy? No doubt tragedy has an emotional aspect; but it also has aesthetic and intellectual aspects.

Aristotle was well aware of those aspects, even if they do not feature prominently in his definition of tragedy. Much of the *Poetics* deals implicitly with aesthetic matters, inasmuch as it discusses the 'well-seasoned language' and the rhythms which tragedy requires. Of the intellectual aspect of art Aristotle has this to say:

everyone enjoys imitation. A sign of that is what happens in actual cases; for we enjoy looking at very accurate likenesses of things which in themselves are painful to see—for example, the forms of the foulest animals, and corpses. The reason for this is that learning is most pleasant not only to philosophers but also to other men, even if they share the pleasure briefly. That is why we enjoy seeing likenesses—as we look, we learn and infer what each thing is, saying 'That's him.'

The pleasure of learning is thus an important ingredient in the productive sciences. Contemplation or the actuality of knowing is the prime component of *eudaimonia*, which is the goal of the practical sciences. Truth and knowledge are the direct aim of the theoretical sciences. The desire for knowledge, which Aristotle thought to be part of every man's nature and which was patently the dominant aspect of his own personality, informs and unifies the tripartite structure of Aristotelian philosophy.

20 *Afterlife*

On Aristotle's death, his friend and pupil Theophrastus assumed his mantle, and under him the Lyceum remained a bright focus of scientific and philosophical study. But in the third century BC the light of Aristotelianism dimmed. Other schools of thought—the Stoics, the Epicureans, the Sceptics— dominated the philosophical stage, and the sciences developed separately from philosophy and became the domain of specialists.

Yet Aristotle was never forgotten, and his work enjoyed more than one renaissance. From the first to the sixth century AD, a sequence of scholarly commentators preserved his writings and revivified his thought. There was a second renewal of interest in Byzantium in the eighth century. Later, in the twelfth century, Aristotle came to Western Europe, where his texts were read by learned men and translated into Latin, and copies were widely disseminated and widely read. Aristotle was known, magisterially, as 'the Philosopher'. His thought was all-pervasive, and the half-hearted attempts by the Church to suppress his writings only confirmed their authority. For some four centuries Aristotle's philosophy and Aristotle's science ruled the West with virtually unchallenged sway.

An account of Aristotle's intellectual afterlife would be little less than a history of European thought. In part his influence was simple and direct: Aristotle's various doctrines and beliefs were purveyed as received truths, and his ideas, or their reflection, can be seen in the pages of philosophers and scientists, of historians and theologians, of poets and playwrights. But the influence also took a subtler form. The structure as well as the content of Aristotle's thought impressed itself upon posterity.

The concepts and the terminology of the Lyceum provided the medium within which philosophy and science developed, so that even those radical thinkers who determined to reject Aristotelian views found themselves doing so in Aristotelian language. When today we talk of matter and form, of species and genera, of energy and potentiality, of substance and quality, of accident and essence, we unwittingly speak the language of Aristotle and think in terms and concepts which were forged in Greece two millennia ago.

It is worth adding that our modern notion of scientific method is thoroughly Aristotelian. Scientific empiricism—the idea that abstract argument must be subordinate to factual evidence, that theory is to be judged before the strict tribunal of observation—now seems a commonplace; but it was not always so, and it is largely due to Aristotle that we understand science to be an empirical pursuit. The point needs emphasizing, if only because Aristotle's most celebrated English critics, Francis Bacon and John Locke, were both staunch empiricists who thought that they were thereby breaking with the Aristotelian tradition. Aristotle was charged with preferring flimsy theories and sterile syllogisms to the solid, fertile facts. But that charge is unjust; and indeed it could only have been brought by men who did not read Aristotle's own works with proper attention and who criticized him for the faults of his successors.

Aristotle undoubtedly had influence. But influence and greatness are not the same thing, and we might yet ask what makes Aristotle a Master—'the master of those who know', as Dante called him—and why he is still worth reading. His greatest single achievement was surely his biology. By the work recorded in the *Researches*, the *Parts of Animals*, and the *Generation of Animals*, he founded the science of biology, Set it on a sure empirical and philosophical basis, and gave it the shape it would retain until the nineteenth century. Second only to his biology is his logic. Here too Aristotle founded a new science, and Aristotle's logic remained until the end of the last century the logic of European thought. Few men have founded one science; Aristotle apart, none has founded more than one.

But in biology and in logic Aristotle is outdated. If we want to learn biology or logic, we no longer turn to Aristotle's treatises: they are now of historical interest only. The same is not true of Aristotle's more philosophical writings. The essays in the *Physics*, the *Metaphysics* and the *Ethics* are less sure, less perfect, less scientific than the logic and the biology; but they are, paradoxically, more alive. For here Aristotle has not yet been overtaken. The *Ethics*, for example, can indeed be read as a historical document—as evidence for the state of practical philosophy in the fourth century BC. But it can also be read as a contribution to current debate, and modern philosophers still treat Aristotle as a brilliant colleague. The philosophical treatises are rich, difficult, exciting: they are still studied as urgent commentary on matters of permanent concern.

Finally, Aristotle set before us, explicitly in his writings and implicitly in his life, an ideal of human excellence. Aristotelian man may not be the sole paragon or the unique ideal, but he is surely an admirable specimen, emulation of whom is no low ambition. I end with a passage from the *Parts of Animals* which expresses some of the best in Aristotelian man.

Of natural substances, some we hold to be for ever free from generation and destruction, others to partake in generation and destruction. The former are worthy and divine, but our studies of them are less adequate; for there is remarkably little evidence available to perception from which we might make enquiries about them and about the things we long to know. But about perishable substances—plants and animals—we are much better off with regard to knowledge, because we are brought up among them; for anyone who is willing to take enough trouble may learn much of the truth about each kind. Each of the groups gives pleasure: even if our grasp of the former is slight, nevertheless because of their worth knowledge of them is more pleasant than knowing everything here about us (just as it is more pleasant to see any small part of the things we love than to see accurately many other large things); and since of the latter we have better and greater knowledge, our grasp of them has the superiority—and again, because they are nearer to us and more akin to our nature, they gain somewhat compared to philosophical study of things divine.

Since we have treated the latter and set down our views, we must now speak of animal nature, as far as is possible omitting nothing whether of less or greater worth. For even in the case of those that are not pleasing to the senses, the nature which fashioned them nevertheless gives immeasurable pleasures to the student who can discern the causes of things and is naturally of a philosophical turn. For it would be irrational and absurd if, while we take pleasure in contemplating the likenesses of those things because we contemplate at the same time the skill of the painter or the sculptor who fashioned them, we should yet fail to enjoy more the contemplation of the natural things themselves, particularly if we can discern their causes. Thus we should not childishly complain against the enquiry into the less worthy animals; for in everything natural there is something marvellous.

Heraclitus is reported to have said to some visitors who wished to meet him and who hesitated when they saw him warming himself at the stove: 'Come in, be bold: there are gods here too.' In the same way we should approach the study of every animal without shame; for in all of them there is something natural and something beautiful.

Chronological table

References and Further Reading

Socrates

Further reading

Ancient Sources

All the dialogues of Plato cited in this book are available in numerous English translations. The most accessible translation of the Socratic writings of Xenophon is that by H. Tredennick and R. Waterfield, *Xenophon, Conversations of Socrates* in Penguin Classics (Harmondsworth, 1990), which has an excellent introduction and notes. The Socratic works are also available as part of the Loeb Classical Library edition of Xenophon (Greek with facing English translation), *Memorabilia* and *Oeconomicus* translated by E. C. Marchant (London and New York, 1923), *Symposium* and *Apology* translated by O. J. Todd (London and Cambridge, Mass., 1961). Diogenes Laertius' *Lives of the Philosophers* is also available in the Loeb edition (2 vols., tr. R. D. Hicks (Cambridge, Mass., 1925)). Aristophanes' *Clouds* is translated by B. B. Rogers (London, 1916 (repr. 1924 as part of the complete Loeb edition of Aristophanes)) and by W. Arrowsmith (Ann Arbor, Mich., 1962). The edition of the play by K. J. Dover (Oxford, 1968, abridged edn., 1970) contains a comprehensive introduction which is very useful even to those who have no Greek.

Most of the fragments of the minor Socratic writers are available in Greek only; the standard edition is that by G. Giannantoni, *Socratis et Socraticorum Reliquiae*, 4 vols. (Naples, 1991). The principal fragments of Aeschines are translated in G. C. Field, *Plato and his Contemporaries* (London, 1930), ch. 11.

J. Ferguson, *Socrates, A Source Book* (London, 1970) contains a comprehensive collection of passages of ancient works (in English translation) referring to Socrates.

Modern Works

The modern literature on Socrates is vast. T. C. Brickhouse and N. D. Smith, *Socrates on Trial* (Oxford, 1989) contains a useful guide to it (pp. 272–316). This note restricts itself to major works in English.

Comprehensive Survey

Guthrie, W. K. C., *A History of Greek Philosophy*, iii, part 2 (Cambridge, 1969). Published separately 1971 under title *Socrates*.

Biography

Taylor, A. E., *Varia Socratica* (Oxford, 1911).

Critical and Analytical Works Concentrating on Plato's Presentation of Socrates

Santas, G. X., *Socrates* (London, Boston, and Henley, 1979).
Vlastos, G., *Socrates, Ironist and Moral Philosopher* (Cambridge, 1991).
—— *Socratic Studies* (ed. M. Burnyeat) (Cambridge, 1994).
Brickhouse, T. C., and Smith, N. D., *Plato's Socrates* (New York and Oxford, 1994).
Irwin, T., *Plato's Ethics* (New York and Oxford, 1995), chs. 1–9.

Works on Socrates' Trial

Stone, I. F., *The Trial of Socrates* (London, 1988). A lively presentation, unreliable in places.
Brickhouse, T. C., and Smith, N. D., *Socrates on Trial* (Oxford, 1989). A heavy work of scholarship.

Collections of Articles

Vlastos, G. (ed.), *The Philosophy of Socrates* (Garden City, NY, 1971).
Benson, H. H. (ed.), *Essays on the Philosophy of Socrates* (New York and Oxford, 1992).
Gower, B. S., and Stokes, M. C. (eds.), *Socratic Questions* (London and New York, 1992).
Prior, W. T. (ed.), *Socrates*, 4 vols. (London and New York, 1996). A comprehensive collection.

Works on Socratic Literature

Vander Waerdt, P. A., (ed.), *The Socratic Movement* (Ithaca, NY and London, 1994).
Rutherford, R. B., *The Art of Plato* (London, 1995).

Kahn, C. H., *Plato and the Socratic Dialogue* (Cambridge, 1996), chs. 1–4.

Socrates in Later Thought

Montuori, M., *Socrates: Physiology of a Myth* (Amsterdam, 1981).

Index of Ancient Works Cited

Plato

Readers who want to study what others have said about Plato will find nearly all the bibliographical information and guidance that they need in the fourth and fifth volumes of W. K. C. Guthrie's *A History of Greek Philosophy* (1962–78), which is also itself both helpful and readable, though enormously long. My own debt to it will be obvious. The earlier volumes, especially that on Socrates, are useful for Plato's predecessors. Those whose taste is for philosophically more sophisticated books might well try I. M. Crombie's *An Examination of Plato's Doctrines* (1962) or J. C. B. Gosling's *Plato* (1973) in the 'Arguments of the Philosophers' series. J. Barnes's *The Presocratics* (1969) in the same series is also good. Sir Karl Popper's *The Open Society and its Enemies* vol. 1 (1945) and Gilbert Ryle's *Plato's Progress* (1966) are two highly readable but also highly controversial books, the first on Plato's politics, the second on his philosophical development. There are a number of good multi-author volumes of essays, among them *New Essays on Plato and Aristotle* (ed. R. Bambrough, 1965), *Studies in Plato's Metaphysics* (ed. R. E. Allen, 1965) and *Plato* (ed. G. Vlastos, 1971). The latter's own *Platonic Studies* (1973) are also to be commended.

All these books are written mainly for specialists. The general reader is better advised to stick to Plato; and for this purpose there is a number of series of translations of single dialogues, some with excellent introductions, and a convenient omnibus volume of all the dialogues (*Plato*, ed. E. Hamilton and H. Cairns, 1961). More advanced, but very useful, are the volumes of translations with commentary in the Clarendon Plato series. However, accurate translation of Plato's Greek is often difficult, and nobody who bases his interpretations on translations, rather than the Greek text, can claim authority.

All references in this book to Plato are to the pages of Stephanus' edition as printed in the margin of the standard Oxford Classical Text of Plato (ed. J. Burnet, 1900–7) and of nearly all translations. In the references below the figures on the left refer to pages of this book. References to Aristotle are to the pages, columns and lines of

312   *Plato*

Bekker's edition, also followed by most modern editions and translations.

Page

108 Thucydides II 35.

109 *The Polity of the Athenians* is wrongly attributed to Xenophon and printed with his works.

110 Herodotus III 38.

111 Thucydides III 82. For persuasive definition see C. L. Stevenson, *Ethics and Language* (1944), ch. 9.

118 Aristotle, *On the Heavens*, 299–300.

119 Heraclitus and Cratylus are discussed by Plato in *Theaetetus* (esp. 179ff.) and *Cratylus* (esp. 439ff.).

122 Aristophanes, *The Clouds*. Xenophon, esp. *Memoirs of Socrates*. Aristotle, esp. *Metaphysics* 987b1, 1078b17, *Eudemian Ethics* 1216b2, *Nicomachean Ethics* 1144b18ff. 1145b23ff. For Socrates' moral influence see Lysias' speech against Aeschines his disciple, fragment xxxviii in Budé edition (ed. Gernet and Bizos, 1955).

128 On Recollection see my 'Philosophical Discoveries', *Mind* 69 (1960), §viii, repr. in *Plato's Meno*, ed. Sesonske and Fleming (1965), *The Linguistic Turn*, ed. R. Rorty (1967), and my *Essays on Philosophical Method* (1971).

129 Lewis Carroll's philosophical use of paradox is delightfully illustrated in P. L. Heath, *The Philosopher's Alice* (1974).

135 J. H. Newman, *The Dream of Gerontius* (1868).

139 On this chapter, see M. Furth, 'Elements of Eleatic Ontology', *Journal of History of Philosophy* 6 (1968), and my own 'A Question about Plato's Theory of Ideas', in my *Essays on Philosophical Method* (1971) (also in *The Critical Approach*, ed. M. Bunge, 1964).

143 For 'Fido' see G. Ryle in *British Philosophy in the Mid-Century*, ed. C. A. Mace (1957).

149 Both sorts of attackers appeal to L. Wittgenstein, *Philosophical Investigations* (1953), esp. §66ff., 242. For the first attack, see J. R. Bambrough, 'Universals and Family Resemblances', *Aristotelian Society Proceedings* 61 (1960/1).

149 For the second attack, see M. Nussbaum, 'Aristophanes and Socrates on Learning Practical Wisdom', *Yale Classical Studies* 26 (1980), and P. T. Geach, 'Plato's *Euthyphro*', *Monist* 50 (1966), repr. in his *Logic Matters* (1972).

150 Wittgenstein, *Philosophical Investigations*, §242.

151 G. Frege, *Foundations of Arithmetic*, trans. J. L. Austin (1959), p. iii.

152 Aristotle, e.g. Categories 1a2.

152 On the two ways of taking the argument, see my 'The Argument from Received Opinion' in my *Essays on Philosophical Method*, pp. 117ff.

154 On the Good, see my 'Plato and the Mathematicians', op.cit. pp. 94–6, repr. from *New Essays on Plato and Aristotle*, ed. R. Bambrough (1965).

158 On this chapter, see my 'Platonism in Moral Education: Two Varieties', *Monist* 58 (1974).

162 Plato in Aristotle, *Nicomachean Ethics* 1104b11.

162 Aristotle, *Nicomachean Ethics* 1094a3, 1172b14.

162 Aristotle, ibid. 1144b17–32.

168 The biblical quotation is from St Paul, *Epistle to the Romans*, ch. vii.

168 Aristotle, 1139a 35; D. Hume, *A Treatise of Human Nature* (1739), III 1 i; II 3 iii.

169 On 'objective prescriptivity' see J. L. Mackie, *Ethics: Inventing Right and Wrong* (1977), ch. 1, commented on in my *Moral Thinking* (1981), pp.78–86.

173 H. Belloc, *The Modern Traveller* (1898).

178 I have tried to sort out the distinction between the meaning of moral words and the criteria for their application in my *The Language of Morals* (1952), esp. chs 6ff.; see also my *Freedom and Reason* (1963), ch. 2.

181 K. R. Popper, *The Open Society and its Enemies*, vol. 1, esp. ch. 7.

Aristotle

Further reading

All Aristotle's works are available in English in the revised 'Oxford Translation':

J. Barnes (ed.), *The Complete Works of Aristotle* (Princeton, 1984)

In addition, let me mention the Clarendon Aristotle series (under the editorship of J. L. Ackrill and L. Judson), each volume in which offers a close translation of a text together with a philosophical commentary.

As for the Greek, the standard edition by Immanuel Bekker (Berlin, 1831) is now out of date from a textual point of view: more recent editions will be found among the Oxford Classical Texts, in the Loeb Classical Library (with facing translation), under the Teubner imprint, or as part of the Budé series.

There is an introductory guide to Aristotle's philosophy:

J. Barnes (ed.), *The Cambridge Companion to Aristotle* (New York, 1995)—which includes a large bibliography.

Out of numerous general books on Aristotle, I mention:

W. D. Ross, *Aristotle* (London, 1923)
J. L. Ackrill, *Aristotle the Philosopher* (London, 1981)
J. Lear, *Aristotle: the Desire to Understand* (Cambridge, 1988)
T. H. Irwin, *Aristotle's First Principles* (Oxford, 1988)

The evidence bearing on Aristotle's life is collected in:

I. Düring, *Aristotle in the Ancient Biographical Tradition* (Göteborg, 1957)

On the Lyceum see:

J. P. Lynch, *Aristotle's School* (Berkeley, 1972)

On Aristotle's 'physics'—his philosophy of science and his general account of the physical world—see:

F. Solmsen, *Aristotle's System of the Physical World* (Ithaca, 1960)

On his *modus operandi* there is a celebrated paper:

G. E. L. Owen, *'Tithenai ta phainomena'*, in his *Logic, Science and Dialectic* (London, 1986)

Note also the papers in:

L. Judson (ed.), *Aristotle's* Physics (Oxford, 1991)

On biology and zoology:

P. Pellegrin, *Aristotle's Classification of Animals* (Berkeley, 1986)
A. Gotthelf and J. Lennox (eds.), *Philosophical Issues in Aristotle's Biology* (Cambridge, 1987)

On psychology let me refer to one book and one anthology:

M. Wedin, *Mind and Imagination in Aristotle* (New Haven, 1988)
M. C. Nussbaum and A. O. Rorty (eds.), *Essays on Aristotle's de Anima* (Oxford, 1992)

On teleology, explanation, causation, and related issues see:

R. Sorabji, *Necessity, Cause and Blame* (London, 1980)

The standard work on Aristotle's logic is:

G. Patzig, *Aristotle's Theory of the Syllogism* (Dordrecht, 1969)

To which add:

K. J. J. Hintikka, *Time and Necessity* (Oxford, 1963)
J. Lear, *Aristotle and Logical Theory* (Cambridge, 1980)

On metaphysics I signal four papers by G. E. L. Owen, all collected in his *Logic, Science and Dialectic* (London, 1986):

'Logic and metaphysics in some earlier works of Aristotle'
'The Platonism of Aristotle'
'Aristotle on the snares of ontology'
'Particular and General'

And note a recent collection:

T. Scaltsas, D. Charles, and M. Gill (eds.), *Unity, Identity and Explanation in Aristotle's Metaphysics* (Oxford, 1994)

As to practical philosophy, on ethics see:

J. O. Urmson, *Aristotle's Ethics* (Oxford, 1987)
D. S. Hutchinson, *The Virtues of Aristotle* (London, 1986)
A. O. Rorty (ed.), *Essays on Aristotle's Ethics* (Berkeley, 1980)

And on politics:

F. D. Miller, *Nature, Justice, and Rights in Aristotle's Politics* (Oxford, 1995)

D. Keyt and F. D. Miller (eds.), *A Companion to Aristotle's Politics* (Oxford, 1991)

On poetry and the arts:

S. Halliwell, *The Poetics of Aristotle* (London, 1987)

A.O. Rorty (ed.), *Essays on Aristotle's Poetics* (Princeton, 1992)

And for rhetoric:

D. J. Furley and A. Nehamas (eds.), *Philosophical Aspects of Aristotle's Rhetoric* (Princeton, 1994)

Finally, on Aristotle's afterlife and the later history of Aristotelianism:

R. Sorabji (ed.), *Aristotle Transformed* (London, 1990)

References

All works cited are by Aristotle unless otherwise stated. References to Aristotle's writings normally consist of an abbreviated title, a book number (in Roman numerals), a chapter number (Arabic), and a specification of page, column and line in the standard edition of the Greek text by Immanuel Bekker. (Most subsequent editions of the Greek and most English translations print Bekker references in their margins at regular intervals.) Thus Mr II 9, 369a31, refers to line 31 of column a on page 369 of Bekker's edition, a line which occurs in the ninth chapter of the second book of Aristotle's *Meteorology*.

Abbreviations

C	*Categories*	PA	*Parts of Animals*
EE	*Eudemian Ethics*	Ph	*Physics*
GA	*Generation of Animals*	Pl	*Politics*
GC	*On Generation and Corruption*	Po	*Poetics*
		PoA	*Posterior Analytics*
H	*On the Heavens*	PrA	*Prior Analytics*
HA	*History of Animals*	Pro	*Protrepticus*
I	*On Interpretation*	R	*Rhetoric*
M	*Metaphysics*	S	*On the Soul*
MA	*Movement of Animals*	SR	*Sophistical Refutations*
Mr	*Meteorology*	T	*Topics*
NE	*Nicomachean Ethics*		

Page 196. (1) all men: M I 1, 980a22

(2) the activity: M XII 7, 1072b27

Page 196. (1) the acquisition: Pro fragment 52 Rose = B 56 Düring, quoted by Iamblichus, Pro 40.20–41.2

(2) we must not: NE X 7, 1177b31–5

(3) he wrote: Diogenes Laertius, *Lives of the Philosophers* V 21

Page 198 (1). In every form: R III 1, 1404a8–12

(2). he surrounds: Atticus, fragment 7 (p. 28 ed. Baudry), quoted by Eusebius, *Preparation for the Gospel* XV ix 14, 810D

Page 201. he did not want: Aelian, *Varia historia* III 36

Page 202. (1) *an inscription:* Ibn Abi Usaibia, *Life of Aristotle* 18, printed in I. Düring, *Aristotle in the Ancient Biographical Tradition* (Göteborg, 1957), p. 215

(2) they drew up: W. Dittenberger (ed.), *Sylloge inscriptionum Graecarum* (3rd ed., Leipzig, 1915), no. 275

(3) as for what: *Letters*, fragment 9 (in M. Plezia (ed.), *Aristoteles: Privatorum scriptorum fragmenta* (Leipzig, 1977)), quoted by Aelian, *Varia historia* XIV 1

Page 204. the city of Assos: S. Mekler (ed.), *Academicorum philosophorum index Herculanensis* (Berlin, 1902), p. 23

Page 206. (1) First, let us: HA I 6, 491a19–21

(2) The octopus: HA IV 1, 524a3–20

Page 207. (1) this is plain: HA V 8, 542a2–6

(2) it defends itself: HA IX 45, 630b8–11

Page 208. (1) are generated: HA V 19, 551a1–7

(2) *an experiment:* HA VI 3, 561a6–562a20

Page 210. the so-called *teuthoi*: HA IV 1, 524a25–8

Page 211. (1) inflamed: Pliny, *Natural History* VIII xvi 44

(2) Their error: GA III 5, 756a31–4

Page 212. (1) he worked: anon., *Vita Aristotelis Marciana* 6 (in Düring, op.cit., p. 98)

(2) he is the first: Strabo, *Geography* XIII i 54

(3) one should make: T I 14, 105b12–15

(4) we have given: M I 3, 983a33–b6

Page 213. (1) in the case: SR 34, 184a9–b9

Page 214. (1) for if the difficulties: NE VII 1, 1145b6–7

(2) In all cases: SR 34, 183b18–27

(3) Investigation: M II 1, 993a30–b5; b11–19

Page 216. why did he: Philodemus, *On Rhetoric* col. LIII 41–2, vol. II, pp. S7–8 Sudhaus

Page 217. at once gave up: *Nerinthus*, fragment 64 Rose, quoted by Themistius, *Oration* XXXIII 295D

Page 218. In the gymnasium: Epicrates, fragment 11 Kock, quoted by Athenaeus, *Deipnosophists* 59D

Page 219. (1) whom it is not right: *Poems*, fragment 3 (in Plezia, op.cit.), quoted by Olympiodorus, *Commentary on the Gorgias* 41.9

(2) Plato used: Aelian, *Varia historia* IV 9

Page 223. (1) The causes: M XII 4, 1070a31–3

(2) all thought: M VI 1, 1025b25

(3) there are three: M VI 1, 1026a18–19

Page 224. (1) If there are: M VI 1, 1026a26–30

(2) the theoretical: M VI 1, 1026a22–3

(3) must be the: M I 2, 982b9–10

(4). there is a science: M IV 3, 1003a21–2

Page 226. (1) is universal: M VI 1, 1026a30–l

(2) the things called: M IV 3, 1005a20; b10; a22–3

(3) assumes the same: M IV 2, 1004b17–18

Page 228. (1) All sentences: I 4, 16b33–17a3

(2) Of statements: I 5, 17a20–2

Page 229. every proposition: PrA I 2, 25a1–2

Page 231. (1) If A: PrA I 4, 25b37–9

(2) A *sullogismos:* PrA I 1, 24b18–20

Page 232. every proof: PrA I 23, 41b1–3

Page 233. we think: PoA I 2, 71b9–12

Page 234. If knowing: PoA I 2, 71b19–25

Page 235. cows: PA III 2, 664a8–11; 14, 674b5–14

Page 236. the conclusion: PoA I 8, 75b22–4

Page 237. (1) poetry: Po 9, 1451b5–7

(2) to say that: M XIII 10, 1087a11, 24

(3). All knowledge: M VI 2, 1027a20–4

Page 239. here as elsewhere: NE VII 1, 1145b2–6

Page 241. Aristotle, accusing: Cicero, *Tusculan Disputations* III xxviii 69

Page 243. (1) Now the question: M VII 1, 1028b2–4

(2) what is really: C 6, 6a26

Page 244. (1) in respect of qualities: C 8, 11a15–16

(2) the classes of the things: Ph I 6, 189a14

Page 245. (1) *sharp:* T I 15, 106a13–20

(2) Something is called: M V 2, 1013a24; 5, 1015a20; 18, 1022a14

(3) things are said to be: M VII 1, 1028a10–13

(4) *'kleis':* NE I 6, 1096b26; V 1, 1129a29–31

(5) things are said: M IV 2, 1003a33–4

Page 246. (1) Everything that is healthy: M IV 2, 1003a34–b4

(2) Thus things: M IV 2, 1003b5–10

Page 247. (1) things are called: M V 7, 1017b23–5

(2) the particular pale: C 2, 1a27–8

Page 249. (1) It is plain: M VII 16, 1040b5–8

(2) all these are defined: Mr IV 12, 390a10–13

Page 251. (1) nature is: Ph III 1, 200b12

(2) things have a nature: Ph II 1, 192b32

Page 252. (1) there is something: Ph V 1, 224a34–b3

(2) there is no change: Ph III 1, 200b32; VI 4, 234b29

Page 253. (1) whatever comes: M VII 8, 1033b12–13

(2) it becomes clear: Ph I 7, 190b1–8

Page 254. change is: Ph III 1, 201a10–11

Page 255. (1) actuality is: M IX 8, 1049b10–12

(2) in all cases: M IX 8, 1049b24–7

Page 257. A thing is called: Ph II 3, 194b23–195a3

Page 258. (1) the because-of-which: M VII 17, 1041a23–7

(2) the cause is: PoA II 2, 90a7

Page 259. what it is: PoA II 2, 90a15–18

Page 260. Why did: PoA II 11, 94a36–b2

Page 261. (1) Why is there: PoA II 11, 94b9

(2) Since things: Ph II 3, 195a4–8

Page 262. both because: PoA II 11, 94b32–4

Page 263. And that there is: M VI 2, 1027a20–2

Page 264. and for that: S III 8, 432a7–9

Page 265. All animals: PoA II 19, 99b35–100a9

Page 266. (1) the cause: GA III 5, 756a2–6

(2) *reliability of the senses*: S III 3, 428b18–25

(3) it is evident: M IV 4, 1008b12–16

Page 267. they are really: M IV 5, 1010b4–9

Page 268. (1) a scribe: Suda, s.v. *Aristoteles*

(2) I have already: Mr I 1, 338a20–7; 339a7–9

Page 270. (1) Of the parts: HA I 1, 486a5–8; 13–14

(2) Circular motion: GC II 11, 338a18–b6

Page 271. (1) Our remote: M XII 8, 1074b1–10

(2) god seems: M I 2, 983a8–9

(3) there is some other: H I 2, 269b14–16

(4) it is the function: PA IV 10, 686a29

(5) we tend: H II 12, 292a19–22; b1–2

Page 272. (1) must there be: MA 4, 699b31–5

(2) initiates change: M XII 7, 1072b3–4

(3) It is because: M I 2, 982b12–13

(4) In what way: M XII 10, 1075a11–8

Page 274. Some things: S II 3, 414a29–b6; b16–18

Page 275. (1) if we are to state: S II 1, 412–6

(2) a soul is: S II 2, 413b11–13

(3) one should not: S II 1, 412b6–8

Page 276. (1) that the soul: S III, 413a3–5

(2) a motion: S III 3, 429a1–2

(3) clearly, those: GA II 3, 736b22–7

Page 277. (1) Hence it remains: GA II 3, 736b27–9

(2) this thought: S III 5, 430a17–18; 22–3

Page 279. (1) if there is so much: PA II 2, 648a33–b1

(2) we might say: GA III 11, 761b13–23

Page 280. (1) as to how many: M XII 8, 1073b10–17

(2) to judge: GA III10, 760b28–33

Page 281. (1) we must first: HA I 6, 491a0–14

(2) empirical science: PrA I 30, 46a17–27

(3) speaking of: H III 7, 306a6–7; 12–18

Page 283. We see more: PA I 1, 639b12–21

Page 284. (1) The cause of: GA II 6, 745a27–b3

(2) Anaxagoras: PA IV 10, 687a8–18

(3) For these causes: PA IV 12, 694b6–12

Page 285. (1) *aphorisms*: e.g. H I 4, 271a33

(2) The bile: PA IV 2, 677a14–18

(3) art imitates: Mr IV 3, 381b6; Pro fragment B 23 Düring, quoted by Iamblichus, Pro 34.8–9

(4) It is particularly: Ph II 8, 199a20–30

Page 286. (1) like a good: GA II 6, 744b16–17

(2) Snakes copulate: GA I 7, 718a18–25

Page 288. the present treatise: NE II 2, 1103b26–8

Page 289. (1) It seems: NE I 7, 1097b22–3

(2) an activity: NE I 7, 1098a16

Page 290. (1) contain something: GA II 3, 737a10–11

(2) the divine: EE VIII 2, 1248a27; NE X 7, 1178a2–3

(3) Thus any choice: EE VIII 3, 1249b16–21

(4) Man is: Pl I 1, 1253a2

(5) Social animals: HA I 1, 488a8–10

(6) What is peculiar: Pl I 1, 1253a15–18

Page 291. (1) A State: NE IX 10, 1170b31–2

(2) is defined by: Pl III 1, 1275a22–3

(3) When either: Pl III 17, 1288a15–19

(4) The view that: Pl III 11, 1281a40–b3

Page 292. (1) It is evident: Pl III 9, 1280b29–34

(2) A fundamental: Pl VI 1, 1317a40; b2–3; 11–13

(3) deal with Greeks: *Letters*, fragment 6a (in Plezia, op.cit.), quoted by Plutarch, *On the Fortune of Alexander* 329B

Page 293. (1) Someone who: Pl I 4, 1254a14–17

(2) Evidently: Pl II 5, 1263a38–40

(3) since the legislator: Pl VII 16, 1334b29–32

(4) No one would: Pl VIII 1, 1337a11–12; 21–4; 26–9

Page 295. (1) Epics: Po 1, 1447a13–16

(2) and it is this: Po 2, 1448a16–18

(3) Tragedy is: Po 6, 1449b24–8

Page 296. (1) the chief means: Po 6, 450a33–5

(2) neither pre–eminent: Po 13, 1453a8–12

Page 297. everyone enjoys: Po 4, 1448b8–17

Page 300. Of natural substances: PA I 5, 644b22–645a23

Index

Expand your collection of
VERY SHORT INTRODUCTIONS

Available now

Available soon

Visit the
VERY SHORT
INTRODUCTIONS
Web site

www.oup.co.uk/vsi

➤ **Information** about all published titles

➤ News of **forthcoming books**

➤ **Extracts** from the books, including titles
not yet published

➤ **Reviews** and views

➤ **Links** to other **web sites** and main
OUP web page

➤ Information about **VSIs in translation**

➤ **Contact** the editors

➤ **Order** other **VSIs** on-line

ANCIENT PHILOSOPHY

A Very Short Introduction

Julia Annas

The tradition of ancient philosophy is a long, rich and varied one, in which a constant note is that of discussion and argument. This book aims to introduce readers to some ancient debates and to get them to engage with the ancient developments of philosophical themes. Getting away from the presentation of ancient philosophy as a succession of Great Thinkers, the book aims to give readers a sense of the freshness and liveliness of ancient philosophy, and of its wide variety of themes and styles.

'Incisive, elegant, and full of the excitement of doing philosophy, Julia Annas's Short Introduction boldly steps outside of conventional chronological ways of organizing material about the Greeks and Romans to get right to the heart of the human problems that exercised them, problems ranging from the relation between reason and emotion to the objectivity of truth. I can't think of a better way to begin.'

Martha Nussbaum, University of Chicago

www.oup.co.uk/vsi/ancientphilosophy

CLASSICS

A Very Short Introduction

Mary Beard and John Henderson

This Very Short Introduction to Classics links a
haunting temple on a lonely mountainside to the glory
of ancient Greece and the grandeur of Rome, and to
Classics within modern culture – from Jefferson and
Byron to Asterix and Ben-Hur.

'The authors show us that Classics is a "modern" and
sexy subject. They succeed brilliantly in this regard …
nobody could fail to be informed and entertained – and
the accent of the book is provocative and stimulating.'

John Godwin, *Times Literary Supplement*

'Statues and slavery, temples and tragedies, museum,
marbles, and mythology – this provocative guide to the
Classics demysties its varied subject-matter while
seducing the reader with the obvious enthusiasm and
pleasure which mark its writing.'

Edith Hall

www.oup.co.uk/vsi/classics

HISTORY

A Very Short Introduction

John H. Arnold

History: A Very Short Introduction is a stimulating essay about how we understand the past. The book explores various questions provoked by our understanding of history, and examines how these questions have been answered in the past. Using examples of how historians work, the book shares the sense of excitement at discovering not only the past, but also ourselves.

'A stimulating and provocative introduction to one of collective humanity's most important quests – understanding the past and its relation to the present. A vivid mix of telling examples and clear cut analysis.'

David Lowenthal, University College London

'This is an extremely engaging book, lively, enthusiastic and highly readable, which presents some of the fundamental problems of historical writing in a lucid and accessible manner. As an invitation to the study of history it should be difficult to resist.'

Peter Burke, Emmanuel College, Cambridge

www.oup.co.uk/vsi/history

MUSIC

A Very Short Introduction

Nicholas Cook

This stimulating Very Short Introduction to music
invites us to really *think* about music and the values
and qualities we ascribe to it.

'A *tour de force*. Nicholas Cook is without doubt one of
the most probing and creative thinkers about music we
have today.'

Jim Samson, University of Bristol

'Nicholas Cook offers a perspective that is clearly influenced by recent writing in a host of disciplines related
to music. It may well prove a landmark in the appreci-
ation of the topic ... In short, I can hardly imagine it being
done better.'

Roger Parker, University of Cambridge

www.oup.co.uk/vsi/music

LITERARY THEORY
A Very Short Introduction
Jonathan Culler

Literary Theory is a controversial subject. Said to have transformed the study of culture and society in the past two decades, it is accused of undermining respect for tradition and truth, encouraging suspicion about the political and psychological implications of cultural products instead of admiration for great literature. In this Very Short Introduction, Jonathan Culler explains 'theory', not by describing warring 'schools' but by sketching key 'moves' that theory has encouraged and speaking directly about the implications of cultural theory for thinking about literature, about the power of language, and about human identity. This lucid introduction will be useful for anyone who has wondered what all the fuss is about or who wants to think about literature today.

> 'It is impossible to imagine a clearer treatment of the subject, or one that is, within the given limits of length, more comprehensive. Culler has always been remarkable for his expository skills, and here he has found exactly the right method and tone for his purposes.'
>
> **Frank Kermode**

www.oup.co.uk/vsi/literarytheory

THEOLOGY

A Very Short Introduction

David F. Ford

This Very Short Introduction provides both believers and non-believers with a balanced survey of the central questions of contemporary theology. David Ford's interrogative approach draws the reader into considering the principles underlying religious belief, including the centrality of salvation to most major religions, the concept of God in ancient, modern, and post-modern contexts, the challenge posed to theology by prayer and worship, and the issue of sin and evil. He also probes the nature of experience, knowledge, and wisdom in theology, and discusses what is involved in interpreting theological texts today.

'David Ford tempts his readers into the huge resources of theology with an attractive mix of simple questions and profound reflection. With its vivid untechnical language it succeeds brilliantly in its task of introduction.'
Stephen Sykes, University of Durham

'a fine book, imaginatively conceived and gracefully written. It carries the reader along with it, enlarging horizons while acknowledging problems and providing practical guidance along the way.'
Maurice Wiles, University of Oxford

www.oup.co.uk/vsi/theology

PSYCHOLOGY

A Very Short Introduction

Gillian Butler and Freda McManus

Psychology: A Very Short Introduction provides an up-to-date overview of the main areas of psychology, translating complex psychological matters, such as perception, into readable topics so as to make psychology accessible for newcomers to the subject. The authors use everyday examples as well as research findings to foster curiosity about how and why the mind works in the way it does, and why we behave in the ways we do. This book explains why knowing about psychology is important and relevant to the modern world.

> 'a very readable, stimulating, and well-written introduction to psychology which combines factual information with a welcome honesty about the current limits of knowledge. It brings alive the fascination and appeal of psychology, its significance and implications, and its inherent challenges.'
>
> **Anthony Clare**

> 'This excellent text provides a succinct account of how modern psychologists approach the study of the mind and human behaviour. ... the best available introduction to the subject.'
>
> **Anthony Storr**

www.oup.co.uk/vsi/psychology

POLITICS

A Very Short Introduction

Kenneth Minogue

In this provocative but balanced essay, Kenneth Minogue discusses the development of politics from the ancient world to the twentieth century. He prompts us to consider why political systems evolve, how politics offers both power and order in our society, whether democracy is always a good thing, and what future politics may have in the twenty-first century.

> 'This is a fascinating book which sketches, in a very short space, one view of the nature of politics … the reader is challenged, provoked and stimulated by Minogue's trenchant views.'
>
> **Ian Davies, *Talking Politics***

> 'a dazzling but unpretentious display of great scholarship and humane reflection'
>
> **Neil O'Sullivan, University of Hull**

www.oup.co.uk/vsi/politics

THE BIBLE

A Very Short Introduction

John Riches

It is sometimes said that the Bible is one of the most
unread books in the world, yet it has been a major force
in the development of Western culture and continues to
exert an enormous influence over many people's lives.
This Very Short Introduction looks at the importance
accorded to the Bible by different communities and
cultures and attempts to explain why it has generated
such a rich variety of uses and interpretations. It explores
how the Bible was written, the development of the
canon, the role of Biblical criticism, the appropriation
of the Bible in high and popular culture, and its use for
political ends.

'John Riches' clear and lively Very Short Introduction
offers a distinctive approach to the Bible ... a distinguished addition to the series.'

Christopher Rowland, University of Oxford

'Short in length, but not in substance, nor in interest. A
fascinating introduction both to the way in which the
Bible came to be what it is, and to what it means and
has meant for believers.'

Joel Marcus, Boston University

www.oup.co.uk/vsi/bible

ARCHAEOLOGY
A Very Short Introduction
Paul Bahn

This entertaining Very Short Introduction reflects the
enduring popularity of archaeology — a subject which
appeals as a pastime, career, and academic discipline,
encompasses the whole globe, and surveys 2.5 million
years. From deserts to jungles, from deep caves to
mountain tops, from pebble tools to satellite photo-
graphs, from excavation to abstract theory, archaeology
interacts with virtually every other discipline in its attempts
to reconstruct the past.

'very lively indeed and remarkably perceptive ... a quite
brilliant and level-headed look at the curious world of
archaeology.'

Barry Cunliffe, University of Oxford

'It is often said that well-written books are rare in archaeology, but this is a model of good writing for a general
audience. The book is full of jokes, but its serious
message – that archaeology can be a rich and fascinating subject – it gets across with more panache than any
other book I know.'

Simon Denison, editor of *British Archaeology*

www.oup.co.uk/vsi/archaeology